UNLOCK

READING & WRITING SKILLS

3

Matt Firth

CAMBRIDGE
UNIVERSITY PRESS

University Printing House, Cambridge CB2 8BS, United Kingdom

Cambridge University Press is part of the University of Cambridge.

It furthers the University's mission by disseminating knowledge in the pursuit of education, learning and research at the highest international levels of excellence.

www.cambridge.org
Information on this title: www.cambridge.org/9781107614048

First published 2014
Reprinted 2016

Printed in Italy by Rotolito Lombarda S.p.A.

A catalogue record for this publication is available from the British Library

ISBN 978-1-107-61526-7 Reading and Writing 3 Student's Book with Online Workbook
ISBN 978-1-107-61404-8 Reading and Writing 3 Teacher's Book with DVD
ISBN 978-1-107-68728-8 Listening and Speaking 3 Student's Book with Online Workbook
ISBN 978-1-107-68154-5 Listening and Speaking 3 Teacher's Book with DVD

Additional resources for this publication at www.cambridge.org/unlock

CONTENTS

UNLOCK UNIT STRUCTURE

The units in *Unlock Reading & Writing Skills* are carefully scaffolded so that students are taken step-by-step through the writing process.

| UNLOCK YOUR KNOWLEDGE | Encourages discussion around the theme of the unit with inspiration from interesting questions and striking visuals. |

| WATCH AND LISTEN | Features an engaging and motivating *Discovery Education™* video which generates interest in the topic. |

| READING 1 | Practises the reading skills required to understand academic texts as well as the vocabulary needed to comprehend the text itself. |

| READING 2 | Presents a second text which provides a different angle on the topic in a different genre. It is a model text for the writing task. |

| LANGUAGE DEVELOPMENT | Practises the vocabulary and grammar from the Readings in preparation for the writing task. |

| CRITICAL THINKING | Contains brainstorming, evaluative and analytical tasks as preparation for the writing task. |

| GRAMMAR FOR WRITING | Presents and practises grammatical structures and features needed for the writing task. |

| ACADEMIC WRITING SKILLS | Practises all the writing skills needed for the writing task. |

| WRITING TASK | Uses the skills and language learnt over the course of the unit to draft and edit the writing task. Requires students to produce a piece of academic writing. Checklists help learners to edit their work. |

| OBJECTIVES REVIEW | Allows students to assess how well they have mastered the skills covered in the unit. |

| WORDLIST | Includes the key vocabulary from the unit. |

This is the unit's main learning objective. It gives learners the opportunity to use all the language and skills they have learnt in the unit.

UNL⊘CK MOTIVATION

UNL⊘CK YOUR KNOWLEDGE

Work with a partner. Discuss the questions below.

1 Is it better to see animals in a zoo or in the wild? Why?
2 Are there more wild animals in your country now or were there more in the past? Why?
3 Why do people keep domestic animals in their homes?
4 What things do we need animals for?
5 Which animals do you think are going to die out in the near future?
6 Can we live without animals?

PERSONALIZE

Unlock encourages students to bring their own knowledge, experiences and opinions to the topics. This motivates students to relate the topics to their own contexts.

DISCOVERY EDUCATION™ VIDEO

Thought-provoking videos from *Discovery Education*™ are included in every unit throughout the course to introduce topics, promote discussion and motivate learners. The videos provide a new angle on a wide range of academic subjects.

> The video was excellent! It helped with raising students' interest in the topic. It was well-structured and the language level was appropriate.
>
> Maria Agata Szczerbik,
> United Arab Emirates University,
> Al-Ain, UAE

UNL🔒CK CRITICAL THINKING

> The Critical thinking sections present a difficult area in an engaging and accessible way.
>
> Shirley Norton, London School of English, UK

BLOOM'S TAXONOMY

CREATE — create, invent, plan, compose, construct, design, imagine

decide, rate, choose, recommend, justify, assess, prioritize — EVALUATE

ANALYZE — explain, contrast, examine, identify, investigate, categorize

show, complete, use, classify, examine, illustrate, solve — APPLY

UNDERSTAND — compare, discuss, restate, predict, translate, outline

name, describe, relate, find, list, write, tell — REMEMBER

BLOOM'S TAXONOMY

The Critical Thinking sections in *Unlock* are based on Benjamin Bloom's classification of learning objectives. This ensures learners develop their **lower-** and **higher-order thinking skills**, ranging from demonstrating **knowledge** and **understanding** to in-depth **evaluation**.
The margin headings in the Critical Thinking sections highlight the exercises which develop Bloom's concepts.

LEARN TO THINK

Learners engage in **evaluative** and **analytical tasks** that are designed to ensure they do all of the thinking and information-gathering required for the end-of-unit writing task.

CRITICAL THINKING

Organizing information
Organizing information from a diagram is an important critical thinking skill.

ANALYZE

1 Look at the diagram of the two sharks and the boxes in Exercise 2. Write a sentence for each feature to explain how the sharks are similar or different.

1 Size: _____
2 Colour: _____
3 Skin pattern: _____
4 Mouth: _____
5 Fins and tail: _____

Large tropical sharks
Whale shark
tail
Tiger shark
fin
no teeth
Human

UNL⊘CK RESEARCH

THE CAMBRIDGE LEARNER CORPUS ⊘

The **Cambridge Learner Corpus** is a bank of official Cambridge English exam papers. Our exclusive access means we can use the corpus to carry out unique research and identify the most common errors learners make. That information is used to ensure the *Unlock* syllabus teaches the most **relevant language**.

THE WORDS YOU NEED

Language Development sections provide vocabulary and grammar building tasks that are further practised in the ⊘ **UNL⊘CK ONLINE** Workbook.
The glossary and end-of-unit wordlists provide definitions, pronunciation and handy summaries of all the key vocabulary.

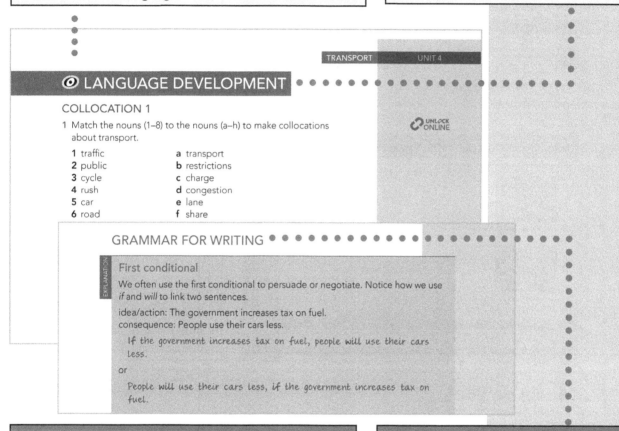

TRANSPORT   UNIT 4

⊘ LANGUAGE DEVELOPMENT

⊘ UNL⊘CK ONLINE

COLLOCATION 1

1 Match the nouns (1–8) to the nouns (a–h) to make collocations about transport.

1 traffic	**a** transport
2 public	**b** restrictions
3 cycle	**c** charge
4 rush	**d** congestion
5 car	**e** lane
6 road	**f** share

GRAMMAR FOR WRITING

EXPLANATION

First conditional

We often use the first conditional to persuade or negotiate. Notice how we use *if* and *will* to link two sentences.

idea/action: The government increases tax on fuel.
consequence: People use their cars less.

If the government increases tax on fuel, people will use their cars less.

or

People will use their cars less, if the government increases tax on fuel.

ACADEMIC LANGUAGE

Unique research using the **Cambridge English Corpus** has been carried out into academic language, in order to provide learners with relevant, academic vocabulary from the start (CEFR A1 and above). This addresses a gap in current academic vocabulary mapping and ensures learners are presented with carefully selected words they will find essential during their studies.

GRAMMAR FOR WRITING

The grammar syllabus is carefully designed to help learners become good writers of English. There is a strong focus on sentence structure, word agreement and referencing, which are important for **coherent** and **organized** academic writing.

> " The language development is clear and the strong lexical focus is positive as learners feel they make more progress when they learn more vocabulary.
>
> Colleen Wackrow,
> Princess Nourah Bint Abdulrahman University, Al-Riyadh, Kingdom of Saudi Arabia "

UNLOCK SOLUTIONS

FLEXIBLE

Unlock is available in a range of print and digital components, so teachers can mix and match according to their requirements.

UNLOCK ONLINE WORKBOOKS

The **UNLOCK ONLINE** Workbooks are accessed via activation codes packaged with the Student's Books. These **easy-to-use** workbooks provide interactive exercises, games, tasks, and further practice of the language and skills from the Student's Books in the Cambridge LMS, an engaging and modern learning environment.

CAMBRIDGE LEARNING MANAGEMENT SYSTEM (LMS)

The Cambridge LMS provides teachers with the ability to track learner progress and save valuable time thanks to automated marking functionality. Blogs, forums and other tools are also available to facilitate communication between students and teachers.

UNLOCK EBOOKS

The *Unlock* Student's Books and Teacher's Books are also available as interactive eBooks. With answers and *Discovery Education*™ videos embedded, the eBooks provide a great alternative to the printed materials.

UNL🔓CK TEACHING TIPS

1 Using video in the classroom

The *Watch and listen* sections in *Unlock* are based on documentary-style videos from Discovery Education™. Each one provides a fresh angle on the unit topic and a stimulating lead-in to the unit.

There are many different ways of using the video in class. For example, you could use the video for free note-taking practice and ask learners to compare their notes to the video script; or you could ask learners to reconstruct the voiceover or record their own commentary to the video. Try not to interrupt the first viewing of a new video, you can go back and watch sections again or explain things for struggling learners. You can also watch with the subtitles turned on when the learners have done all the listening comprehension work required of them.

See also: Goldstein, B. and Driver, P. (2014) *Language Learning with Digital Video* Cambridge University Press and the *Unlock* website www.cambridge.org/unlock for more ideas on using video in the classroom.

2 Teaching reading skills

Learners who aim to study at university will need to be comfortable dealing with long, complex texts. The reading texts in *Unlock Reading & Writing Skills* provide learners with practice obtaining meaning quickly from extensive texts. Discourage your learners from reading every word of a text line-by-line and instead focus on skimming and scanning:

- Skimming – help promote quick and efficient reading. Ask learners to pass quickly over the text to get the basic gist, an awareness of the organization of the text and the tone and intention of the writer.

- Scanning – help learners locate key data and reject irrelevant information in a text. Ask learners to run their eyes up, down and diagonally (from left to right) across the text looking for clusters of important words. Search for names, places, people, dates, quantities, lists of nouns and compound adjectives.

The reading texts in *Unlock Reading & Writing Skills* demonstrate different genres such as academic text, magazine article or learner essay.

The *Reading between the lines* sections make learners aware of the different conventions of each genre. Understanding text genre should help prepare learners for the kind of content to expect in the text they are going to read. Ask learners to use *Reading 2* as a writing frame to plan their sentences, paragraphs and essays for the *Writing task*.

3 Managing discussions in the classroom

There are opportunities for discussion throughout *Unlock Reading & Writing Skills*. The photographs and the *Unlock your knowledge* boxes on the first page of each unit provide the first discussion opportunity. Learners could be asked to guess what is happening in the photographs or predict what is going to happen, for example. Learners could investigate the *Unlock your knowledge* questions for homework in preparation for the lesson.

Throughout the rest of the unit, the heading *Discussion* indicates a set of questions which can be an opportunity for free speaking practice. Learners can use these questions to develop their ideas about the topic and gain confidence in the arguments they will put forward in the *Writing task*.

To maximise speaking practice, learners could complete the discussion sections in pairs. Monitor each pair to check they can find enough to say and help where necessary. Encourage learners to minimise their use of their own language and make notes of any error correction and feedback after the learners have finished speaking.

An alternative approach might be to ask learners to role-play discussions in the character of one of the people in the unit. This may free the learners from the responsibility to provide the correct answer and allow them to see an argument from another perspective.

4 Teaching writing skills

Learners work towards the *Writing task* throughout the unit by learning vocabulary and grammar relevant for the *Writing task*, and then by reading about the key issues involved in the topic. Learners gather, organise and evaluate this information in the *Critical thinking* section and use it to prepare the *Writing task*. By the time learners come to attempt the *Writing task*, they have done all the thinking required to be able to write. They can do the *Writing task* during class time or for homework. If your learners require exam practice, set the writing task as a timed test with a minimum word count which is similar to the exam the learners are training for and do the writing task in exam conditions. Alternatively, allow learners to work together in the class to do the writing task and then set the *Additional writing task* (see below) in the Teacher's Book as homework.

Task and Language Checklists

Encourage your learners to edit their written work by referring to the *Task checklist* and *Language checklist* at the end of the unit.

Model answers

The model answers in the Teacher's Book can be used in a number of ways:

- Photocopy the *Writing task* model answer and hand this to your learners when you feedback on their writing task. You can highlight useful areas of language and discourse structure to help the learners compose a second draft or write a response to the additional writing tasks.

- Use the model answer as a teaching aid in class. Photocopy the answer and cut it up into paragraphs, sentences or lines then ask learners to order it correctly.

- Use a marker pen to delete academic vocabulary, key words or functional grammar. Ask learners to replace the missing words or phrases. Learners can test each other by gapping their own model answers which they swap with their partner.

Additional writing tasks

There are ten *Additional writing tasks* in the Teacher's Book, one for each unit. These provide another opportunity to practice the skills and language learnt in the unit. They can be handed out to learners or carried out on the Online Workbook.

5 Teaching vocabulary

The *Wordlist* at the end of each unit includes topic vocabulary and academic vocabulary. There are many ways that you can work with the vocabulary. During the early units, encourage the learners to learn the new words by setting regular review tests. You could ask the learners to choose e.g. five words from the unit vocabulary to learn. You could later test your learners' use of the words by asking them to write a short paragraph incorporating the words they have learned.

Use the end-of-unit *Wordlists* and the *Glossary* at the back of the book to give extra spelling practice. Set spelling tests at the end of every unit or dictate sets of words from the glossary which follow spelling patterns or contain common diagraphs (like *th, ch, sh, ph, wh*) or prefixes and suffixes (like *al-, in-, -tion, -ful*). You could also dictate a definition from the Glossary in English or provide the words in your learner's own language to make spelling tests more challenging.

6 Using the Research projects with your class

There is an opportunity for students to investigate and explore the unit topic further in the *Research projects* which feature at the end of each unit in the Teacher's Books. These are optional activities which will allow your learners to work in groups (or individually) to discover more about a particular aspect of the topic, carry out a problem-solving activity or engage in a task which takes their learning outside the classroom.

Learners can make use of the Cambridge LMS tools to share their work with the teacher or with the class as a whole. See section 5 above and section 8 on page 11 for more ideas.

7 Using UNL⌀CK digital components: Online workbook and the Cambridge Learning Management System (LMS)

The Online Workbook provides:

- additional practice of the key skills and language covered in the Student's Book through interactive exercises. The **UNLOCK ONLINE** symbol next to a section or activity in the Student's Book means that there is additional practice of that language or skill in the Online Workbook. These exercises are ideal as homework.

- End-of-unit *Writng tasks* and *Additional writing tasks* from the Teacher's Books. You can ask your learners to carry out both *writing tasks* in the Writing tool in the Online Workbook for homework. Then you can mark their written work and feed back to your learners online.

- a gradebook which allows you to track your learners' progress throughout the course. This can help structure a one-to-one review with the learner or be used as a record of learning. You can also use this to help you decide what to review in class.

- games for vocabulary and language practice which are not scored in the gradebook.

The Cambridge LMS provides the following tools:

- Blogs

The class blog can be used for free writing practice to consolidate learning and share ideas. For example, you could ask each learner to post a description of their holiday (or another event linked to a topic covered in class). You could ask them to read and comment on two other learners' posts.

- Forums

The forums can be used for discussions. You could post a discussion question (taken from the next lesson) and encourage learners to post their thoughts on the question for homework.

- Wikis

In each class there is a Wiki. You can set up pages within this. The wikis are ideal for whole class project work. You can use the wiki to practice process writing and to train the students to redraft and proof-read. Try not to correct students online. Take note of common errors and use these to create a fun activity to review the language in class. See www.cambridge.org/unlock for more ideas on using these tools with your class.

> **How to access the Cambridge LMS and setup classes**
>
> Go to **www.cambridge.org/unlock** for more information for teachers on accessing and using the Cambridge LMS and Online Workbooks.

8 Using *Unlock* interactive eBooks

Unlock Reading & Writing Skills Student's Books are available as fully interactive eBooks. The content of the printed Student's book and the Student's eBook is the same. However, there will be a number of differences in the way some content appears.

If you are using the interactive eBooks on tablet devices in the classroom, you may want to consider how this affects your class structure. For example, your learners will be able to independently access the video and audio content via the eBook. This means learners could do video activities at home and class time could be optimised on discussion activities and other productive tasks. Learners can compare their responses to the answer key in their eBooks which means the teacher may need to spend less time on checking answers with the whole class, leaving more time to monitor learner progress and help individual learners.

9 Using mobile technology in the language learning classroom

By Michael Pazinas, Curriculum and assessment coordinator for the Foundation Program at the United Arab Emirates University.

The presiding learning paradigm for mobile technology in the language classroom should be to create as many meaningful learning opportunities as possible for its users. What should be at the core of this thinking is that while modern mobile technology can be a 21st century 'super-toolbox', it should be there to support a larger learning strategy. Physical and virtual learning spaces, content and pedagogy all need to be factored in before deciding on delivery and ultimately the technological tools needed.

It is with these factors in mind, that the research projects featured in this Teacher's Book aim to add elements of hands-on inquiry, collaboration, critical thinking and analysis. They have real challenges, which learners have to research and find solutions for. In an ideal world, they can become tangible, important solutions. While they are designed with groups in mind, there is nothing to stop them being used with individuals. They can be fully enriching experiences, used as starting points or simply ideas to be adapted and streamlined. When used in these ways, learner devices can become research libraries, film, art and music studios, podcast stations, marketing offices and blog creation tools.

Michael has first-hand experience of developing materials for the paperless classroom. He is the author of the Research projects which feature in the Teacher's Books.

1 ANIMALS

UNLOCK YOUR KNOWLEDGE

Lead-in

Ask learners for examples of typical weekend activities for families with small children. Elicit *a trip to the zoo* (or similar) and ask one or two of the learners for their early memories of such trips.

Learners discuss the questions in pairs. If you have a class with different nationalities, ask them to work with someone from a different region or country. If time is short, ask the learners to choose the 3 or 4 questions they find most interesting. Allow 3–5 minutes for discussion and then invite feedback from the class. Raise your hand to indicate when you would like the discussion to stop. This will allow the learners time to finish off their sentences and is less abrupt than simply asking them to stop talking. When the class is silent, ask for a summary of one pair's discussion of question 1. Invite comment from the class. Continue through to question 6. Keep the discussions brief.

Possible answers

1 Many people think it is better to see animals in the wild because they can then be appreciated in their natural habitat. However, seeing animals in a zoo means that people who cannot travel can still see animals from other parts of the world.
2 Answers will vary.
3 People keep domestic animals for companionship; some research has suggested that stroking a cat can reduce stress; dogs can help owners feel more secure when walking or living alone; pets can help children develop a sense of responsibility.
4 Many regions rely on animals for heavy work, such as pulling ploughs or transporting goods or people. Animals can provide materials such as wool, suede and leather. Animals also provide meat and dairy produce, such as milk and cheese.

5 Endangered animals include the blue whale, the giant panda, the great white shark and the white rhinoceros. Do not spend too much time on this question as it will be discussed in greater detail later in the unit.
6 A world without animals is unimaginable. The consequences for the global ecosystems, economies and societies would be severe, in many cases catastrophic.

Optional activity

As a follow-up activity, have the pairs/groups research their answers to questions 2 and 5 online to see to what extent their suggestions are correct. They could also research question 4 to see if they can find any uses not suggested by the class. This could be done in class (if internet access is available) or as a homework task.

WATCH AND LISTEN

Videoscript

SHARKS

The great white shark is known for its size. The largest sharks can grow to six metres in length and over 2,000 kilograms in weight. Great white sharks are meat-eaters and prey on large sea creatures like tuna, seals and even whales. Great whites have also been known to attack boats. This researcher is lucky to escape with his life when a shark bites into his boat. Three people are killed on average each year by great white sharks.

This is False Bay, South Africa, one of the best places in the world to see a great white. The sharks come to hunt the 60,000 seals that live here. In order to find fish, the seals have to cross the deep water of the bay – this is where the sharks wait. Great whites are expert hunters and take prey by surprise from below. They wait underneath the seals and then swim up and crash into them at 40 kilometres per hour, killing them with one bite.

These scientists are trying to find out how sharks choose what to attack. Will a shark attack something that looks like food? See how the sharks react when researchers put carpet in the shape of a seal in the water. At high speeds the shark can't tell the difference.

Can a shark choose between a plant and a fish? When scientists put tuna and seaweed in the water, the shark bites into both. Even though sharks eat meat, if a plant looks like an animal, the shark attacks.

Will a shark prefer to eat a human or a fish? When the shark has a choice between humans and tuna, it is the fish that attracts the shark's attention. Great white sharks clearly prefer fish to humans.

The research these scientists are doing shows that great white sharks are dangerous hunters which will attack anything that looks and acts like a fish. Unfortunately, that means humans can also get bitten by mistake.

PREPARING TO WATCH

USING YOUR KNOWLEDGE TO PREDICT CONTENT

1 👥 Learners discuss the questions in pairs. Allow 5 minutes for discussion and then invite feedback from the class. Don't comment on learners' answers at this point as the questions will be answered when you play the video in Exercise 2.

2 ▶ Play the video and then go through the answers with the class. Allow 10 minutes for this.

> **Answers**
> 1 The great white shark.
> 2 The largest great white sharks can grow to 6 metres in length and over 2,000 kilograms in weight.
> 3 Large sea creatures like tuna, seals and even whales.
> 4 Sharks usually attack humans by mistake.
> 5 Yes, they do sometimes.

UNDERSTANDING KEY VOCABULARY

3 👤👥 Learners work individually. Give them 3–5 minutes and then go through the answers with the class. Explain *prey* if necessary by telling the learners that mice are the prey of cats and owls and eliciting the possible prey of sharks (suggested answers will vary). Ask the learners to quickly complete the paragraph using the words in the box and to check their answers with a partner (3–5 minutes). Quickly go through the answers with the class.

> **Answers**
> 1 dangerous 2 hunters 3 attack 4 prey 5 mistake 6 fatal

WHILE WATCHING

UNDERSTANDING MAIN IDEAS

4 ▶ Before you play the video again, you could ask the learners to read the three possible topics, and to choose which topic they would

find the most interesting. Get a quick show of hands for each, then play the clip and ask the class to circle the actual topic. Allow 5 minutes for this exercise.

> **Answer** c

UNDERSTANDING DETAIL

5 ▶👤👥 Allow the learners 2 minutes to match the sentence halves either individually or with a partner (stronger learners may need less time). Play the video a second time and tell the learners to check their answers. Quickly go through the answers with the class.

> **Answers**
> 1d 2f 3a 4c 5g 6e 7b

MAKING INFERENCES

6 👥 Point out that it is important to be able to *infer* (=to form an opinion or guess that something is true because of the information that you have) answers to questions, as such answers will not always be provided explicitly. Tell the learners to answer the questions according to what they now know about sharks. Refer them to the Video script in the Student's Book, if they would like to review the information provided in the video. Give them 3 minutes to complete the activity and encourage them to discuss as many ideas as possible. Monitor the class and take notes on language use. Go through the possible answers with the class and give feedback on the language notes you took during the learners' discussions.

> **Possible answers**
> 1 The narrator says that at high speeds the shark can't tell the difference between a seal and a carpet in the shape of a seal. The narrator later says that great white sharks are dangerous hunters which will attack anything that looks and acts like a fish. From this, we can infer that perhaps the shark mistook the boat for a seal, a fish or whale.
> 2 The narrator says that in order to find fish, the seals have to cross the deep water of the bay. From this we can infer that seals risk swimming in the bay because they need to hunt for food.
> 3 The video doesn't answer this question specifically. However, given the choice, animals are more likely to eat their natural prey. As humans are not the natural prey of sharks, sharks will prefer to eat fish.

DISCUSSION

7 👥 👥👥 Ask learners to work with a different partner and give them 1 minute to discuss questions 1 and 2. Elicit ideas from the class. Then ask the pairs to join with another pair and give them a further 2 minutes to discuss question 3 in small groups. Elicit ideas from the class.

> **Possible answers**
>
> 1 There are 60 shark attacks reported each year, mainly in warm water, so how much we should worry depends on where we are swimming.
> 2 Great white sharks are now rarer than tigers, with only 3,500 left, so perhaps they should be protected.
> 3 Research into animal behaviour is useful to prevent cruelty to animals and to monitor population size to see whether they are endangered. Studying animals for medical research helps the development of human medicine.

READING 1

PREPARING TO READ

USING YOUR KNOWLEDGE TO PREDICT CONTENT

> **Optional lead-in**
>
> On the board, write the words *China* and *Oman*, with plenty of space between each. Write the word *oryx* next to *Oman* and connect the two words with a short line. Do the same with the words *Chinese alligator* and *China*. Ask the class if anyone has heard of either of these animals. It is unlikely that many (if any) will have. Ask the class why so few people have heard of these animals (=possibly because they are endangered, and therefore extremely rare).

1 👤 Ask the learners to complete the first column of the table with all the endangered animals they can think of. Then ask them to complete the second column with the names of all the extinct animals that they can think of. Go through the answers with the class. Where there is uncertainty as to whether an animal is either endangered or extinct, note the name of the animal in question. You could ask the learners to check online as a homework research task, using English language websites.

> **Possible answers**
>
> Endangered animals: blue whale, giant panda, Chinese alligator, great white shark, Indian elephant, white rhinoceros, Arabian oryx, sea turtle
> Extinct animals: *Tyrannosaurus rex*, woolly mammoth, dodo, Caspian tiger, sabre tooth tiger, woolly rhinoceros, Asiatic lion, Arabian ostrich

2 👤 Tell the learners to quickly scan the factsheet and give them a strict time limit of 90 seconds to add any animals that they have not already included in the table. Go through the answers with the class.

> **Answers**
>
> Oryx, seals, tigers, crocodiles, whales, tuna, sharks

WHILE READING

READING FOR MAIN IDEAS

3 👤 With a strong class you could ask learners to decide on the best order for the ideas before they read the text. Then tell them to quickly read the text and to match the main ideas with the paragraphs in which they are mentioned. Set a time limit of 1 minute, and tell them that they need only match the ideas to the paragraphs; they do not need to understand everything at this stage. Go through the answers with the class. Encourage discussion on any differences between learners' initial suggestions and the actual order of the paragraphs.

> **Answers**
>
> 1C 2A 3D 4B

> **Reading for the main ideas**
>
> Ask the learners to read the box. Then ask them how many main ideas there should be in each paragraph and where we would normally find them.

READING FOR DETAIL

4 👤 👥 Tell the learners that they only need to decide in which paragraphs they would find the answers. They do not need to find the actual answers yet. Tell them to do this task individually, and then to check their answers with a partner. Set a time limit of 3 minutes (2 minutes for a stronger class).

> **Answers**
>
> 1A 2B 3C 4C 5D 6D 7D

5 Learners read the factsheet again and find the answers individually. Allow 4–5 minutes for them to complete the task. Then check the answers quickly with the whole class.

Answers

1 Humans.
2 Their habitats are destroyed.
3 For food, for fur to make coats, and skin to make bags and shoes, for sport, to make medicines and teas from their bones.
4 Whales, tuna and sharks.
5 We can take care not to pollute natural areas and refuse to buy any products which are made from animals' body parts.
6 Governments can make it against the law to hunt, fish or trade in endangered species.
7 They can provide funding for animal sanctuaries and zoos where endangered animals can be bred and then released back into the wild.

READING BETWEEN THE LINES

WORKING OUT MEANING FROM CONTEXT

6 Ask the learners what they do if they can't understand a word when they are reading a text in English. Elicit ideas from the class. Point out that working out meaning from context is an essential skill, and is one of the ways we learn not only a second language, but also our first. This may also be an important skill to develop when it comes to preparing for an end of course exam. Tell the learners to read the last paragraph of the factsheet and to underline the words and phrases that mean the same as the words in bold. Do the first sentence with the class. Then tell the learners to do the rest individually and to check their answers in pairs. Allow 5 minutes in total for this activity.

Answers

1 face a financial penalty 2 refusing to buy 3 against the law
4 provide funding for 5 cooperate by taking these steps

DISCUSSION

7 Learners work in pairs or small groups. If possible, have them work with a new partner. Allow 2–3 minutes for the discussion. Elicit answers from two or three pairs/small groups and encourage class discussion of question 2.

Answers will vary.

Optional activity

Ask the learners to find out what their own local or national governments are doing to conserve animal habitats. Is this seen as a controversial issue?

READING 2

PREPARING TO READ

USING VISUALS TO PREDICT CONTENT

Optional lead-in

Ask learners to close their books. Draw a quick outline of the British Isles (=a group of islands off the coast of northwestern Europe that include the islands of Great Britain, Ireland and over six thousand smaller islands). Elicit the names of the five countries in your map on the board Scotland, Northern Ireland, Ireland, Wales, England.

Background note: The United Kingdom or The British Isles?

There is often confusion about these two names. Some people use England, the United Kingdom and Great Britain synonymously but this is incorrect. Great Britain (GB) comprises Scotland, England and Wales. The United Kingdom (UK) comprises Great Britain and Northern Ireland. The term *British Isles* is a purely geographical term.

1 Allow learners 5 minutes to complete the task in pairs. Quickly elicit some ideas from the class but do not spend too much time at this stage to avoid pre-empting the work which follows.

Answers

1 squirrels 2 and 3 Answers will vary.

WHILE READING

SKIMMING

2 Ask the class to skim the article and find 3 reasons why the red squirrel is losing the battle for survival.

Answers

Red squirrels are smaller and weaker than grey squirrels. The parapox virus is fatal to red squirrels. They are affected by the loss of their natural woodland habitat.

READING FOR MAIN IDEAS

3 👤 Remind learners that at this stage they do not need to understand all the words in the text. They only need to find the answers to the 3 questions. Allow them 3–4 minutes to complete the task individually (stronger classes may be able to complete this in under 2 minutes). Go through the answers quickly with the class. Ask the class what type of text it is, and elicit the term *article*. Tell the learners to pay close attention to the structure of the texts throughout the course. It would be useful for them to note down, or highlight, useful chunks of language as they work with these texts. The language can then by adapted for use in the learners' own essays.

Answers

1 Fewer than 140,000.
2 The grey squirrel.
3 Grey squirrels are larger and therefore stronger. They live on the ground so they are not so badly affected by loss of habitat, they use food provided by humans and they are not killed by the parapox virus.

READING FOR DETAIL

Language note

You might want to tell your learners that we can talk in general about a subject in two ways:

1 Grey squirrels are more common than red squirrels. (Using the plural noun and no article.)
2 The grey squirrel is more common than the red squirrel. (Using the singular noun and the definite article.)

1 is more informal and conversational than 2, which is more academic and often written rather than spoken.

4 👤👥 Learners read the text again and complete the summary individually or in pairs (this should take about 3 minutes). With stronger classes, tell the learners to complete the summary first and then to check their answers against the text. Go through the answers quickly with the class.

Answers

1 grey 2 fewer 3 pest 4 fatter 5 able 6 kills 7 Few 8 aren't

READING BETWEEN THE LINES

MAKING INFERENCES FROM THE TEXT

5 👤👥 Elicit the meaning of *inference*, reminding the learners that they first encountered the term in Exercise 6, page 17. Learners answer the questions individually, referring back to the text as necessary, and check their answers with a partner (4–6 minutes in total). Go through the answers with the class.

Possible answers

1 Because they damage trees, they eat humans' waste food and they carry a virus that kills red squirrels.
2 Red squirrels.
3 Perhaps for nostalgic reasons, because they see them as traditionally 'British'.
4 Because they are islands, and the sea acts as a natural defence against alien species.

DISCUSSION

6 👥 Learners discuss question 1 in pairs (2 minutes). Get a quick show of hands for each of the three options. Then ask if anyone thinks that Britain shouldn't bother trying to save red squirrels (if anyone agrees with this idea, find out why). Put the learners into groups of 4 and ask them to discuss questions 2 and 3. Conduct a class feedback session and encourage learners to give examples of similar problems in either their own country or in another country.

Answers will vary.

Optional activity

With stronger groups you might want to introduce other terms similar to *introduced animal species* such as *non-indigenous species* and *invasive species* (though these do not only refer to those that have been deliberately introduced). Such plants and animals threaten native wildlife by competing with them for the same ecosystem.

Background note: Introduced species

Introduced species are often successful because they have no natural predators. Examples of introduced animal species that have caused problems include: the American signal crayfish (in the UK), the cane toad (in Florida, USA), the dromedary camel (in Australia) and the common raccoon (in Germany and France). For a more complete *list of introduced species*, type list of introduced species into your search engine.

◉ LANGUAGE DEVELOPMENT

ACADEMIC ADJECTIVES 1

1 👤 Give learners 2–3 minutes to complete the exercise individually and to check their answers in pairs. Go through the answers quickly with the class. Then ask learners in pairs to try using some of the adjectives in a sentence (e.g. *The red squirrel is now endangered in the UK, because the grey squirrel is so aggressive*). Allow a maximum of 2 minutes. Then elicit some ideas from the class. Give feedback as appropriate.

Answers
1d 2g 3b 4a 5c 6e 7f

Comparative adjectives

Ask learners to read the box. If you have a strong class, you could ask them what form of the adjective is used if there are more than 2 things (we use the superlative form).

Language note

As the table shows, one-syllable adjectives normally have comparatives ending in -er, e.g. *tall/taller*. Some two-syllable adjectives also take -er in their comparative form, especially adjectives that end with an unstressed vowel, e.g. *clever/cleverer*. Two syllable adjectives ending in -y have -ier e.g. *happy/happier*.

With many two-syllable adjectives, both -er and *more* are possible. However, the structure *more* is now more common than -er. You could ask your learners to research current common usage by looking for examples of two-syllable adjectives in news websites. Other websites may also be useful for this task, but the constantly updating nature of news websites makes them an excellent source of information on how language is used today. Online corpora can also be useful for such tasks. You can find online corpora by typing *English corpus* into your search engine.

2 👤👥 Tell the learners to complete the task individually. Allow enough time for most of the class to complete the task. Then tell them to check their answers with a partner. Go through the answers with the class. Challenge the class to complete this exercise in under 2 minutes.

one-syllable adjective	two- (or more) syllable adjective	two-syllable adjective ending with -y
adjective + -er + than	*more* + adjective + *than*	adjective + -ier + *than*
2 smaller than	4 more common than 5 more endangered than 6 more aggressive than	8 healthier than

3 👤👥 Tell the learners to complete the sentences using comparative forms from the table, either individually or in pairs (4–5 minutes).

Possible answers

1 The red squirrel is smaller and weaker than the grey squirrel.
2 Grey squirrels are generally healthier than their smaller cousins because they are not affected by the parapox virus.
3 Great white sharks are more endangered than tiger sharks, which are not at risk of extinction.
4 Whale sharks are less aggressive than tiger sharks and do not attack humans.

CRITICAL THINKING

At this point in each unit learners are asked to begin to think about the Writing task they will do at the end of the unit (2 comparison paragraphs, *Compare and contrast the two sharks in the diagram*). Give them a minute to read the box and to look at the diagram below it.

ANALYZE

Organizing information

Ask learners to read the box and point out that texts are not the only source of information. Organizing information from a diagram is an important critical thinking skill. Tell the learners that they will be writing formal sentences, paragraphs and essays throughout the course.

1 👤👥 This exercise is designed to prepare learners for the Writing task at the end of the unit. Tell them to complete the exercise individually (7–10 minutes), and to compare their sentences with a partner (3–5 minutes). They should make any corrections necessary. Elicit 5 sentences from the class, inviting alternative suggestions and giving feedback as appropriate.

Possible answers

1 The whale shark is larger than the tiger shark.
2 Both sharks have the same grey colour and a lighter underside.
3 The tiger shark has stripes on its back and the whale shark has dots.
4 The whale shark has a larger mouth but the tiger shark has many sharp teeth.
5 The whale shark has a longer tail and wider fins but the fin on the back of a tiger shark is larger in relation to its body size.

EVALUATE

2 👤 Give the learners 4–5 minutes to complete the task individually. Quickly check through the answers with the class.

Answers

1 the tiger shark 2 the whale shark 3 the tiger shark 4 the whale shark 5 the tiger shark 6 the tiger shark 7 The tiger shark eats human-sized animals only but the whale shark eats very small animals so it will not mistake humans for its normal prey.

WRITING

GRAMMAR FOR WRITING

Word order

👤👥 Tell the learners to read the box and to compare the usual word order in English with that of their first language. Ask them to compare their ideas with a partner, and to discuss any typical word order errors that people learning their first language(s) sometimes make.

1 👤👥 Learners complete the exercise individually (7–10 minutes) and check their answers with a partner. Go through the answers carefully with the class.

Answers

subject	verb		prepositional phrase	
1 The tiger shark	doesn't hunt		in fresh water.	
linker	**subject**	**verb**	**adjective**	
2 However,	the whale shark	isn't	aggressive.	
subject	**verb**	**object**	**prepositional phrase**	
3 The tiger shark	has	markings	on its skin.	
subject	**verb**	**object**	**verb**	**object**
4 The whale shark	has	a large mouth and	eats	plankton

Optional activity

If it seems that further practice is needed, tell the learners to choose 5 sentences from the earlier texts and to label the different parts of grammar.

Using *and, or, but* and *whereas*

Tell the learners to read the box and point out that joining sentences is an important feature of academic writing in many languages, not just English. You could ask them to discuss any differences in use between *and, or, but* and *whereas*. with a partner. If you have access to the internet, they could go to a news website, or any other website you know of that has good examples of contemporary usage, and ask them to search for instances of *and, but* and *whereas* online. You could then ask them to work in pairs, to try to identify any general patterns and be ready to discuss their ideas with the class.

Language note

Depending on the level of the group, it may be easier at this stage to simply say that the word *whereas* is more formal than *but*. However, with a stronger group you might want to say that *whereas* is used to balance two ideas that contrast, but which do not contradict each other. It is a fairly formal word, and has a high frequency in academic and other formal texts. *But* is often used to join two clauses in a similar way to *whereas*. However, the clause following *but* often contains a surprising contrast. Compare the two sentences:

The red squirrel is under threat, whereas the grey squirrel is thriving.

The red squirrel is much loved in the UK, but has been known to attack humans.

2 👤👥 Give learners 5 minutes to complete the task individually. They should then compare their ideas with a partner. Go through the answers carefully with the class, giving further support where necessary (see Language note above).

Answers

1 a Has two positive sentences.
  b The two positive sentences have been joined with *and*.
  c The sentences have been joined with *and* and the unnecessary repeated subject (the tiger shark) and verb have been removed.
2 *And* joins two positive sentences. *Or* joins two negative sentences.

3 👤👥 Learners complete the exercise individually and compare their ideas with a partner. Allow up to 5 minutes for this task, including the pairwork discussion. Go through the answers quickly with the class.

Answers

1 The whale shark is light blue and has dots on its body.
2 The tiger shark is dark blue and has a stripe pattern on its body.
3 The tiger shark eats large sea creatures and is dangerous to humans.
4 The whale shark is not aggressive or dangerous to swim with.
5 The tiger shark is not an endangered or protected species.
6 The whale shark is an endangered species and protected from fishing.

4 👤👥 Tell the learners to read the example sentence and to notice the use of *whereas*. Then ask them to replace *whereas* with *but*, and elicit ideas about possible differences in nuance. If necessary go back over the information in the language box above. Once learners are clear about the differences, ask them to complete the exercise individually using *whereas* or *but* (4–5 minutes). If you highlighted the difference between *but* and *whereas* in the box above, as learners complete the task, ask them to find examples where either word could be used, as well as examples where only one of the words sounds correct. Learners then discuss their ideas in pairs. Go through the possible answers together, allowing time to discuss any differences in nuance when using *whereas* or *but* in any of the sentences.

Possible answers

The whale shark is light blue and has dots on its body whereas the tiger shark is dark blue and has a stripe pattern on its body.
The tiger shark eats large sea creatures and is dangerous to humans but the whale shark is not aggressive or dangerous to swim with.
The tiger shark is not an endangered or protected species whereas the whale shark is an endangered species and is protected from fishing.

Using *both* and *neither*

Ask the learners to read the box and ask questions to check that they have understood the concept and the form.
Does the grey squirrel carry the parapox virus? (Yes)
Does the red squirrel carry the parapox virus? (Yes)
So - *Both the red squirrel and the grey squirrel carry the parapox virus.*
Is the grey squirrel found in the far north of Scotland? (No)
Is the red squirrel found in the far north of Scotland? (No)
So - *Neither the grey squirrel nor the red (squirrel) are found in the far north of Scotland.*

5 👤👥 Learners complete the exercise individually or in pairs (allow 3 minutes). Monitor their work as they complete the sentences, clearing up any confusion. Go through the answers with the class.

Possible answers

1 Both the red (squirrel) and the grey squirrel have long tails. OR Both red (squirrels) and grey squirrels have long tails.
2 Neither the red (squirrel) nor the grey squirrel live on the Isle of Man. OR Neither red (squirrels) nor grey squirrels live on the Isle of Man.
3 Neither species of squirrel are meat-eaters. OR Neither red (squirrels) nor grey squirrels are meat-eaters.
4 Neither the grey nor the red squirrel is an endangered species.
5 Both species of squirrel live in forests. OR Both red (squirrels) and grey squirrels live in forests.

Optional activity

Ask the learners to each write down two sentences, one using *neither* and one using *both*. Elicit examples and lead a discussion on the differences between the two. Then ask them to check their ideas against the Using *neither* and *both* language box.

ACADEMIC WRITING SKILLS

Punctuation

Ask learners to read the box and emphasize that punctuation is an extremely important part of writing clear, efficient texts. Ask questions to check that they have understood the concepts. Use this as an opportunity to clear up any confusion concerning the use of full stops, capital letters and commas. Be aware that their use may be very different in the learners' first language, so there may be some interference from the learners' first and other languages. For more information on interference from learners' other languages, as well as lots of useful examples and teaching tips, see *Learner English: A Teacher's Guide to Interference and Other Problems (2nd Edition)* (CUP 2001).

Optional lead-in

Ask the learners to close their books, and have or write the first sentence from Exercise 1 on the board (=*however the whale shark has to be protected in countries in asia like the philippines because it is so slow and easy to catch*). Put the learners into small groups and ask them to punctuate the sentence. Ask the groups if any of them are 100% certain that they have the correct punctuation. If one of the groups is certain, invite one person in that group to correct the sentence on the board. Ask the class if any of the groups have punctuated the sentence differently and lead a discussion on any difficulties learners have with punctuation (this could also be done in small groups if learners are reluctant to discuss problems they have with punctuation). Then ask the learners to read the Punctuation box again and to check how they punctuated the sentence. Make sure the sentence on the board is correctly punctuated. Then ask the learners to do the remaining sentences in small groups. Allow 5 minutes for the learners to complete and discuss the remaining sentences.

1 ⚊ Learners work individually. Monitor their work and offer help where necessary. Then go through the answers with the class, writing each sentence on the board as you go through them. Allow 10–15 minutes for this.

Answers
1 However, the whale shark has to be protected in countries in Asia like the Philippines because it is so slow and easy to catch.
2 The whale shark is a large, slow-moving fish with wide fins, a long tail and huge mouth.
3 This gentle giant is not dangerous to humans, and divers can swim with it, touch it and even ride on its back fin.

4 It does this by ram feeding, which means it swims fast to force water and animals into its mouth.
5 It uses this mouth to eat very small plants and animals like krill, plankton and algae.

Paragraph structure

Tell the learners to read the box, and stress how important clear paragraph structure is in written English. As will be discussed in later units, each paragraph should begin with a clear topic sentence, which is then developed with examples and illustrations. There should only be **one** main idea per paragraph. This is fundamental to academic writing, but is something that learners find difficult if it is not addressed at paragraph level before they are required to write complete essays.

2 ⚊ Learners complete the exercise individually. Quickly go through the answer with the class.

Answers
2, 5, 4, 3, 1

WRITING TASK

WRITE A FIRST DRAFT

1 ⚊ Ask the learners to read the introduction and conclusion of the essay *Compare and contrast the two sharks in the diagram*. They then use their notes from the Critical thinking and Writing sections above to complete the first draft of the 2 supporting paragraphs. Allow up to 20 minutes for this first stage.

EDIT

2 & 3 ⚊⚊ Learners work individually to check the content and structure of their work against the Task checklist and make any changes necessary. Monitor and help with any problems. Allow up to 10 minutes. If the class is comfortable with peer reviews, tell them that they will be checking each other's work once they have checked their own, so they must make sure it is as good as it can be before passing it on to a partner to review. Then ask them to swap their work with a partner and review each other's work. They should amend their work as necessary before going on to the next stage. Allow 10–15 minutes for the peer review, depending on the level of the class.

4 & 5 👤 Learners do the same with the Language checklist and make any changes necessary. Again monitor and help with any problems. If there is time and if you think it will be helpful, ask them to peer review their work. Allow 10–15 minutes, depending on the level of the class.

As this is the first full essay the learners write, it is important to allow them to work steadily and at their own pace. Inevitably, some learners will finish this task sooner than others. Have some useful supplementary work available.

Answers

Model answer: see page 133 of the Teacher's Book

OBJECTIVES REVIEW

See Introduction, page 9 for ideas about using the Objectives review with your learners.

WORDLIST

See Introduction, page 9 for ideas about how to make the most of the Wordists with your learners.

REVIEW TEST

See page 97 for the photocopiable Review test for this unit and page 93 for ideas about when and how to administer the Review test.

RESEARCH PROJECT

Educate people about endangered species in your region.

Divide the class into groups and ask them to research these questions:

1 What endangered animals are there in their part of the world?

2 Why are they endangered? How can we help them?

3 Why are animals important to us?

Learners should make a documentary film to answer the questions. Learners should include footage of endangered species, and overlay the footage with their answers to the questions.

2 CUSTOMS AND TRADITIONS

Learning objectives

Before you start the Unlock your knowledge section ask the learners to read the Learning objectives box so that they have a clear idea of what they are going to learn in this unit. Tell them that you will come back to these objectives at the end of the unit when they review what they have learned. Give them the opportunity to ask you any questions they might have.

UNLOCK YOUR KNOWLEDGE

Lead-in

Find out from the class which learner has had the most recent birthday by asking these questions: *Is it anyone's birthday today? Have any of you had a birthday this week? Who has had a birthday recently?* If appropriate, ask the learner with the most recent birthday if they did anything to celebrate: *What did you do to celebrate?* Then ask the class *Who will be the next learner to celebrate a birthday? What will you do to celebrate?* Finally tell the learners to *Find one person whose birthday is nearest to yours and sit with that person.*

Background note: Name days and birthdays

Useful information on the celebration of name days, birthdays and official birthdays (e.g. Britain's Queen Elizabeth II has both an official birthday and an actual birthday) can be found by going to your search engine and typing in *birthday*.

1 👥 Ask the learners to discuss question 1 in pairs. Allow up to 2 minutes for discussion. Then elicit ideas from the class. Ask the learners to work in pairs and discuss questions 2 and 3. Encourage them to discuss their own experiences of birthdays and other celebrations. Give them 3 minutes to discuss the questions.

> **Answers**
> 1 a wedding in Japan 2 and 3 Answers will vary.

WATCH AND LISTEN

Background note

The term *cultural awareness* is often used in English language teaching to describe the process of sensitizing our learners to the impact that behaviour resulting from socialization into a particular culture has on language use and communication. It is useful for learners to be aware not only of English-speaking cultures, but also of the cultures of other groups with whom they may use English as a lingua franca, as well as their own cultures. Cross-cultural interaction when using English as a lingua franca is a rapidly developing area of research. While it is important to avoid clichés and stereotypes when discussing foreign cultures, it is probably true to say that we all exhibit evidence of culturally-conditioned behaviour. Awareness of this can help our learners better understand the influence that cultural attitudes towards, for example, work, art, social class, age and sex can have on the ways in which people communicate.

Videoscript

CUSTOMS AND TRADITIONS

Dagestan is a land of towering mountains, rushing rivers and ancient stone villages. Dagestan is an amazing mix of ethnic and cultural diversity. About thirty-five separate groups live side by side in this republic, which is the size of Scotland or the UAE.

Dagestan is the southernmost region of the Russian Federation, where the people speak an amazing 12 languages. Traditions are respected all over Dagestan, and particularly in the rural areas, where little has changed for generations.

These women are making traditional Dagestani carpets. Everything is done by hand, with designs that are hundreds of years old. All the materials are local, from the wool used to make thread to the dyes made from local roots and vegetables. The carpets are sold around the world and can be seen in many major museums.

Respecting the elderly members of the community is very important in Dagestani culture. Older people are local leaders in the special system of family networks in Dagestan.

The population is growing fast in Dagestan. People have large families.

Even though many Dagestanis now live outside the country, it is common for people to return to their family home when they get older. Most Dagestanis say they would like to be buried in their home village in the mountains, as their families have been for hundreds of years.

PREPARING TO WATCH

USING VISUALS TO PREDICT CONTENT

1 👥 Ask the learners to discuss question 1 in pairs. Encourage them to go into some detail by asking *Why do you think that? What clues are there? Where else might it be?* Elicit suggestions from the class. Then ask the learners to discuss the other 4 questions in their pairs. Again, encourage them to go into detail. Allow 4 minutes for discussion. Then elicit 2 or 3 ideas for each question but don't give the correct answers yet as the learners check their work in Exercise 2.

2 ▶ Play the video and ask the learners to check their answers. Then ask the class to try to agree on the best description of the topic.

> **Answers**
>
> 1 1 Dagestan 2 a rural area 3 a traditional region 4 carpet making, agriculture 5 extended families
> 2 c

WHILE WATCHING

UNDERSTANDING MAIN IDEAS

3 ▶ 👤👥 Before you play the video again you could ask the learners to work individually and put the ideas in the order in which they remember hearing them. Then ask them to check their answers with a partner and to try to agree on the order. Play the video again and ask the class to check their first answers with a partner and to make any changes necessary. Go through the answers with the class. Allow 10 minutes (including the third viewing).

> **Answers**
>
> 1b languages 2e traditional industry 3d family networks 4f marriage 5g migration

UNDERSTANDING DETAIL

4 ▶ 👤👥 Ask the learners to read sentence 1 and tell you if it is correct or not (=no, Dagestan is the same size as Scotland). Tell them that each of the statements contains a factual mistake. Ask the learners to correct the statements individually and to check their answers with a partner. Then play the video

a final time and ask the class to check their answers. Go through the answers quickly with the class. Allow up to 10 minutes, including a final viewing of the video.

> **Answers**
>
> 1 Dagestan is the same size as Scotland.
> 2 Dagestan is in the Russian Federation.
> 3 12 languages are spoken in the region.
> 4 Carpet-making is done by hand.
> 5 Older people are local leaders.
> 6 The population of Dagestan is growing.
> 7 Dagestanis want to be buried in their home village in the mountains.

LISTENING FOR KEY INFORMATION

5 👥 Ask the class to close their books and tell you what they can remember about carpet-making in Dagestan. Elicit suggestions and write any key vocabulary that comes up on the board. Then ask the learners to do Exercise 6 in pairs. Go through the answers quickly with the class. If necessary, play the video again. However, beware of playing it too often with stronger classes. Allow up to 5 minutes (up to 10 minutes if playing the video again).

> **Answers**
>
> a traditional c local e wool f thread g vegetables i museums

MAKING INFERENCES

6 👥 Learners discuss the questions in pairs. Allow 2 minutes for discussion. Then quickly go through the answers with the class.

> **Possible answers**
>
> 1 Perhaps because they are handmade and the designs haven't changed over the centuries.
> 2 More jobs are available in Russia and Ukraine than in Dagestan.

DISCUSSION

7 Learners discuss the questions in pairs. If possible, try to have learners sitting either with someone from a different country or region, or with someone who has spent a fair amount of time in a different country or region. Allow up to 5 minutes. Then lead a class feedback session.

READING 1

Background note

Most cultures have some form of wedding ceremony in which two people commit to remain faithful to each other for life. One of the most common forms of such a commitment is marriage, which in most cultures involves the uniting of one woman with one man. Other examples of similar institutions include the civil partnership, which in some countries is available to couples of the same sex. Marriages and civil partnerships are usually intended to be life-long partnerships, and can only be ended on death, dissolution (i.e. divorce) and annulment, which is when the marriage is deemed not to have ever existed.

One famous example of an annulment was the English King Henry VIII's 1527 appeal to the Pope for an annulment of his marriage with Catherine of Aragon on the grounds that the marriage was against the biblical prohibition of a union between a man and his brother's widow (Catherine had been married to Henry's elder brother, Arthur, who had died). This was refused, leading to the English Reformation. On 23 May 1533, five months after Henry married Anne Boleyn, his earlier marriage was annulled by the Archbishop of Canterbury.

If you think it would be appropriate, you could ask the class about any famous historical marriages or divorces in their countries.

PREPARING TO READ

Optional lead-in

Tell the class to imagine that a foreign student is coming to spend a several months in their country. The student wants to avoid making any cultural gaffes (=embarrassing mistakes) when meeting new people. What should the student know that would help them make a good impression?

SCANNING TO PREDICT CONTENT

1 👤 Learners work individually. Challenge them to find all the words in under a minute. Remind them that they need not read and understand the text; all they need do at this stage is to find the words in the box.

2 👤👥 Learners work individually and then check their answers with a partner. Go through the answers with the class. Allow 5 minutes for this. Challenge the learners to do the task in under 5 minutes if possible, and to let you know when they have found all of the answers.

Answers

1 Japan and India 2 Brazil and India and sometimes in Japan 3 Brazil 4 Japan 5 India

WHILE READING

READING FOR MAIN IDEAS

3 👤👥 Learners complete the task individually and then check their answers with a partner. Allow 5 minutes for this exercise. Again, you could challenge the learners to do the task in under 5 minutes if possible, and to let you know when they have found the answers.

Answer e table manners

Optional activity

👥 If you have a mix of nationalities in your class or if many of your learners have lived in different countries, you could divide the class into small groups and assign each group a country from the reading (Brazil, Japan or India). Ask the groups to discuss differences and similarities between their own cultures and what they have read about the target culture. Give them 3–5 minutes discussion time and then ask each group to report back. Finish by asking the class if they know anything else about the three cultures represented in the text, e.g. *What else do you know about Brazilians?*

READING FOR DETAIL

4 👤👥 Learners complete the exercise individually and then check their answers with a partner. Quickly go through the answers with the class.

Answers

1d 2a 3g 4f 5c 6e 7b

Reading for detail

Ask learners to read the box. You could ask them to tell you about times when they have looked for key words in texts in English or in their own languages.

READING BETWEEN THE LINES

MAKING INFERENCES FROM THE TEXT

5 👥👥 Learners discuss the questions in pairs or small groups. Allow up to 5 minutes for discussion. Encourage the learners to discuss

the questions in depth and to think of possible examples, using the text as a starting point, e.g. *Why might it be useful for a foreigner to know that Indians do not like to say 'no'?* Go through the answers with the class, eliciting any examples that the learners may have discussed.

Answers

1 It may look as if you are paying or bribing them.
2 It may make them feel their action is inappropriate.
3 So they know if you are the boss and how much respect to show you.
4 In case they upset or annoy you.
5 To show respect to your hosts and to impress clients in a business situation.

DISCUSSION

6 👥 👥👥 Learners discuss the questions in pairs or small groups. Allow 3–5 minutes for discussion. Finish off by asking the group what people should know about the customs of the country in which the class is taking place so if you are teaching in Oman, for example, ask the class what foreigners should know about Omani customs.

Answers will vary.

READING 2

PREPARING TO READ

UNDERSTANDING KEY VOCABULARY

1 👤👥 Learners complete the exercise individually and check their answers with a partner. With very strong groups, tell the class to cover the definitions on the right and to go through the 7 words with a partner to see how many they can define. They should then compare their ideas with the definitions on the right, and complete the task.

Answers

1f 2d 3h 4b 5i 6a 7c 8e 9g

PREVIEWING

2 👥 Learners discuss the questions with a partner. Set a strict time limit of 1 minute. Then quickly elicit ideas from the class. Avoid commenting on any of the ideas at this stage,

as the learners will read the text to find the answers for themselves in Exercise 3.

3 👤 Learners read the text and check their answers. Tell the learners to focus on the answers to the 3 questions in Exercise 2. Remind them that they do not need to understand all the words at this stage.

Answers

1 The average age of people who get married in the UK is about 30.
2 About a hundred guests are invited.
3 Yes, attitudes to marriage are changing and they have been changing over the last 20–30 years.

WHILE READING

SKIMMING

4 👤 Tell the learners to tick (✓) the best description from what they can remember of the text. You could then ask them to quickly read through the text a second time and check their answer. You could also turn this in to a competitive game by telling the learners to raise their hands as soon as they are sure they know the answer.

Answer a

READING FOR DETAIL

5 👤 Learners correct the factual mistakes individually. They could then check their answers with a partner. With a stronger group, tell the learners to correct the sentences with page 40 covered. They should then check their answers by reading the text again. Allow up to 5 minutes for this task. Then go through the answers quickly with the class.

Possible answers

1 Weddings in the UK are expensive and take a long time to organize.
2 Most people get married at about 30.
3 All couples have to sign a marriage certificate.
4 Divorced men and women cannot always remarry in a church.
5 When a couple get engaged, the man gives the woman a ring.
6 The bride's father gives his daughter away and the bridesmaids help her with her dress.
7 After the wedding ceremony, the guests give wedding presents for the couple's new home.
8 Nowadays, the couple's parents pay for the reception and the couple pay for everything else.

READING BETWEEN THE LINES

UNDERSTANDING DISCOURSE

6 👤👥 Tell the class to quickly find the number 16 in the text and to read the sentence in which it is written. Then tell them to look at question 1 and to tell you to what the word *this* refers in the sentence they have just read (=the age of [legal] marriage). Then tell them to do the rest of the questions individually and to check their answers with a partner.

> ### Answers
> 1 the age of (legal) marriage
> 2 a marriage certificate
> 3 the remarriage of divorced men and women
> 4 getting engaged

DISCUSSION

7 👥 Learners discuss the questions in pairs or small groups. Encourage them to discuss their personal experiences of any weddings they have attended. How different were these weddings from each other, or from the weddings they have just read about? Allow 5 minutes for discussion, taking notes on the language you hear as the learners share their ideas. Elicit some example answers from the class and give feedback on the language you noted during the discussions.

> ### Answers will vary.

⊙ LANGUAGE DEVELOPMENT

Avoiding generalizations

Ask the learners to read the box. While they read you might like to write on the board the following quote from Alexandre Dumas, the French dramatist and novelist (1802-1870): 'All generalizations are dangerous, even this one.' This clever little quote neatly illustrates the problem with generalizations, and will give your learners something to think about as they work on improving their written English! Tell learners that if they make broad generalizations and skip over details that should be included in their work, this can give the impression that they have not put in the thought and research necessary to form, support and explain their ideas. If your learners are unused to academic writing, either in English or in their first language, this needs to be highlighted. Generalizations can significantly reduce the quality of their work, and are likely to leave a negative impression on the reader.

The Student's Book gives some useful tips on avoiding generalizations. If you think that your learners could benefit from more work on avoiding generalizations, you can find information online by typing *avoiding generalizations in academic English* into your search engine.

1 👤👥 Learners rewrite the 5 sentences individually and then compare their answers in pairs. Allow 4 minutes for the task. Then go through the answers with the class.

> ### Answers
> 1 We tend to tip the waiter in restaurants.
> 2 Weddings tend to be less common these days.
> 3 Birthdays can be important.
> 4 Blowing your nose in public can be rude in Japan.
> 5 Shaking hands tends to be how most people greet you in India.

Adverbs of frequency

Ask the learners to read the box. They should be familiar with frequency adverbs but the position of them with the verb *be* can cause problems.

Adverbs of frequency tell us how often something happens and as the box illustrates, they can be used to help avoid generalizations (e.g. *sometimes, often, rarely*). However, remind learners that they can also be used to make generalizations, rather than to avoid them (e.g. *always, never*).

Compare the following examples:

1 You **always** say that!

2 You **often** say that!

The first example is clearly not literally true, and is an example of an adverb of frequency being used to make a generalization. The second example is probably more accurate, and the adverb of frequency makes the sentence less general and closer to the truth.

2 👤👥 Learners rewrite the 5 sentences individually and compare their answers in pairs. Allow 4 minutes for the task. Then go through the answers with the class.

> ### Answers
> 1 The bride's family usually pays for the wedding.
> 2 People often go for picnics in the countryside at weekends.
> 3 Professionals can sometimes get upset if you don't use their correct title.
> 4 Cultural knowledge is frequently important in business situations.
> 5 It is usually best to arrive on time for an appointment.

ACADEMIC ADJECTIVES 2

Academic adjectives

In academic language, it is important to write clearly and use appropriate adjectives. For example, the sentence *Illiteracy is a **serious** problem in this country* is more likely to be found in an academic text than *Illiteracy is a **bad** problem in this country*. Exercise 3 helps illustrate the differences between words that would be found in an academic text and their more colloquial equivalents.

3 👤👥 Learners rewrite the 7 sentences individually and compare their answers in pairs. Allow 5 minutes for the task and then go through the answers with the class.

Answers

1 brief 2 serious 3 separate 4 certain 5 important
6 obvious 7 common

Optional activity

👥 Ask the learners in small groups to think about cultural stereotypes and to discuss positive and negative things that people say about the British (e.g. that they are polite, that they have bad teeth). Allow 2 or 3 minutes for discussion and then elicit ideas from the class. Write some of the examples on the board, and ask the class whether these statements are true of all British people. Elicit ways that the statements can be made more accurate, e.g. *The British are polite* could become one of the following: *People say that the British are polite*; *The British are seen as being polite*; *People in Britain have a reputation for politeness, but sometimes they can seem a little cold.*

You can personalize this task by asking the learners to discuss positive and negative things that people say about people from their own country.

CRITICAL THINKING

Give the learners a minute to read the Writing task they will do at the end of the unit (3 descriptive paragraphs, *Describe the laws and traditions concerning weddings in your country. Have there been any changes in recent years?*) and keep it in mind as they do the next exercises.

ANALYZE

1 👤👥 Learners complete the task individually and then compare their answers in pairs. Go through the answers with the class. Allow 10 minutes for the whole task.

Answers

1 16 with parental permission, 18 without parental permission 2 about 30 3 marriage certificate
4 registry office or church 5 father (for permission)
6 ring 7 100 8 the bride's father 9 the groom's father 10 the groom's surname 11 hotel
12 a meal 13 speeches 14 honeymoon

2 👥 Learners read the last paragraph of Reading 2 on page 40 and discuss in pairs what has changed. Allow 2 minutes for the reading and discussion. Then do a brief class feedback.

Answers

The way people propose has changed. It is now old-fashioned for the groom to ask the bride's father for permission to marry his daughter, and sometimes the woman will ask the man to marry her, rather than the man asking the woman.
The locations have changed. People may marry in many different places, e.g. at a town hall or a hotel or even a on tropical beach. Who pays for the wedding has also changed. These days the couple pay most of the costs.
It is now quite common for married women to keep their maiden name rather than taking the husband's surname.

Optional activity

This activity is particularly suited to younger learners who may not have given marriage much thought. It will also help prepare weaker learners for the Writing task. Tell the learners to read the Writing task (*Describe the laws and traditions concerning weddings in your country. Have there been any changes in recent years?*) again and in pairs or small groups to discuss the ideas that could go into the 3 descriptive paragraphs. Give them 5–10 minutes to discuss their ideas and to take notes. Tell them that they do not need to write full sentences but they should rather focus on the more general ideas, vocabulary and short phrases that could go into the final writing task.

You could also do this as a pyramid task. Once the pairs or small groups have discussed their ideas and taken notes, put each pair/group together with another pair/group and ask them to compare their ideas. If appropriate (e.g. if the class is big enough, or if more fluency practice is needed) repeat this stage. Then lead a class discussion, inviting ideas from each group.

APPLY

3 👥 Learners work in pairs and discuss weddings in their countries. They then add notes in the 3rd column (Your country) of the table.

4 👥👥 Learners circle in a different colour in column 3 the customs and traditions in their countries that have changed recently. You could then ask them to say how things have changed.

WRITING

GRAMMAR FOR WRITING

Optional lead-in

👥 👥👥 Find two texts on the same topic. The topic need not necessarily be weddings. You could try to find another topic that will also engage your learners. Both texts should be correctly written. However, one should be rather dull, the other more interesting. Give the learners the two texts to read and discuss in pairs or groups of 3, but do not tell them where you got the texts from or who the intended audience is. Instead, ask them to discuss which text is more interesting, and why. Tell them to go into as much detail as possible when analyzing and comparing the two texts. Allow 5 minutes for discussion. Then lead a class feedback session noting down the differences in style. Do not comment too much at this stage, as the next task will cover some of the ideas your learners are likely to have identified.

Adding detail for interest

Ask the learners to read the box. If you did the Optional
lead-in above, remind them about why they found one text more interesting than the other. Was it to do with the amount of detail?

1 👤👥 Learners complete the task individually. Then ask them to compare their answers in pairs. Allow 2 minutes for the task. Then go through the answers with the class.

> ### Answers
> 1e 2d 3b 4c 5a

2 👤 Do the first sentence with the class. Then ask the learners to complete the next 2 sentences individually and compare their answers in pairs. Allow 2 minutes for the task and then go through the answers with the class. As more than one answer may be possible, elicit any alternative suggestions that the learners may have. Give feedback as appropriate, commenting on how likely/correct the alternative suggestions are.

Possible answers

1 After the ceremony, there is often a large wedding reception with hundreds of guests.
2 The man may give an expensive diamond ring to his fiancée to show they are engaged.
3 At the reception, the guests usually bring wrapped wedding gifts for the bride and groom.

ACADEMIC WRITING SKILLS

Essay structure

Ask the learners to read the box. You might want to go into more detail about the structure and purpose of each of the parts of an essay. An essay should have an introduction, a number of main body paragraphs (often 3) and a conclusion. The introduction should begin with an interesting sentence to introduce the topic, and should include a clear thesis statement that outlines what the writer will argue or express in the essay. Each main body paragraph should start with a topic sentence that contains one main idea. The rest of the paragraph should then support or argue against that idea using illustrations and examples. The final paragraph is the conclusion, which should briefly restate the main ideas of the body paragraphs and then restate the thesis statement. The essay should end with an appropriate final sentence, for example a prediction based on what has been discussed in the essay. However, the conclusion should not introduce any new arguments used to support the initial thesis statement.

1 👤 Tell the learners to read the essay question and model introduction and answer the question.

> ### Answers
> 1 the law concerning marriage 2 typical wedding customs and traditions 3 how weddings have changed in recent years

2 👤👥 Learners complete the task individually (15–20 minutes) and compare their answers in pairs, making any amendments that might be necessary (5–10 minutes).

WRITING TASK

WRITE A FIRST DRAFT

1 👤👥 Learners use their notes from the Critical thinking and Writing sections above to write the 3 paragraphs for their essay *Describe the laws and traditions concerning weddings in your country. Have there been any changes in recent years?* Monitor and help with any problems. Allow 10–15 minutes for this.

EDIT

2 & 3 👤👥 Learners work individually to check the content and structure of their work against the Task checklist and make any changes necessary. Monitor and help with any problems. Allow up to 10 minutes. If there is time and if you think it will be helpful, ask them to peer review their work.

4 & 5 👤 Learners do the same with the Language checklist and make any changes necessary. Again monitor and help with any problems. If there is time and if you think it will be helpful, ask them to peer review their work. Allow up to 10 minutes including the peer review. Have something ready for those learners who finish early.

Optional activity

Learners could complete the task for homework. If the learners write their essays on a computer, encourage them to use an English language spelling and grammar checker to proofread the first draft. If the task is done as a homework task, tell the learners to keep a copy of the first draft and then to work through the task and language checklists before writing a second draft. If possible, the learners should email their essays to you in e.g. Word/Pages format so that you can give feedback using track changes and comments. Extensive feedback is extremely useful at this stage. Once the learners have received useful feedback from the teacher for one or two essays, their essay writing skills will soon start to improve.

Answers

Model answer: see page 134 of the Teacher's Book

OBJECTIVES REVIEW

See Introduction, page 9 for ideas about using the Objectives review with your learners.

WORDLIST

See Introduction, page 9 for ideas about how to make the most of the Wordlists with your learners.

REVIEW TEST

See page 101 for the photocopiable Review test for this unit and page 93 for ideas about when and how to administer the Review test.

RESEARCH PROJECT

Find a way to share different cultural traditions within your country.

Divide the class into groups asking them to think about their own cultural traditions. They can list and discuss them. Then ask them to think of other minority groups of people within their country and to research, compare and contrast the traditions of these other cultures.

Learners could interview people from other countries in their educational environment or use video conferencing to interview people from other cultures outside their country. Classes can create a slideshow presentation about the people they have researched.

HISTORY

Learning objectives

Before you start the Unlock your knowledge section ask the learners to read the Learning objectives box so that they have a clear idea of what they are going to learn in this unit. Tell them that you will come back to these objectives at the end of the unit when they review what they have learned. Give them the opportunity to ask you any questions they might have.

UNLOCK YOUR KNOWLEDGE

Lead-in (1)

👥 👥👥 Have a slide with the following words ready (or write them on the board): *a tennis ball, a mobile phone, an electric guitar, a Roman coin, a newspaper from last year, a Coca-Cola bottle, a dinosaur bone, a dress once worn by Princess Diana, a CD.* Ask the learners which ones they would expect to find in a museum, and why. This can also be done as a pair or group work activity followed by a class feedback session. Point out to learners that although museums are often associated with ancient artefacts (such as the Roman coin in the list above), there are so many different types of museums that good arguments could be made for finding all of the above items in one museum or another. As an extension, you could encourage the learners to discuss the type of museum in which the items in the list would be found, and whether or not they would be interested in visiting such a museum.

Lead-in (2)

For a shorter warmer, simply ask the class what is the strangest/oldest/most valuable/smallest/biggest etc. thing they have ever seen in a museum. Elicit a few ideas from the class, encouraging discussion.

👥 👥👥 Learners discuss the questions in pairs or small groups. Monitor to check that they are using correct language, giving feedback during or after the task as appropriate. Allow 5 minutes for the task and then lead a class feedback session.

> Answers will vary.

WATCH AND LISTEN

Videoscript

ARCHAEOLOGY

Wonderful artwork, ancient writing, and huge stone monuments. These are the remains of ancient Egyptian civilization which have amazed the world for centuries.

Egyptology was born in 1799, when the ancient Egyptian writing system – hieroglyphics – was first translated. Today, the archaeological season in Egypt starts in October, when a small number of archaeologists are allowed to start excavations. It is illegal to excavate or remove artefacts without permission, and security is tight.

These are the tombs of the ancient kings of Egypt. Down the dark passages, there are many clues about ancient Egyptian society. Complicated rituals surrounded death, and fantastic treasure was buried for use in the afterlife. Hidden underground, these painted tombs and fragile artefacts have been preserved by the dry air of the desert.

Before any discoveries can be made, there is always a large amount of earth and sand to move first. In the ancient city of Thebes, a team of archaeologists work to remove the sand that has hidden a tomb for two and a half thousand years. It is a time-consuming task but the site is so delicate, heavy machinery is not allowed and the earth must be moved by hand.

On the other side of the river Nile, in the Valley of the Kings, another team of archaeologists use the latest X-ray equipment to examine a mummy. The equipment can show the age, gender and cause of death of the mummy without damaging the fragile remains. The excavation is examined very closely. Every new artefact must be carefully recorded and nothing can be moved until it is photographed and preserved by experts. Every year, archaeologists continue to look for more evidence of this advanced culture under the hot Egyptian sun.

PREPARING TO WATCH

USING VISUALS TO PREDICT CONTENT

1 You could write the following phrases on the board: *The first one...; I'm pretty sure that...; I think that's...; That has to be...; That's obviously...; The one on the right could be...*.

Then ask the learners to look at the photos from the video. Elicit possible answers to the 3 questions from the class. Encourage class discussion and speculation on the possible answers. Allow 3–5 minutes before going on to Exercise 2.

Answers

1 The Valley of the Kings in Luxor, Egypt
2 They are doing archaeology: excavating and cataloguing archaeological finds.
3 Many people are interested in ancient Egypt because there are many remains, which are extremely old and very well preserved.

UNDERSTANDING KEY VOCABULARY

2 Learners complete the sentences individually and then compare their ideas with a partner. Allow
3 minutes (including the pair work) and then quickly check the answers with the class.

Answers

1 hieroglyphics 2 archaeologist 3 remains 4 tomb
5 excavation 6 artefact

WHILE WATCHING

UNDERSTANDING MAIN IDEAS

3 Tell the class to close their books. Say that you are going to play a short video and ask them what they think will be included. Elicit ideas. Then tell them to open their books and compare what was just discussed with the main ideas listed in Exercise 3. Play the video and tell the learners to number the main ideas (a–f) in the order in which they hear them. Allow 10 minutes for this exercise.

Answers

1a the archaeological season
2e excavation on the site
3c ancient Egyptian kings
4f the Valley of the kings
5d modern X-ray equipment
6b examining and recording

4 Learners match the sentence halves and then check their ideas with a partner. Play the video a second time and ask the learners to check their answers. Then go through the answers quickly with the class. Allow 5 minutes for this exercise.

Answers

1c 2e 3d 4a 5f 6b

MAKING INFERENCES

5 Give the learners 5 minutes to discuss the questions in pairs or small groups. Invite ideas from each group, but tell the groups they need only add any points that have not yet already been made. This will avoid repetition and keep things more interesting and less predictable for the rest of the class.

Possible answers

1 It is autumn so it is then cool enough to begin work in the desert.
2 The artefacts and ruins are very delicate.
3 Thieves steal from archaeological sites.
4 A lot of information can be found by studying an object where it was buried. This information might be lost or the artefact might fall apart if it was removed before it had been recorded, photographed, and preserved.

DISCUSSION

6 Learners work in pairs, ideally with people they have not worked with before. Then do feedback with the class. Allow up to 5 minutes for discussion or less if you feel discussion is drying up.

Possible answers

1 Answers will vary. If learners are slow coming up with ideas, ask them to do some research for homework. If Internet access is available, a list of historical sites can be found by typing *world heritage* into your search engine.
2 Historical sites have great educational value. They can often give people a more vivid experience of former cultures than is possible from books or the Internet. Such sites are also important tourist attractions, and can benefit both a country's reputation and its economy.

READING 1

PREPARING TO READ

USING YOUR KNOWLEDGE TO PREDICT CONTENT

1 Put the learners into new pairs or small groups to keep things fresh. Give them 3–5 minutes to discuss the questions. Encourage them to use examples from their own experience if possible.

> **Possible answers**
>
> 1 Science museums, maritime museums, natural history museums, military museums, open-air museums, zoos, art galleries
> 2 Museums inspire and stimulate young minds and help children learn together in an informal environment.
> 3 Hands-on activities, audio-visual and interactive exhibits, actors in historical costumes and play areas make museums fun.

UNDERSTANDING KEY VOCABULARY

2 🧍 🧑‍🤝‍🧑 You could tell the learners not to look at the definitions (1–9) yet but just to look at the words and to put a tick next to the words they know, a cross next to the words they don't know and a question mark next to the words they can guess. Once they have considered the words, they should go through them with one or two other people and try to turn all of the crosses and question marks into ticks. They should then check their answers by matching the words in the box with the definitions. Do a quick class feedback. Alternatively just ask the learners to work individually and then check the answers with the class.

> **Answers**
>
> 1 fossils 2 archaeology 3 exhibit 4 natural history 5 exhibition 6 ancient 7 field 8 knight 9 sword

WHILE READING

SCANNING TO FIND INFORMATION

3 🧍 Learners complete the task individually. This is a scanning activity, so stress that they do not need to read or understand every word. Set a limit of 60–90 seconds, depending on the level of the group. Quickly go through the answers with the class.

> **Answers**
>
> 1B 2C 3D 4A

4 Elicit ideas from the class.

> **Answers**
>
> The museums produced the brochures to advertise their exhibitions and services to the public.

SKIMMING

5 🧍 🧑‍🤝‍🧑 Learners complete the task individually and check their answers with a partner. If they disagree on any of the answers, tell them to show each other the part of the text in which that answer can be found. Allow 5–10 minutes to complete the task, including pair discussion. Then go through the answers with the class.

> **Answers**
>
> 1B 2C 3D 4A 5C 6D 7A

READING FOR DETAIL

6 🧍 🧑‍🤝‍🧑 Learners complete the task individually and check their answers with a partner. With stronger groups, tell the learners to answer the questions from memory first and then to read through the texts again to check their answers. Then go through the answers quickly with the class. Allow 3–5 minutes, depending on the level of the group.

> **Answers**
>
> 1c 2c 3a 4b

READING BETWEEN THE LINES

IDENTIFYING PURPOSE AND AUDIENCE

7 🧑‍🤝‍🧑 👥 Encourage the learners to discuss the merits of each possible answer. They should then choose one answer for each question, based on their understanding of the text. This can be done either as pair work or in small groups. Allow 5 minutes for discussion. Then go through the answers quickly with the class.

> **Answers**
>
> 1a 2c 3b 4c

> ### Identifying purpose and audience
>
> Ask learners to read the box. With a stronger class you might want to expand on this and tell learners that the writer-reader relationship is a two-way relationship. Writers must consider why they are writing a particular text, and who the likely readers will be. Readers must try to think about the writer's purpose in writing that text. A basic empathy between writer and reader will help the reader get more out of a text, and will also help the reader when it comes to understanding difficult vocabulary and sentence structures. Once the reader has some appreciation

of what the writer's intentions were, the reader will be probably be prepared to invest more in trying to understand a text and as a result will find the reading process much more rewarding. Questions that help learners identify the writer's purpose include:

1 Read the title. Why do you think the writer wrote this text?

2 What is the writer's point of view? Why did the writer adopt this point of view?

3 Did the writer explicitly state his/her purpose?

4 Did the writer achieve his/her purpose? How effective was the text?

5 Was the writer able to influence your response to the text? How?

6 Which examples from the text best support your ideas about the writer's purpose?

Optional activity

Remind the class that a writer will always have a purpose for writing. Ask them what the author's purpose was in the following situations:

1 You have read an article, and enjoyed reading it very much.

2 You have read an article and have learned something from it.

3 You have read an article and as a result have changed your opinion about the topic.

The author's purpose may have been to 1 entertain, 2 inform/educate, 3 persuade/influence. You could point out that a writer will often have more than one purpose in writing, e.g. to educate and persuade; to entertain, educate and persuade.

DISCUSSION

8 👥 Learners discuss the questions in pairs or small groups. Encourage them to share their experiences. If appropriate, ask them to discuss the worst/most boring/most pointless museum they have visited, as well as their more positive experiences. Lead a quick class feedback session. Try to call on learners who were discussing any particularly entertaining stories during the pair/group work stage. Allow up to 5 minutes for the task.

| Answers will vary.

READING 2

PREPARING TO READ

UNDERSTANDING KEY VOCABULARY

1 👤👥 Learners complete the exercise alone and check their answers with a partner. Alternatively, they could use the same procedure as outlined in Understanding key vocabulary Exercise 2 (page 30 above). Quickly go through the answers with the class.

Answers

1 tuition 2 ongoing discussion 3 compulsory 4 less obvious 5 economic benefits 6 knowledgeable 7 beyond

WHILE READING

SCANNING TO FIND INFORMATION

2 👤 Tell the learners to quickly scan through the essay on page 58 and count the number of times the word *should* appears in each paragraph. Tell them to raise their hands as soon as they are sure they have the correct number of *shoulds*. Wait until two or three learners have finished, then elicit the number of *shoulds* in each paragraph from the first learner to have their hand up. Ask the other learners if this is the correct number. If yes, go on to question 2. If no, elicit the correct number from the class. Then ask them to tell you what they think the answer to question 2 is but avoid commenting on their answers yet. Allow 5–10 minutes for questions 1 and 2 and a further 5–10 minutes for the reading and follow up discussion with the whole class of question 3. Ask learners to justify their answers. This text is quite a personal piece of writing rather than an objective academic text. Point out to the learners that there are times when a more personal approach is appropriate (e.g. in a blog or in a newspaper column), and times when a more objective approach is preferred (e.g. in an academic essay or paper to be published in an academic journal). You could ask the learners to scan the text for examples of subjective, personal writing (examples include *it seems to me*; *we should*; *I would say*).

Answers

1 Paragraph A: 3 Paragraph B: 1 Paragraph C: 1
Paragraph D: 1
2 The writer thinks we should teach History.

3 👤👥 Learners work individually and then compare their answers with a partner. Go through the answers with the class.

Answers

1C 2D 3B 4A

READING FOR DETAIL

4 👤👥 Learners complete the chart individually and check their answers with a partner. Go through the answers quickly with the class. Allow 5 minutes including the feedback.

Answers

1 We should focus on Maths and English.
2 Science benefits the economy.
3 This knowledge creates better citizens.
4 Pupils learn about culture.
5 Pupils improve reading and writing skills.

5 Do this as a class discussion. The writer includes more reasons in favour of teaching History than against because he/she supports the teaching of History and wants to strengthen the case by putting forward more arguments that support his/her opinion.

READING BETWEEN THE LINES

MAKING INFERENCES FROM THE TEXT

6 👤👥 Ask the learners to read through the 5 claims. From memory, they should quickly decide on whether the writer would agree or disagree with each. They should then check their answers against the essay, underline the sections that support them and discuss their answers briefly with a partner. Allow 5 minutes for the task.

Answers

1 disagree 2 agree 3 disagree 4 agree 5 disagree

Optional activity

👥👥 Put each pair of learners together with another pair and ask them to discuss their thoughts on the 5 statements. This could also be done as a pair work activity, but it is good for the learners to

take part occasionally in slightly larger discussions. Allow 5–10 minutes for the task and then ask each group to report back on their ideas to the class.

DISCUSSION

7 👥👥 Learners discuss the 2 questions in pairs or small groups. Allow 3–5 minutes.

Answers will vary.

Background note

Your learners might be interested to know that in 2012, the most popular subjects at UK universities were Law, Design, Psychology, Business Management, Computer Science, English, Medicine and Social Science.

Optional activity

👤 As a research task, learners could choose two or three UK universities and find out what subjects they offer. Which subjects seem to be the most popular? Are there any differences in the subjects offered in the UK and those offered in the learners' country?

⊙ LANGUAGE DEVELOPMENT

ACADEMIC VOCABULARY

1 👤👥 Learners complete the 5 pairs of sentences individually and then check their answers with a partner. Go through the answers with the class. You could point out that *research*, *document* and *display* can all be used as both nouns and verbs. Challenge the learners to try and finish this exercise in under 3 minutes.

Answers

1 research 2 financial 3 document 4 period 5 display

Making suggestions

Tell the learners to read the box and be prepared to deal with the grammar of *should* + infinitive without *to*, adjective + infinitive with *to* and –*ing* forms as nouns. Point out that when used to make suggestions, *should* and *ought to* are very similar:
- History **should** be taught in schools.
- History **ought to** be taught in schools.

Both terms can be used to make suggestions, and can usually replace each other. You could ask the class to look at the 3 different ways to make suggestions in academic essays and to tell you which one they think is the most objective (=the least influenced by personal feelings or opinions) and which is the least. Point out that when writing in most academic contexts, it is important to remain as objective as possible. Of the different ways outlined in the box, *Teaching History in schools is a good idea* is probably the least objective, and *It is important to teach History in schools* is probably the most objective.

You could point out that *must* has a similar meaning to *should* and *ought to*, but is much stronger. It expresses the idea that something is absolutely necessary, rather than simply a very good idea or strong suggestion. You could give these sentences as examples and elicit the difference in meaning:

- *History **should/ought to** be taught in schools.*
- *History **must** be taught in schools.*

In an academic context, the example using *must* seems much more subjective than the example using *should/ought to*.

Making suggestions in academic essays

With a stronger group, you could present some alternative ways of making suggestions in academic English. You could also point out that while *should* is quite common in essays written at school and in English language exams, such as IELTS, later on in their academic careers learners will need to consider ways of writing in a more objective style. *Should* suggests a value judgment, which can detract from the objectivity of an essay, in favour of a more subjective approach. Compare the following:

- *History is of crucial importance and should be taught in schools.* (=the writer's personal, subjective opinion).
- *History is of crucial importance. Evidence suggests that children who study History beyond the age of 14 are better able to articulate their opinions, have a stronger sense of cultural identity and achieve better in other research based courses.* (=the writer's opinion supported by research).

Other ways to make suggestions in academic essays include:

One way to *deal with this issue would be to...;* **Another way to** *address this problem is to...;* **This can be solved by...;* **The evidence strongly suggests that...**

2 👤 Allow up to 5 minutes for learners to do this exercise and then go through the answers with the class.

Answers

1 a It is important to pay to visit museums.
   b Paying to visit museums is a good idea.
2 a It is important to protect ancient objects from theft.
   b Protecting ancient objects from theft is a good idea.
3 a It is important to learn from past mistakes.
   b Learning from past mistakes is a good idea.

3 👤 Ask the learners to do this exercise alone. Allow 3–5 minutes, depending on the level, then go through the answers with the class.

Answers

1 it is important 2 is a good idea 3 we should 4 it is important 5 we should 6 it is important

Optional activity

As a research task, you could ask the class to find examples of academic essays and note down other ways that writers can introduce suggestions. Examples of academic writing can be found on the Internet, and *Google Scholar* is a good collection of essays and other examples of academic writing. You can also find *Cambridge Language IELTS sample candidate writing scripts and examiner comments* online, another useful source for both learners and teachers.

CRITICAL THINKING

Optional lead-in

Give each learner two pieces of card/paper, one green and one red, about 5cm x 5cm. Ask the learners to read the Writing task in the box, and to consider the arguments that they have read so far, both for and against. Ask those who agree that museums should be free to hold up the green card. Quickly count the number who agree that museums should be free. Then ask those who think that we should have to pay for museums to hold up the red card. Quickly count the learners and then elicit reasons from both sides. Avoid too much comment at this stage as the arguments will be considered in more depth in the next exercises.

Give the learners a minute to read the Writing task they will do at the end of the unit (a balanced opinion essay, *Should museums be free or should visitors pay for admission? Discuss.*) and keep it in mind as they do the next exercises.

Organizing ideas

Ask the learners to read the box. Tell them that it is very important for ideas to be well organized in an academic essay, otherwise the writing will appear unstructured and difficult to follow. You could also point out that it is worth taking a few minutes at the start of a written exam to draft a quick outline of the essay, including details on which arguments will go where.

ANALYZE

Optional lead-in

Elicit ideas from the learners as to where they might be able to find arguments for and against the topic of the Writing task. If few ideas are suggested, ask the learners to discuss their ideas in pairs and then elicit ideas from the class.

Some possible answers are:

Essays on the subject (it is often possible to find good examples of academic essays through your search engine); newspaper opinion columns; news websites; museum websites; transcripts of parliamentary debates.

1 👤 Tell the learners to read the opinions a–f and to decide which people think that museums should be free, and which people think that visitors should pay for admission. Allow 1 minute for this task, then go through the answers with the class.

Answers

1 People should pay to visit a museum.
2 Museums should be free.
3 People should pay to visit a museum.
4 Museums should be free.

EVALUATE

2 👤👥 Tell the learners to complete the table with the opinions from Exercise 1 and then to check their answers with a partner. Allow up to 5 minutes for this. If some learners finish early, ask them to discuss which arguments they think are strongest, and why, with a partner. Quickly invite feedback on this after first going through the answers to Exercise 2 with the class.

Answers

b The public should help pay for the staff, security and building costs.
c It makes History so much more interesting than reading about it in a book.
d The state should keep its treasures safe from theft and maintained in good condition.

WRITING

GRAMMAR FOR WRITING

Stating opinions

Ask the learners to read the box. Point out that these notes apply to a more personal style of writing, such as that required in some English language exams, rather than the more formal style that would be suitable for an academic essay.

1 👤👥 Go through the first example with the class. Then ask the learners to complete the exercise alone and check their answers with a partner. Allow 5–10 minutes, depending on the level of the class, and then go through the possible answers with the class. When discussing the suggested answers, point out that many variations are possible. Invite alternative suggestions from the class and give feedback as appropriate.

Possible answers

2 A number of people suggest that museums should make people pay for entry.
3 It seems to me that it would be better to teach foreign languages instead of History.
4 Some people feel that students should be made to learn History.
5 I would say that we need to make museums more interesting for young people.

Linking contrasting sentences

Ask the learners to read the box. While it is important for learners to vary their language to avoid repetition, be wary of modelling clichéd language. Point out that phrases such as *but, however* and *although* are all common in written English. However, more idiomatic phrases such as *on the other hand* can sound predictable if used too often in the same text. The construction *On the one hand ... on the other hand* is best avoided altogether. To show contrast with the previous sentence or idea, it is enough simply to use *On the other hand* as a synonym for *However* at the start of a sentence.

2 👤👥 This is a very useful language awareness exercise that encourages learners to notice patterns so try to do such tasks as often as possible and make sure you allow enough time for the learners to benefit from them. Tell the learners to study the 5 sentences on their own and to notice any patterns. If necessary, go through the first 2 sentences with the class so that the learners understand exactly what they have to do. Then ask them to go through the remaining 3 sentences alone and to compare their ideas with a partner. Go through the answers carefully with the class. Keep a record of what they have problems with.

Answers
1 no comma
2 a comma before the linking word *although*
3 a full stop before the linking word and a comma after it
4 a full stop before the linking phrase and a comma after it
5 a capital letter for the linking word at the start of the sentence and a comma after the first part of the statement

Optional activity
Punctuation can cause difficulties at this level, especially if the learners' first language has a very different system, so you could ask learners to look for examples of formal writing online and notice the punctuation patterns. Tell them to bring any useful examples of language they have found to the next class. This will give you time to prepare some more detailed exercises that address the learners' specific needs based on the notes you made of their problems with Exercise 2. It will also give the learners further valuable noticing practice. Allow 5–15 minutes on this, depending on how detailed the post-task class feedback session is. You can find examples of academic writing by typing *academic papers* into your search engine.

Optional lead-in
Tell the learners to close their books. Write the example sentence 1 on the board (*Museums are free but they cost a lot of money to maintain*). Ask the learners to rewrite the sentence using the word *although*. Give them enough time to do this. Then ask them to open their books and compare what they wrote with the example in Exercise 3.

3 🔍👥👥 Learners work individually to rewrite the sentences. Point out that more than one answer is possible. Allow 3–5 minutes, and then ask them to compare their ideas with a partner. Go through the answers quickly with the class, eliciting alternative suggestions and giving feedback as appropriate.

Answers
2 Although museums are free to allow all children to visit them, many children never go to one/a museum.
3 Although it is a good idea for governments to pay for museums, there are many other more important things that a government should spend its money on.

4 Although some museums may be quite boring for children, nowadays many of them are very interactive.
5 Although museums are great places for schools to visit, sometimes they are very expensive.

ACADEMIC WRITING SKILLS

Writing an introduction
Tell the learners to read the box and to find out what a thesis statement is.

Elicit from the class the importance of the thesis statement in an essay. If the class is struggling, ask the following questions to help them understand the function of the thesis statement:

1 Where is the thesis statement in the learner essay? (= in the introduction)

2 Does the thesis statement tell you what the writer thinks? (=yes)

3 Does the thesis statement tell you what the writer's conclusion is? (=yes)

4 Does the thesis statement tell you why the writer came to that conclusion? (=yes)

5 Is the thesis statement a vague, general sentence or a detailed and specific sentence? (=detailed and specific)

Once you are sure that the learners understand exactly what a thesis statement is, go on to the Exercise 1.

1 🔍 Ask the learners to do the exercise quickly, alone. Remind them of the importance of a clear thesis statement in formal and academic writing. Set a strict time limit of 2 minutes, 90 seconds for a stronger group, and then go through the answers with the class.

Answers
a2i b3ii c1iii

2 Elicit the answer from the class.

Answer
a2i

WRITING TASK

WRITE A FIRST DRAFT

1 🔍 Learners use their notes from the Critical thinking and Writing sections above to write their essay *Should museums be free or should visitors pay for admission? Discuss.* By this stage, they will have had the opportunity to rehearse their ideas and to study the structure

of the essay. Give them 5 minutes to write the Introduction from page 66, and 15–20 minutes to write the 2 main paragraphs. Monitor the class carefully, and when it seems that most people have finished or are finishing, give them 2 minutes more to complete the paragraphs. Ask those learners who have finished to check that the paragraphs have clear topic sentences that are then developed further, and make sure their work leads in to it well.

EDIT

2 & 3 👤👥 Learners work individually to check the content and structure of their work against the Task checklist and make any changes necessary. Monitor and help with any problems. Allow up to 10 minutes. If there is time and if you think it will be helpful, ask them to peer review their work.

4 & 5 Learners do the same with the Language checklist and make any changes necessary. Again monitor and help with any problems. If there is time and if you think it will be helpful, ask them to peer review their work. Allow up to 10 minutes including the peer review. Have something ready for those learners who finish early (e.g. part of the Review test for this unit on page 91 or the Additional writing task for this unit on page 119).

Optional approach to the Writing task

👤 In earlier units, learners have been encouraged to give each other feedback on their writing task before writing the final draft. Now might be a good time to find out what each learner is capable of when working alone. Rather than guiding the learners through Exercises 1–5 in class, you could present the Writing task (Exercises 1–5) in one of the following three ways:

1 Semi-exam conditions Set a time limit of 45 minutes for learners to complete Exercises 1–5 on their own with no further resources. Then tell them to hand their essays in for correction (or email them to you if they have written the essays using a computer). If using email, tell the learners to save the essay using the following filename: *Surname_First name_Museums_essay* and to write *Museums essay* in the subject line of the email.

2 Open learning Set a time limit of 45–60 minutes, and allow the learners to use whatever resources they have available (e.g. dictionaries, grammar books, the Internet etc.). They should then submit the essays for correction as above.

---

3 Homework task Tell the learners that they can decide whether to set themselves the challenge of writing the essay under semi-exam conditions, or whether they would like the support of a dictionary, the Internet and their class notes etc.

Answer

Model answer: see page 135 of the Teacher's Book

OBJECTIVES REVIEW

See Introduction, page 9 for ideas about using the Objectives review with your learners.

WORDLIST

See Introduction, page 9 for ideas about how to make the most of the Wordlists with your learners.

REVIEW TEST

See page 105 for the photocopiable Review test for this unit and page 93 for ideas about when and how to administer the Review test.

RESEARCH PROJECT

Recreate a scene from local history.

Explain to your learners that they are going to research a period of local history. Ask them to find out about the people of the time including trade, government, traditions and culture, food, clothing, household objects, technology, education and health.

With this information, learners may want to create a museum exhibition with information, food or historical artifacts with descriptions. They can supplement this with posters, websites and informative videos.

4 TRANSPORT

UNLOCK YOUR KNOWLEDGE

Lead-in

Ask the class how they usually get to school. Write the different forms of transport mentioned on the board, e.g. on foot (walking), by bike, by bus, by car etc.

1 👥 Learners work in pairs and brainstorm modes of transport. You could ask them to think about private and public transport. Do a quick feedback with the class. Allow 3–5 minutes.

> **Possible answers**
>
> **Air:** plane, helicopter, seaplane, glider, microlight;
> **Sea:** rowing boat, ferry, motorboat, yacht, canoe, ship;
> **Land (private):** car, motorbike, bicycle, scooter, lorry;
> **Land (public):** bus, train, underground (train), coach, tram, trolleybus

Optional activity

👥 An alternative approach to Exercise 1 would be to tell the learners in pairs to write down as many forms of transport as they can in 90 seconds. Tell them that they will get one point for each form of transport that no one else thinks of. The winning team is the pair with the most points. Ask the first pair to read their list slowly, and ask the class to call out if they have written down the same form of transport. Award points for any forms of transport no one else has thought of, e.g. a helicopter, a skateboard, a space shuttle etc. Repeat this procedure with each pair. Ask the learners to total their scores and declare one pair the winner. This activity should take around 5 minutes.

2 👤👥 Learners answer the questions individually or in pairs. Do feedback with the class. You could find out which mode of transport is the most popular.

Background note: Underground trains

You might point out that the London Underground train system is also called *The Tube*, the Paris underground system is called *The Metro*, as are other underground systems in various parts of the world, and New York underground train system is usually referred to as *The Subway* (in British English, a *subway* is a passage under a road or railway for people to walk through).

Optional activity

👥 Ask the learners to work in small groups and discuss any modes of transport that they would never use, and why? For example, I would never travel in a submarine because I don't like the idea of being underwater. Quickly elicit ideas from each group.

WATCH AND LISTEN

Videoscript

INDIAN TRANSPORT

For a country with a population of 1.2 billion, there are only 13 million cars in India. Some traditional forms of transport have been in use in India for centuries. Water taxis take thousands of passengers along the river Ganges every day. The wooden boats they use are handed from father to son, and the boatmen repair them themselves.

Ox carts have been traditionally used for transport, especially in rural India. In recent years, some cities have banned the movement of ox carts and other slow-moving vehicles on the main roads because of traffic problems.

Bicycles are a common mode of travel in much of India. More people can now afford to own a bicycle than ever before. In 2005, more than 40% of Indian households owned a bicycle. But for long journeys, public transport is essential and India's public transport systems are among the most heavily used in the world.

Railways were first introduced to India in 1853. By 1947, there were forty-two rail systems. In 1951, the systems were nationalized as one unit, becoming one of the largest networks in the world. With 65,000 kilometres of rail routes and 7,500 stations, the railway network in India is the fourth biggest in the world after Russia, China and the USA. Indian trains carry over 30 million passengers and 2.8 million tonnes of freight daily. Indian Railways are the world's biggest employer, with over 1.4 million staff. Generally, Indian Railways are very efficient, but trains do run late, and sometimes it's hours rather than minutes. However, at the moment, they are a much better option than a traffic jam.

PREPARING TO WATCH

USING YOUR KNOWLEDGE TO PREDICT CONTENT

1 👥 You could put the learners into groups of 3 and ask them to discuss the answers to questions 1–6. Tell the groups to decide on the answers and get a quick show of hands for the different answers. Avoid commenting at this stage as learners will check their answers in Exercise 2.

2 ▶ 👤 Learners watch the video and check their answers. Quickly go through the answers with the class. Allow 10 minutes for Exercises 1 and 2 including feedback.

> **Answers**
> 1c 2b 3a 4a 5d 6c

WHILE WATCHING

LISTENING FOR KEY INFORMATION

3 ▶ 👤👥 Play the video again while the learners complete the exercise individually. They should then check their answers with a partner. Go through the answers with the class. Allow up to 10 minutes for this exercise.

> **Answers**
> 1 centuries 2 passengers 3 father 4 rural 5 ban
> 6 transport 7 afford 8 systems 9 stations
> 10 freight 11 efficient

UNDERSTANDING DETAIL

4 👤👥 Learners complete the table individually and then check their answers in pairs or small groups. Elicit ideas from the class and comment on any particularly original or surprising ideas (e.g. ideas not given below). Allow 10 minutes for this task, including discussion time and feedback.

> **Possible answers**
>
> | | mode of transport | advantages | disadvantages |
> |---|---|---|---|
> | 1 | water taxis | environmentally friendly | need a river |
> | 2 | ox carts | inexpensive | cause traffic congestion |
> | 3 | bicycles | inexpensive | dangerous in traffic |
> | 4 | trains | large rail network | can be late |

DISCUSSION

5 👥 👥👥 Learners discuss the 2 questions in pairs or small groups. Allow 3 minutes for discussion and then elicit ideas from the groups. Try to get at least one idea from each of the groups.

> **Answers will vary.**

READING 1

PREPARING TO READ

USING VISUALS TO PREDICT CONTENT

1 👥 Learners discuss their answers in pairs. Tell them to try to work out the answers in under a minute. Then go through the answers with the class. As there has been a lot of pair and group work so far, you could elicit ideas from the class rather than having the learners first discuss their ideas with a partner.

> **Background note: Gridlock**
>
> You could point out that extreme traffic congestion is known as *gridlock*. In such a situation, no traffic can move due to continuous queues of traffic blocking intersecting streets, bringing traffic to a complete standstill. Gridlock can occur during periods of peak traffic, when the entire traffic infrastructure fails completely. This is especially true of large cities and towns where cars are one of the main means of transport and is made worse, as well as more dangerous, when there is inadequate provision for buses, ambulances, police cars and other such vehicles.

> **Answers**
> 1 The problem is traffic congestion.
> 2 The vehicle in the second photograph is an electric car. It could be a solution because it would cause less pollution and be quieter than cars are now.
> 3 Its transport system has been designed to reduce traffic congestion.

UNDERSTANDING KEY VOCABULARY

2 👤👥 Ask the learners to complete the exercise individually and then check their answers in pairs. Go through the answers with the class. Allow 3 minutes for the exercise. You could then tell the learners that they are going to read a text that includes the words in the box and ask them what they think the text will be about. Elicit ideas, then go on to Exercise 3.

Answers

1 outskirts 2 route 3 commuting time
4 traffic congestion 5 major issue 6 vandalism
7 carbon-neutral 8 vehicle 9 rapid transit

WHILE READING

READING FOR MAIN IDEAS

3 Give the learners 2 minutes to read the text quickly and ask them to put their hands up as soon as they have the answers to the 5 questions. Elicit the answers to the questions, ideally from the first 5 learners with their hands up (one answer from each learner).

Answers

1 A Personal Rapid Transit system
2 Masdar City is carbon-neutral. It will get all of its electricity from renewable energy sources.
3 There will also be an underground metro system and a Light Rail Transit system.
4 The cost is substantial.
5 The PRT system is powered by solar energy. The podcars are pulled by magnets along the route and are controlled wirelessly.

READING FOR DETAIL

4 Ask the learners to complete the exercise individually and then check their answers in pairs. Remind them to use no more than 3 words in each gap. Go through the answers with the class. Allow 3–5 minutes for the exercise.

Answers

1 traffic congestion/jams 2 45 minutes
3 the environment / renewable energy sources
4 not allowed 5 public transport
6 global financial crisis

READING BETWEEN THE LINES

MAKING INFERENCES FROM THE TEXT

5 Learners answer the 3 questions in pairs or small groups if you have an uneven number of learners. Allow a very short time for discussion. Then elicit ideas from the pairs/groups once it looks as though most learners have the answers.

Possible answers

1 The global financial crisis meant the government ran out of money and had to delay the project.
2 The PRT has no driver or guards so vandals could easily damage the podcars.
3 If there was a problem with the software, the pods could crash. Podcars could hit people or be a target for robbers or vandals.

DISCUSSION

6 Learners discuss the 3 questions in pairs or small groups. Allow 3–5 minutes for discussion. Then elicit ideas from the pairs/groups. Encourage class discussion, especially when learners offer opposing ideas. If all or most of the learners are from (or live near) the same city, take a vote on question 3.

Answers will vary.

Optional activity 1

Ask the class if any of them have read a book or seen a film that gives a fictional vision of how people might deal with the problem of traffic congestion in the future. Films include *Bladerunner* and *Brazil*, both of which feature flying cars in virtual traffic lanes high above the ground. Ask them to work in groups of 5 and to discuss any visions of future transport that they have seen or read about. They should make brief notes on each one, and then rank them, with 1 being the most likely to become a reality. They could also discuss which of these forms of transport/solutions to traffic congestion they think are best, and why. Allow 5–10 minutes for discussion and then ask each group to report back to the class.

Optional activity 2

Tell the learners that there are many examples of academic essays, scientific research papers and government-related documents online that deal with the issue of possible solutions to current traffic congestion. Ask the learners in pairs to discuss what keywords they would use to find this information, what search engine they would use and whether they know of any websites (other than a search engine) that might be useful. Allow the learners 2–4 minutes to plan their research and then elicit suggestions from the class. If you have internet access in class, give the learners 20 minutes to conduct their research in pairs. Then ask each pair to report back. When eliciting suggestions from the class, tell them that they need only discuss ideas not already put forward by another pair. This task could also be set as an individual research task for homework.

READING 2

PREPARING TO READ

USING VISUALS TO PREDICT CONTENT

1 👥 Pair the learners with someone they have not yet worked with during the lesson. Ask them to discuss the first 2 questions in their new pairs. Allow a couple of minutes for discussion. Then elicit ideas from the group. Avoid commenting as this will be the topic of the reading which follows. Tell the learners to quickly scan the essay (no more than 90 seconds) and to see what solutions are mentioned. Go through the answers quickly with the class.

> **Answers**
>
> 1 The photographs show bicycle lending, a gas-powered bus and an underground train in London, UK.
> 2 Building bridges and tunnels under the city, congestion charging, a park and ride system (= people park their cars in car parks on the edges of cities and then take buses to the city centre), a monorail, an underground railway, a PRT system, trams, trolley buses, road pricing, bus lanes. Building more roads with wider lanes, building tunnels and bridges, increasing fuel tax, introducing tolls (=making people pay to travel on certain roads), encouraging other forms of transport (e.g. cycling), persuading people to use buses.

> **Using visuals to predict content**
>
> Ask the learners to read the box and tell you what sort of visuals can be particularly helpful, e.g. photographs, graphs, tables.

WHILE READING

SKIMMING

2 👥👥 Ask the learners to complete the exercise individually and then discuss their answers in pairs. Where learners have different answers from their partners, encourage them to support their choice of title by referring to the text. Allow a short time for discussion. Then elicit the correct answer from the class. If the class is not sure why the answer is correct, ask one or more of the learners who had the correct answer to support their choice with

references from the text. This is an important skill, and will be useful when it comes to supporting their thesis statements and topic sentences when writing essays.

> **Answer**   b

3 Quickly elicit the 4 effects from the class. If the answers don't come quickly, give the learners 60 seconds to look back at the text and find the answers.

> **Answers**
>
> Traffic congestion causes stress, reduces productivity, means that emergency services are caught in traffic and wastes fuel (which contributes to global warming).

4 👥👥 Ask the learners to complete the exercise individually and then check their answers in pairs. Remind them to use only one word in each gap. Allow 3–5 minutes for the exercise. Once most learners have completed the table, go through the answers with the class.

> **Answers**
>
> 1 tunnels 2 travel 3 encourage 4 fuel 5 jobs
> 6 health 7 traffic 8 bus 9 congestion 10 night

READING BETWEEN THE LINES

MAKING INFERENCES FROM THE TEXT

5 👥 Learners answer the 3 questions in pairs. Allow 3–5 minutes for discussion. Then elicit the answers from the class.

> **Possible answers**
>
> 1 Health problems caused by stress may include high blood pressure, headaches, heart attacks and depression.
> 2 A government would not want an unpopular tax because people might not vote for them at the next election.
> 3 Many people think that only the poor (who cannot afford a car) use buses.

DISCUSSION

6 👥 Learners discuss the questions in pairs. If possible, try to have learners sitting with someone from a different city or region. Allow up to 5 minutes. Then lead a class feedback session.

> **Answers will vary.**

8

Optional activity

Elicit from the class when it might be useful to summarize a piece of text. Suggestions could include writing an abstract of a research paper, taking notes on a longer paper as part of your research for an essay or writing a short blog entry based on a piece of longer research. Ask the learners to individually write a summary of Reading 2 in *exactly* 100 words (contractions such as *can't* count as two words). Before they begin writing, they should first discuss what parts of the text should remain and how they can best summarize the text in exactly 100 words so that the key points still remain. Set a strict time limit of 10 minutes, including discussion time, and then ask the learners to compare their summaries in pairs. If you have access to one, or can create one, you could also ask the learners to display their summaries on a class wiki for peer correction. If the learners know that their written work will get a wider audience than just the teacher, they will often respond by putting more effort into the first draft.

◉ LANGUAGE DEVELOPMENT

COLLOCATION 1

1 Elicit the meaning of *collocation* from the learners (=a word or phrase that sounds natural and correct when it is used with another word or phrase). If this might be too difficult, or if they are slow in answering, then write the word *traffic* on the left hand side of the board and the words *congestion* and *transport* underneath each other on the right. Then ask the learners which one of the two words on the right collocates with *traffic* (=congestion). Learners then complete the exercise individually and check their answers in pairs. Encourage them to discuss the meanings of the collocations they suggest. Then go through the answers with the class. Allow 5 minutes for the exercise.

Answers

1d 2a 3e 4h 5f 6g 7c 8b

2 Learners complete the sentences individually and check their answers with a partner. Allow 2–3 minutes. Then go through the answers with the class.

Answers

1 traffic congestion 2 public transport 3 cycle lane
4 Parking restrictions 5 rush hour 6 car share
7 road rage 8 congestion charge

ACADEMIC SYNONYMS

3 Learners replace the verbs with their synonyms individually and check their answers with a partner. Allow 2–3 minutes and then go through the answers with the class.

Answers

1 require 2 attempt 3 select 4 realize 5 organize
6 consider 7 prevent 8 convince

CRITICAL THINKING

Give the learners a minute to read the Writing task they will do at the end of the unit (a problem-solution essay, *Describe the traffic problems in this city and outline the advantages and disadvantages of the suggested solutions. Which of the solutions is the most suitable?*) and keep it in mind as they do the next exercises.

ANALYZE

1 Learners work in pairs and read about the first problem. They then discuss the 3 remaining problems. Elicit ideas from the class and then go through any answers below which have not already been suggested by the class. They may well come up with different problems from the ones in the Student's Book.

Possible answers

2 Although there is a bus service joining the residential and economic areas, this may increase the congestion on the main route into and out of the city centre as the buses have to make frequent stops.
3 The fact that the majority of people start and finish work at the same time means that there is a lot of congestion as everyone is going into the city or going home at the same time.
4 There is a junction with traffic lights at one end of the bridge, which may also cause/add to the congestion problems.

APPLY

2 Learners complete the exercise individually, depending on their answers to Exercise 1 above. They then compare their suggestions with a partner. Remind them that they will use their ideas in an essay later, so they should pay close attention to their spelling and grammar. Monitor the class as they write, giving feedback and suggesting corrections as appropriate. Allow 10 minutes for the exercise. Then go through the learners' ideas with the whole class.

Possible answers

2 Cycling: It is far too hot to expect people to cycle. It can be dangerous.
3 Park and ride system: Such a system is designed to keep traffic out of the centre but the problem is getting to the centre not getting around the centre.
4 Banning cars: The problem is getting to the centre, not getting around the centre.
5 Underground: Expensive as the network would have to go under the river.
6 More roads: Expensive because it would require new bridges.
7 Fuel tax: Unpopular with the public. People may buy cheaper fuel in a neighbouring country or city.
8 Car share: Difficult to set up and run. Not always a practical solution.
9 Buses: They would still use the crowded road. Buses have an image problem with the public.
10 Trains: Would require a bridge and a railway line to be built so tickets would be expensive to cover the cost.
11 Rapid transit system: This would also be expensive because it would need bridges and vehicles. There may be safety problems.
12 Ferries: These cause queues as cars wait to board. They don't run very frequently.
13 Relocate the residential area: This is an expensive, long-term solution. Many people may not want to live next to an industrial area.

WRITING

GRAMMAR FOR WRITING

First conditional

The *if* + *will* + infinitive construction is sometimes referred to as the first conditional. It is used when talking about a real possibility that a particular condition will happen in the future, and what the reaction to that condition will be. We use the Present simple to talk about the possible future condition. For example, *If the train is delayed, I will be late for my meeting.*

A conditional sentence consists of two clauses, an *if* clause and a main clause:

If the government increases tax on fuel, people will use their cars less.

If the *if* clause comes first, a comma is usually used. However, If the *if* clause comes second, there is no need for a comma:

People will use their cars less if the government increases tax on fuel.

APPLY

1 👤 👥 Learners answer the questions individually. Ask them to check their answers with a partner and if necessary go through the grammar notes again together. Elicit the answers from the class and check whether the learners have any questions about conditional clauses. Once you are sure that the learners have understood the grammar notes, go on to Exercise 2. Allow up to 5 minutes for this including time for the learners to go through the grammar notes a second time if necessary.

Answers

1a 2b 3 *can* changes to *be able to* when it follows another modal verb *(will)*.

2 👤 👥 Learners complete the exercise individually and then check their ideas with a partner. Allow 3–5 minutes for the learners to write the five sentences. Then go through the answers with the class.

Answers

1 If we move the offices and schools next to the houses, we will have fewer traffic problems.
2 If we have a ferry over the river, fewer people will use the bridge.
3 If we increase the price of fuel, fewer cars will use the roads.
4 If we change the office hours, the cars will not all use the road at the same time.
5 If we build a railway line, people will be able to use the train instead of their cars.

Using *if...not* and *unless*

Point out that *if ... not* and *unless* both mean *except if*:
Take the bus unless you can get a lift. (=if you can't get a lift. / **except if** you can get a lift.)
Try to get a lift. If not, take the bus. (**If** you can't get a lift / **Except if** you can get a lift, take the bus.)
if not is always followed by a comma:
I hope to get the job. If not, I'll look for something else.
Unless is often preceded by a comma, but not always.
*I'll be back this evening, **unless** there's a train strike.*
*I'll be back this evening – **unless** there's a train strike.*
*I'll be back this evening **unless** there's a train strike.*
The comma is often left out and is sometimes replaced by a dash. It might be best simply to tell your learners that they should use a comma before *unless* when it is used to mean *except if*, but not to be surprised if they see examples where there is no comma.

3 👤👥 Learners answer the questions individually. Ask them to check their answers with a partner and if necessary go through the grammar box again together. Elicit the answers from the class and check whether the learners have any questions. Allow up to 10 minutes for this exercise, including time to go through the grammar box a second time if necessary.

> **Possible answers**
>
> 1 The traffic won't improve unless we build more roads. OR If we don't build more roads, the traffic won't improve.
> 2 Pollution won't be reduced if we do not use cleaner transport. OR Unless we use cleaner transport, pollution won't be reduced.
> 3 People won't get to work on time unless we provide a solution. OR If we don't provide a solution, people won't get to work on time.
> 4 We won't solve the traffic problem if we don't build houses closer to the business areas. OR Unless we build houses closer to the business areas, we won't solve the traffic problem.
> 5 Unless the city invests in a PRT, there won't be less congestion. OR If the city doesn't invest in a PRT, there won't be less congestion.

ACADEMIC WRITING SKILLS

> **Optional lead-in**
>
> 👥 Ask the learners to close their books and discuss what should go into the conclusion of an academic essay. Give them a minute or two to discuss their ideas.

> **Writing a conclusion**
>
> Ask learners to read the box. Remind them that their personal opinion on the question must also be stated in the introduction in the form of a thesis statement. The writer states their opinion in the introduction and supports that opinion with illustrated arguments in the main body. The conclusion then brings together all the points from the main body and shows how these support the initial thesis statement, which should be restated. The writer can then make a final comment (such as some speculation as to what might happen in the future), but no new information in support of the thesis statement should be included in the conclusion.

1 👤👥 Learners complete the exercise individually and check their ideas with a partner. Allow up to 5 minutes for this exercise and then go through the answers with the class.

> **Answers**
>
> 1ci 2 biii 3 aii

2 👤 Ask the learners to quickly read the sentences again and to underline or highlight the phrases used to introduce opinions and conclusions. Set a time limit of a minute and then go through the answers with the class.

> **Answers**
>
> 1 To sum up, In conclusion, Overall
> 2 In my opinion, I would say that, It is my view that

WRITING TASK

PLAN

1 👤👥 Ask the learners to read the title of the problem-solution essay *Describe the traffic problems in this city and outline the advantages and disadvantages of the suggested solutions. Which of the solutions is the most suitable*? They should review the problems and solutions they discussed earlier in the Critical thinking and Writing sections and choose the 3 they think are most important. Then they should complete the essay plan with notes. Allow 5–10 minutes for the exercise. When the learners seem to be finishing their notes, ask them to work with a partner and go through their notes together, making any changes necessary. Go through the learners' ideas with the whole class.

> **Answers will vary.**

WRITE A FIRST DRAFT

2 👥👥 Ask the learners to write the 3 paragraphs in groups of 3. If possible, try to make sure that each group has a good balance of stronger and weaker learners (i.e. make sure that no one group is significantly stronger or weaker than the other groups). They could either produce one essay together (in which case, appoint a writer but stress that all 3 learners should contribute to the essay), or they could each write the essay individually based on the ideas they discuss in their groups. Allow 15–20 minutes for this exercise.

EDIT

3 & 4 👤 👥 Learners work individually to check the content and structure of their work against the Task checklist and make any changes necessary. Monitor and help with any problems. Allow up to 10 minutes. If there is time and if you think it will be helpful, ask them to peer review their work.

5 & 6 👤 Learners do the same with the Language checklist and make any changes necessary. Again monitor and help with any problems. If there is time and if you think it will be helpful, ask them to peer review their work. Allow up to 10 minutes including the peer review. Have something ready for those learners who finish early.

Answers

Model answer: see page 136 of the Teacher's Book

OBJECTIVES REVIEW

See Introduction, page 9 for ideas about using the Objectives review with your learners.

WORDLIST

See Introduction, page 9 for ideas about how to make the most of the Wordlists with your learners.

REVIEW TEST

See page 109 for the photocopiable Review test for this unit and page 93 for ideas about when and how to administer the Review test.

RESEARCH PROJECT

Improve the transportation in your area.

Explain to your class that they are going to write a proposal to the local council explaining ways they could improve transport in the area. They should focus on two areas: road safety and the improvement and promotion of public transportation. The proposal needs to discuss the current situation and state where any problems exist. It should also contain a description of improvements to the transport network and the advantages these improvements.

Learners could extend this activity by developing a public transport promotion focusing on awareness of the issues through promotional products, leaflets, logos, slogans and videos.

THE ENVIRONMENT

Learning objectives

Before you start the Unlock your knowledge section ask the learners to read the Learning objectives box so that they have a clear idea of what they are going to learn in this unit. Tell them that you will come back to these objectives at the end of the unit when they review what they have learned. Give them the opportunity to ask you any questions they might have.

UNLOCK YOUR KNOWLEDGE

Lead-in

Ask the learners in pairs to discuss the single most important environmental issue that either affects their country now, or which might affect their country in the future. Give the learners 2 minutes to discuss their answers and then put pairs together to discuss their ideas. Allow 3–5 minutes for discussion. Then go on to Exercise 1.

1 Learners discuss the questions in pairs or small groups. If some of these issues have already been discussed during the lead-in, ask them to focus on the question or questions that most interest them. Tell them to go into as much detail as possible, offering possible solutions where they can. Allow 3–5 minutes for the exercise. Then lead a brief class discussion.

Answers will vary.

Background note: Climate change

It is difficult to think of a country that is not experiencing some degree of environmental change. Whereas in the 1980s and 1990s, the impact of climate change was more commonly discussed in terms of its effect on developing countries, increasingly all countries are having to face up to the realities of our changing climate. Parts of the UK were hit by a series of floods in 2012 and many countries regularly face drought (=long periods with no rain). Countries such as Austria, where skiing is a major industry, are responding to the retreating glaciers by building ski runs at altitudes previously unheard of. There is a growing consensus that climate change is a reality.

WATCH AND LISTEN

Videoscript

GLOBAL WARMING

The frozen glaciers of Alaska have remained unchanged for millions of years. But now the ice is melting and the impact on our environment will be huge. These ice sheets start life as snow, turn to glaciers, and eventually crash into the sea. A single glacier can move up to a metre every hour.

An astonishing 20,000 trillion tonnes of ice move across Alaska every day. Alaska's 100,000 glaciers are under threat of disappearing because they are very sensitive to the effects of global warming. To understand why, adventurer Will Gadd is going where few have gone before: to follow one of the melt streams running through the glacier.

These fast rivers of freezing water are formed as glaciers melt, and they are an important measure of its health. Every glacier is in balance. The amount of snow falling in winter must equal the amount that melts in the summer. If that balance changes, the glacier will disappear. Right now, that's what's happening. These glaciers are melting faster than they are growing.

Alaskan glaciers have been here for over three million years. They are currently losing ice at the rate of eighty billion tonnes a year. It's the end of the road for this glacier as it tumbles off the mountains and into the sea.

Alaska's glaciers are retreating at an increasing rate. Every year, 19 trillion tonnes of melt water are pouring away and not being replenished. As the glaciers melt away, it's the rest of the world that's affected. Alaskan glaciers are melting so fast, they are accounting for ten per cent of the world's rising sea levels. It's the most dramatic transformation this area has undergone since the ice age and shows how global warming is changing our environment. It's hard to believe all this could soon be gone.

PREPARING TO WATCH

USING YOUR KNOWLEDGE TO PREDICT CONTENT

1 Do this either as a pairwork or as a class activity. If pairwork, allow 2–3 minutes for discussion and then elicit the answers from the

class. As a class activity, elicit ideas from the class. Make sure that a good variety of learners are able to share their ideas. You could ask some follow-up questions, such as *Has anyone ever been to a glacier? What kind of sports can you do on glaciers in mountainous regions?* (in some countries, for example Austria, it is possible to ski on glaciers all year round).

> **Answers**
> 1 A large mass of ice which moves slowly, usually down a slope or valley.
> 2 At the North and South Poles and in mountain ranges (on Earth), and on Mars.
> 3 It is melting and falling into the sea.
> 4 Probably global warming.

UNDERSTANDING KEY VOCABULARY

2 👤 Give the learners one minute to complete the exercise individually, and then go through the answers with the class.

> **Articles**
>
> After you have gone through the answers, ask the learners if they notice the differences in the articles taken by the nouns 1–6. Point out that while most take the indefinite article (=a), *environment* takes the definite article (=the) and *global warming* is a mass/uncountable noun and does not take an article at all.

> **Answers**
> 1d 2a 3f 4b 5c 6e

WHILE WATCHING

UNDERSTANDING MAIN IDEAS

3 ▶️👤 Learners watch the video and complete the exercise individually. Go through the answers with the class. With a stronger group, you could ask them to complete the gaps with the best answers before they watch the video to see if they were right. Allow 10 minutes for this exercise.

> *effect* vs. *affect*
>
> You could point out the difference between the noun *effect* (=a change, reaction, or result that is caused by something) and the verb *affect* (=to influence someone or something, or cause them to change).

> **Answers**
> 1 glaciers 2 formed 3 melt 4 effects
> 5 global warming 6 environment

UNDERSTANDING DETAIL

4 ▶️👤👥 Learners complete the exercise individually and check their answers with a partner, completing the gaps in the labels.

> **Answers**
> 1 snow 2 one 3 streams 4 eighty 5 crashes

MAKING INFERENCES

5 👥 Learners complete the exercise in pairs. Allow 3 minutes for discussion. Then elicit ideas from the groups.

> **Answers**
> 1 Global warming means that the ice is melting faster than the snow replacing it. The amount of snow that falls on the glacier in winter is not enough to replace the ice that melts in higher temperatures in summer.
> 2 No.
> 3 They have been there for three million years.

DISCUSSION

6 👥👥👥 Learners discuss the 3 questions in pairs or small groups. Allow 3 minutes for discussion. Then elicit ideas from the groups. Try to get at least one idea from each group.

> **Possible answers**
> 1 Most scientists agree that global warming is probably affected by human activity.
> 2 Individuals, corporations, governments, in fact everyone has a responsibility.
> 3 They can reduce carbon emissions and invest in alternative energy sources.
> 4 We can buy fewer products, use local products and services, use less energy and recycle materials.

READING 1

PREPARING TO READ

USING YOUR KNOWLEDGE TO PREDICT CONTENT

1 👥👥👥 Learners discuss the 4 questions in pairs or small groups. Allow 3 minutes for discussion. Then elicit ideas from the pairs or groups. Try to get at least one idea from each of them.

Answers

1 It has melted (away).
2 76 years.
3 Some water has stayed as a lake but most has flowed into the sea.
4 Sea levels are rising.

WHILE READING

READING FOR MAIN IDEAS

2 Give the learners 2 minutes to quickly read through the text and order the main ideas individually. Go through the correct order together with the class.

Answers

1c 2b 3d 4a

> **Optional activity**
>
> With a stronger group, you could ask them to try and put the main ideas in the most likely order with a partner, then to quickly read through the text to see if they were right. If you try this, start them off by asking *Which of the 4 main ideas is most likely to come at the end?* (=a solution to the problem). This will help them think about the possible structure of the text which was dealt with in Unit 4.

SCANNING TO FIND INFORMATION

3 Give the learners 2–3 minutes to complete the gaps with the best answers. Then ask them to read the leaflet a second time to see if they were right. Go through the answers with the class.

Answers

1 CO_2 levels 2 Global sea levels 3 mangrove forests
4 global temperatures 5 agriculture 6 extinction
7 coral reefs

> **Scanning to find information**
>
> Ask the learners to read the box and to find what example is given when we might need to scan to find information (=in an examination). Ask them to discuss in pairs other situations in which they might need to find detailed information quickly in a text. Allow a couple of minutes for discussion. Then quickly go around the class and elicit as many ideas as possible.

READING FOR DETAIL

4 Ask the learners to complete the exercise individually and then check their answers in pairs. Remind them to use no more than three words in each of the gaps. Go through the answers with the class. Allow 3–5 minutes for the exercise.

Answers

1 Argentina 2 The Northwest Passage
3 food/agriculture 4 asthma 5 greenhouse gases
6 cut down trees 7 renewable energy

READING BETWEEN THE LINES

IDENTIFYING PURPOSE

5 Elicit the answer from the class.

Answer c

DISCUSSION

6 Learners discuss their answers to the 3 questions in pairs or small groups. Allow a very short time for discussion. Then elicit ideas from the groups once it looks as though most learners have the answer.

Answers

1 It will be an important global shipping route. At the moment ships have to sail via the Panama Canal to get between the Atlantic and the Pacific Oceans.
2 Solar panels are most effective in direct sunlight as there is a higher concentration of photons in this type of light, so they are not ideal in overcast or wintry conditions. Wind power requires a lot of wind so the turbines are installed on mountains or near the coast, and some people complain they are ugly.
3 Unless global warming has an immediate effect on our way of life, there is little to motivate us to do more to prevent global warming.

READING 2

PREPARING TO READ

PREVIEWING

1 Learners answer the 3 questions in pairs or small groups. Allow 2–3 minutes for discussion and then elicit ideas from the groups as soon as it looks as though most learners are ready. Avoid giving the correct answers at this stage,

as the learners will read the journal and find the answers for themselves in Exercise 3.

Possible answers

1 Trees absorb CO_2 and produce O_2 which helps reduce global warming. They also maintain biodiversity, which can help provide food and medicines. Trees also prevent erosion and landslides and so reduce flooding.
2 People cut down trees for fuel, timber and to clear land for agriculture or construction.
3 The climate will become warmer. There will be many fewer animal species, more soil erosion and more flooding. There will be less fresh water.

UNDERSTANDING KEY VOCABULARY

2 👤 Ask the learners to complete the exercise individually and then check their answers in pairs. Allow 2 minutes for the exercise. Then quickly go through the answers with the class.

Answers

1d 2i 3a 4g 5h 6c 7e 8b 9f

WHILE READING

READING FOR MAIN IDEAS

3 👤 Learners complete the summary individually and then check their answers in pairs. Allow 3–5 minutes for the exercise. Then quickly go through the answers with the class.

Answers

1 deforestation 2 effects 3 livestock 4 crops
5 decade 6 erosion 7 fires 8 habitats 9 protected
10 environment

READING FOR DETAIL

4 👤 Do this either with learners working individually or as a class activity. If learners work individually, allow 2–3 minutes for discussion and then elicit the answers from the class. As a class activity, go straight to eliciting ideas from the class.

Answers

1 palm oil *not* olive oil 2 2–3 years *not* 10 3 UK *not* USA
4 destroys *not* protects 5 carbon dioxide *not* oxygen
6 large-scale *not* small-scale

READING BETWEEN THE LINES

MAKING INFERENCES

5 👥 Ask the learners to form new pairs or small groups, and to discuss the 3 questions. Allow 3–5 minutes for discussion. Then elicit ideas from the class.

Possible answers

1 The writer is suggesting these are large-scale business operations, not small subsistence farms.
2 The trees will become fire risks so they will need to be cut down.
3 There may be many plant and animal species which remain undiscovered in the rainforests. These could provide new medicines and crops, if they do not become extinct first.

DISCUSSION

6 👥 Ask the learners to work with a new partner and to discuss the 3 questions in pairs. If you began the lesson with the Optional lead-in, your learners may already have discussed question 3. If so, this will give them the chance to consider the question in more depth and to use some of the vocabulary presented in this unit. Allow 3–5 minutes for discussion and then lead a class discussion.

Answers will vary.

⊙ LANGUAGE DEVELOPMENT

ACADEMIC VOCABULARY

1 👤 Learners complete the exercise individually and check their answers with a partner. Allow 2–3 minutes and then go through the answers with the class.

Answers

1 issue 2 predict 3 consequences 4 trend 5 areas
6 annual 7 challenge

TOPIC VOCABULARY

2 👤👥 Elicit the meaning of *collocation* from the class. If necessary, remind them that collocations are words that sound natural and

correct when used with another word. Ask the learners to complete the exercise individually, without looking back at the reading texts. Allow 2 minutes and then ask the learners to try and complete any gaps with a partner. Once it looks as though the learners have got as far as they can, ask them to look back at the texts on pages 91 and 94 to check their answers and to complete any missing collocations. Quickly go through the answers with the class.

Answers

1 renewable energy, fossil fuels 2 Global warming, greenhouse gases 3 natural environment, human activity 4 Deforestation, climate change 5 logging, rainforest 6 Subsistence farming 7 environmental disasters

CRITICAL THINKING

Give the learners a minute to read the Writing task they will do at the end of the unit (a cause-effect essay *Outline the human causes of climate change. What effects will these have on the planet?*) and keep it in mind as they do the next exercises.

Optional lead-in

This is a fun way of preparing the learners for the Writing task. Ask the learners to read the description of the writing task for this unit. On the board, write: *increasing demand for beef – increasing levels of methane.* Tell the learners that intensive cattle production has lead to increased amounts of methane, which is one of the contributing factors to climate change. Then ask them to make notes on as many examples of how human activity is changing the climate as they can in two minutes. Ask all of the learners to stand and form a horseshoe shape around the class. Tell them that you will ask one learner to read out one example of human activity, and the next learner has to say how that is affecting the planet. For example, the first learner might say 'We are increasing livestock production', the next learner could continue with 'This has led to increased methane, which contributes to climate change'. Continue round the class until all ideas are exhausted. As soon as a learner is unable to think of a new idea, or think of how the example of human activity given is affecting the planet, tell them to sit down. The winner is the last learner standing.

If you think your learners will need more preparation for the above exercise, use it as a follow-up to Exercises 1 and 2 instead.

Selecting

Ask the class to read the box. Point out that it is important for learners to be selective to make sure that the information included in their essays is relevant to the title. They should avoid focusing on one or two key words in an essay title and simply writing everything they know about the topic. The information they include, as well as the way in which they use that information, will depend on the specific wording of the title. A classic mistake that learners make is not answering the specific essay title. An essay will always have a particular focus, and learners must be sure they understand what is required before they start the selecting their material. An essay will lose marks for containing information that is irrelevant. When researching an essay, learners are bound to come across a certain amount of interesting material. However, this material should only be included if it helps the learner respond to the essay title.

EVALUATE

1 ♟ Learners complete the exercise in pairs. Allow 2–3 minutes and then go through the answers with the class.

Answers

Causes: factory emissions, deforestation, petrol cars, an increase in the population, power stations, livestock
Effects: melting glaciers, storms, rising sea levels, loss of habitat, species extinction, flooding, droughts

2 & 3 ♟♟ ♟♟♟ Learners complete the exercises in pairs or small groups. Monitor the groups and take notes on their language for feedback at the end of the exercise. Remember to take notes on good use of language as well as on any errors that need to be addressed. Allow 5–10 minutes for discussion and then elicit suggestions from the class. If you began this section with the Optional lead-in above, don't spend too much time covering ideas already discussed. Instead, use this as a quick reinforcement exercise to help learners remember the ideas they suggested during the lead-in. Give the class feedback on the language notes you took while you monitored the group discussions. Again, remember to both praise good language use as well as correcting errors. When correcting errors, as far as possible try to elicit the corrections from the learners. This can be done either orally, e.g. *During your discussions, several learners said X. What should they have said?* or on the board by writing the error down and eliciting

the corrections. It is a good idea to anonymize the errors, especially with mixed ability groups or where learners are concerned about losing face. Do this by constructing a new sentence that includes the error you heard. Then elicit the corrections from the class.

2 Possible answers

Causes: heating homes and buildings; growing, transporting and cooking food; travelling (e.g. by car, plane, bus and train); treating water to make it drinkable; heating water, transporting water into homes; manufacturing, using and transporting products.
Effects: The cost of insurance will rise as the weather becomes more extreme. Water availability will become a problem as temperatures rise. Tropical diseases like malaria will spread north into northern Europe and the north of the USA. Low-lying islands will become submerged if sea levels rise.

3 Possible answers

Solutions: Reduce greenhouse gas emissions by reducing the number of cars, power stations and factories that use energy generated by burning fossil fuels. Invest in alternative, non-polluting energy sources. Use less transport and energy in manufacturing. Reduce the number of livestock on farms. Plant more trees.

Optional activity

If you did not use the Optional lead-in above, you could use it here.

WRITING

GRAMMAR FOR WRITING

Cause and effect

Ask the class to review their notes on the Critical thinking exercise they have just done and what they discussed if you began or ended that section with the Optional lead-in. Remind them that what they discussed during those exercises was cause and effect: the causes of certain problems and their effect on the environment. Then ask them to read the Cause and effect box. You could ask them to close their books after they have studied the box and elicit the cause of the habitat destruction referred to in it (=*deforestation*).

Language note

In academic writing it is considered bad style to repeat words too often so it is very useful for learners to have a wide range of functional language, such as the variety of ways of writing about cause and effect presented here.

1 👤 Give the learners 1–2 minutes to complete the exercise individually and check their answers with a partner. Go through the answers with the class.

Answers

2 causes / results in 3 caused by / due to / the result of 4 caused by / due to / the result of

2 👤 Give the learners 2 minutes to complete the exercise individually and check their answers with a partner. Go through the answers with the class.

Answers

1 results 2 due 3 causes 4 caused 5 result 6 result 7 lead

Optional activity

If you think your learners need more practice with the language of cause and effect, you could refer them back to the environmental issues they discussed at the start of the unit and write cause and effect sentences for each, using the structures outlined in the Cause and effect box.

Using *because* and *because of*

You might want to tell learners the following:
- *Because* can be used at the beginning of a clause before the subject and the verb.
- *Because of* can be used before either a noun or a pronoun.

Compare the following:
- *Forests are being cut down to provide land for food because the population is growing at such a rapid rate.* (NOT … ~~because of the population is growing at such a rapid rate.~~)
- *The glaciers are melting because of global warming.* (NOT *The glaciers are melting* ~~because global warming.~~)

Many people still believe that it is incorrect to start a sentence with *Because*. However, this usage is both common and acceptable, and is typically used for rhetorical effect in both spoken and written English, e.g. *Because humans are so selfish, the planet is dying.*

3 👤 Give learners 2 minutes to complete the exercise individually and check their answers with a partner. Go through the answers with the class.

Answers

1 because of 2 because 3 because of 4 because of 5 because 6 because of 7 because of

ACADEMIC WRITING SKILLS

1 👤👥 Give learners 2–3 minutes to complete the exercise individually and check their answers with a partner. Go through the answers with the class.

> ### Answers
> 1 a c 2 b d 3 two 4 three

2 👤 Give the learners 2 minutes to complete the exercise individually and check their answers with a partner. Go through the answers with the class.

> ### Possible answers
> 1 using fossil fuels, deforestation, an increase in the population
> 2 species extinction, melting glaciers
> 3 a number of ways
> 4 Rising sea levels, flooding
> 5 in three main ways

WRITING TASK

WRITE A FIRST DRAFT

1 👤 Ask the learners to read the title of the essay *Outline the human causes of climate change. What effects will these have on the planet?* and the introduction and conclusion. They should then write the 2 paragraphs about the human causes of climate change and their effects using the ideas they worked on in the Critical thinking and Writing sections above. Monitor and help with any problems. Allow 10–15 minutes for this.

EDIT

2 & 3 👤👥 Learners work individually to check the content and structure of their work against the Task checklist and make any changes necessary. Monitor and help with any problems. Allow up to 10 minutes. If there is time and if you think it will be helpful, ask them to peer review their work.

4 & 5 👤 Learners do the same with the Language checklist and make any changes necessary. Again monitor and help with any problems. If there is time and if you think it will be helpful, ask them to peer review their work. Allow up to 10 minutes including the peer review. Have something ready for those learners who finish early.

> ### Answers
> Model answer: see page 137 of the Teacher's Book

OBJECTIVES REVIEW

See Introduction, page 9 for ideas about using the Objectives review with your learners.

WORDLIST

See Introduction, page 9 for ideas about how to make the most of the Wordlists with your learners.

REVIEW TEST

See page 112 for the photocopiable Review test for this unit and page 93 for ideas about when and how to administer the Review test.

RESEARCH PROJECT

Help stop global warming by reducing your use of fossil fuels.

Divide the class and ask them to find out:
1 what fossil fuels are
2 why fossil fuels cause global warming
3 how fossil fuels are used by the learners in their homes and school
4 what the alternatives are for fossil fuels in their environment.

Explain that the learners are responsible for recording the class consumption of fossil fuels. They will create data and analyze the data. They can then research and write about how to reduce their consumption as a way to educate others.

6 HEALTH AND FITNESS

Learning objectives

Before you start the Unlock your knowledge section ask the learners to read the Learning objectives box so that they have a clear idea of what they are going to learn in this unit. Tell them that you will come back to these objectives at the end of the unit when they review what they have learned. Give them the opportunity to ask you any questions they might have.

UNLOCK YOUR KNOWLEDGE

Background note: Handling the topic of obesity sensitively

Governments across the globe are trying to find ways to improve their citizens' health. One cost-effective way is through preventative initiatives, such as banning smoking in public places and encouraging healthier lifestyles. However, despite such efforts, many countries are now facing an obesity epidemic that could have disastrous consequences on their economies and societies if left unchecked. In the UK, a 2013 report by the Academy of Medical Royal Colleges called for a range of measures from taxing sugary drinks to improving food in hospitals; and in the USA, with obesity rates approaching 35% in adults and associated healthcare costs on the rise, many doctors have urged health regulators to approve radical new weight-loss treatments. According to the World Economic Forum (WEF), obesity kills 2.8 million adults every year, and in many countries more people die from obesity-related diseases than as a result of undernourishment.

Obesity is clearly a matter for concern, and few countries remain untouched by its consequences. Health and fitness are interesting and important topics, and can lead to some excellent language work. However, the topic does need to be dealt with sensitively in class. While it is tempting to blame overweight people for their apparently poor diet and fitness, such issues are often linked with poverty, lack of education and limited access to healthy food. In a 2012 paper published in the respected scientific journal *Plos One*, scientists reported finding changes around the DNA at birth which may result from a mother's diet or exposure to pollution or stress, linking the environment in the womb with increased body weight in later life. With these considerations in mind, take care when leading discussion sessions that some of the class might find difficult. Be careful not to alienate any of your learners, and make sure that a good range of different views are put forward during pair, group and class work, possibly feeding in some of the ideas mentioned here to encourage a balanced approach to the topic.

Lead-in

To engage learners in the topic you could write the the following questions on the board and ask them to work in pairs and discuss: *What can people do keep fit and healthy? Why is it important for people to watch their weight? What should people eat in a balanced diet?* Get feedback from the class but don't give feedback or go into much detail as these and other issues to do with health and fitness will be dealt with in this unit.

1 ⬤⬤⬤ Learners complete the exercise individually or in pairs. Go through the answers quickly with the class.

Answers

1 e 2 f 3 c 4 d 5 b 6 a

2 ⬤⬤⬤ As these questions could well generate some heated discussion, they would be a useful basis for a pyramid discussion. Start the learners off discussing the three questions in pairs and then join each pair with another pair after 3–5 minutes. Continue joining the groups every few minutes until finally the whole class is involved in one discussion. This is a good way to get the whole class involved in a lively discussion, and can be a useful way of maintaining good classroom dynamics.

Answers will vary.

WATCH AND LISTEN

Videoscript

CYCLING

The world's top road cyclists manage to ride for over three and a half thousand kilometres, at an average speed of 40 kilometres per hour in each race. How do they manage this amazing physical achievement?

Teams who compete at the highest level in the Tour de France put their success down to training. The riders in the team treat their training for any sport as if it is a job. For example, they set goals for each day's training and, like a regular job, they stop when they reach those goals. This means even though they might cycle 700 kilometres a week, they don't train too hard and get injured before their race.

The way they train means that they are much fitter than a normal person. The best riders extract twice as much oxygen from each breath as an average healthy person, so they are able to generate twice as much energy. Riders like this train their hearts to pump nine gallons of blood to their muscles per minute, whereas you or I could only manage five.

The team of riders is built entirely around helping the team leader win the race. The team work together to make sure that the leader is fresh to cycle fastest at the end of the race.

The team's job is to block the wind that he rides into. They ride in a V-shape, so that the leader can save a quarter of the energy he would normally spend riding into the wind. In a side wind, the team ride in a wing shape to protect him.

The team also make sure that their equipment and food is the most advanced. Modern bicycles use space technology and weigh 1.3 kilograms. A wind tunnel is used to analyze a rider's position on the bike and reduce drag. To get the most energy for the race, cyclists train their body to burn fat by not eating too many carbohydrates, but as they start to race, they eat a lot more. During a race, a cyclist can consume up to 4,000 calories per day in carbohydrates alone.

This kind of preparation is the key to winning a race that can last up to three weeks. Even the smallest aspect of a rider's performance could be the difference between winning and losing.

PREPARING TO WATCH

USING YOUR KNOWLEDGE TO PREDICT CONTENT

1 You could ask the learners to get into groups of 3. If possible, try to make sure that each group has at least one person in it who either cycles regularly or who knows something about cycling. Ask the groups to discuss the answers to the 2 questions. Lead a brief class discussion on each of the questions, adding any facts not already covered by the learners from the possible answers below. You could ask the class what the plural of *sportsperson* is (=sportspeople). Point out that the usual plural of *person* is *people*, and that *persons* is normally only used in legal documents or other very formal texts.

Possible answers

1 Professional sportspeople must train very hard and very regularly. This builds up physical stamina and power. They also need to eat the correct food, both during training and before a race. They will usually consume lots of carbohydrates in the run up to a race. This is called carbohydrate loading, more commonly known as carb-loading.

2 By having better equipment, by team tactics, diet, or even by being naturally gifted with a strong heart and lungs. Some professional sports people have been banned from their sports and stripped of their awards for using illegal drugs to improve their performance.

UNDERSTANDING KEY VOCABULARY

2 Learners complete the exercise individually and check their answers with a partner. Go through the answers with the class.

Answers
1 remove 2 pump 3 set 4 burn 5 generate

WHILE WATCHING

UNDERSTANDING MAIN IDEAS

3 Before you play the video you could ask the learners to go through the words and phrases a–i with a partner and to check that they understand them all. Allow 2–3 minutes for discussion and then check whether the class needs help with any of the vocabulary. Play the video and ask the learners to circle the points that are discussed.

Answers
b d e h i

NOTE TAKING

4 Before you play the video again you could ask the learners to complete the notes based on what they can remember from the video. Where they are unsure of an answer, ask them to guess or to make a note of the kind of word that is missing (i.e. *Is it a number, a noun, a verb* etc.?). Allow 2–3 minutes for the exercise, then play the video a second time and ask the learners to check their answers with a partner and complete any remaining gaps. Go through the answers quickly with the class.

Answers
1 3,500 2 40 3 oxygen 4 9 5 5 6 wind 7 space
8 1.3 kilograms 9 4,000

MAKING INFERENCES

5 👥 👥👥 Learners complete the exercise in pairs or small groups. Allow a very short time for discussion and then elicit ideas from the groups once it looks as though most learners have the answer. As there has been a lot of discussion on the topic of cycling, you might like to assign each pair or group just 1 of the 3 questions to discuss before leading a quick class feedback.

Possible answers

1 They are able to train effectively and use oxygen better than most people to produce more power.
2 To reduce drag and air resistance so that they can ride faster.
3 To protect the team leader from the wind so that he/ she is fresh to cycle fastest at the end of the race.

DISCUSSION

6 👥 Learners discuss the questions in pairs. Allow 3–5 minutes for discussion, and make a note of some of the more interesting responses to the questions during the learners' discussions. Use your notes as the basis of the follow-up class feedback session. Again, you might like to assign each pair or group just one of the questions to discuss before leading a class feedback session. When discussing the learners' responses to question 3, try to elicit examples of good and bad role models from the world of sports.

Answers will vary.

> **Background note: Professional sportspeople as role models**
>
> Examples of good and bad role models from the world of cycling could be: Bradley Wiggins, seven-time Olympic medallist and winner of the Tour de France in 2012, is an example of a good role model, while Lance Armstrong, whom the United States Anti-Doping Agency labelled a 'serial cheat' who led 'the most sophisticated, professionalized and successful doping programme that sport has ever seen' is a bad one. Armstrong was stripped of all his Tour de France titles in 2012.

> **Optional activity**
>
> Ask the class if they can remember the name of the cycle race mentioned in the video (=the Tour de France). Ask the learners if they know the names of any of the regions or cities through which the Tour de France passes. Tell the class that the route changes every year, but that it always includes a passage through the mountains of the Pyrenees and the Alps, and the finish is always on the Champs-Élysées in Paris. Point out that the Tour also sometimes includes countries other than France, and ask the class if they can guess the names of some of the countries that have been included in the Tour (=Andorra, Belgium, Germany, Ireland, Italy, Luxembourg, Monaco, Netherlands, Spain, Switzerland and the UK have all hosted stages or part of a stage). As a research task, you could ask learners to use the Internet to find the route of the Tour de France in the year in which they were born. They could then compare the routes in pairs or small groups and then plan an alternative route together, including all of the areas they would most like to visit.

READING 1

PREPARING TO READ

UNDERSTANDING KEY VOCABULARY

1 👤 👥 Learners complete the exercise individually and check their answers with a partner. Go through the answers with the class.

> **Answers**
>
> 1 d 2 e 3 a 4 c 5 b 6 h 7 g 8 f

USING VISUALS TO PREDICT CONTENT

2 Elicit the types of exercise from the class. As a follow up, you could get a quick show of hands for each type of exercise to find out which are the most popular with your class.

> **Answers**
>
> 1 (playing) rugby 2 (playing) squash 3 (doing) housework 4 football 5 gardening 6 running 7 swimming 8 cycling

> **Optional activity**
>
> 👥 To further personalize this section of the unit, ask the learners to quickly discuss their favourite sports with a partner. You could also ask them each to think of one sports or exercise related anecdote (=personal story) to share with a partner.

WHILE READING

SKIMMING

3 👤 Give the learners 15 seconds to answer question 1 and identify the type of text, and tell them to raise their hand as soon as they are certain of the answer. Elicit the correct answer from the first learner with their hand up. If the answer is incorrect, ask the next learner and continue until you have the right answer. Ask the learner that gave you the correct answer how they were able to tell what type of text it was. What clues were there? Then get them to do question 2. Allow up to 5 minutes and then go through the answers quickly with the class.

> **Answer**   c

READING FOR MAIN IDEAS

4 👤👥 Learners complete the exercise individually and check their answers with a partner. Allow 5 minutes and then elicit the answers from the class. When a learner gives you the correct answer, ask that learner how they were able to match the correct heading. What clues are there in the text?

> **Answers**
> 1 C 2 A 3 E 4 not needed 5 B 6 D

READING FOR DETAIL

5 👤👥 Learners complete the exercise individually and check their answers with a partner. Allow 5 minutes and then elicit the answers from the class. With a stronger class, you could first ask them to try and answer the questions, before they read the leaflet again to check their answers.

> **Answers**
> 1 heart disease, type two diabetes, stroke and cancer
> 2 mood, self-esteem, sleep quality 3 seven hours
> 4 the pitch 5 off-peak times 6 (a pair of) trainers
> 7 the park 8 getting fit

USING KEY VOCABULARY

6 👤👥 Learners complete the phrases individually and check their answers with a partner. Allow 3–5 minutes for this and then quickly elicit the answers from the class

> **Answers**
> 2 burn (fewer) calories 3 strengthen muscles
> 4 join a sports club 5 book a court 6 go for a run
> 7 get off the bus one stop early 8 live longer

7 To vary things you could ask the class to close their books and to tell you if more or fewer than 15 different ways of getting fit are mentioned in the leaflet. Ask the learners to open their books and then elicit the exact number from the class. Once you have established that a total of 13 different ways were mentioned, call on individual learners to give you one of these each. Write the learners' suggestions down as you hear them, writing those mentioned in the leaflet on the left hand side of the board and those suggested by learners but not in the leaflet on the right. Try to involve those learners who haven't spoken much during the class feedback sessions during this lesson. Don't stop calling on individual learners until you have elicited all of the 13 ways. Then ask the learners to go through the other ways of getting fit (on the right hand side of the board) together to make sure they know what all of the words and phrases mean. As a follow-up exercise, you could ask the learners to work in pairs and agree on their top ten. Such ranking exercises provide useful language practice, and can often be used when you have a suitable list of related words and phrases.

> **Answers**
> 1 13
> 2 walking, cycling, football, rugby, cricket, squash, gym, swimming, running, getting off the bus one stop early, going to the park (for football / running games), gardening, housework

READING BETWEEN THE LINES

MAKING INFERENCES FROM THE TEXT

8 👥 👥👥 Learners discuss the questions in pairs or small groups. Elicit ideas from the class and comment on any particularly original or surprising ideas.

> **Possible answers**
>
> 1 Two and a half hours (150 minutes) of exercise, i.e. you have done your exercise for the week.
> 2 It makes you feel better about your body, yourself and your willpower. Exercise also releases adrenalin and endorphins in the brain, which increase the rates of blood circulation, breathing and carbohydrate metabolism, preparing the muscles for exertion and making you feel happy.
> 3 Fewer people use leisure centres during office hours, so the prices are lower.
> 4 The leaflet is written for adults. It asks the reader to think back to their childhood and talks about offices and work.

DISCUSSION

9 👥 Allow 5 minutes for the discussion, then elicit ideas from the class. Encourage discussion if the class seem interested in the topic.

> **Answers will vary.**

READING 2

PREPARING TO READ

USING YOUR KNOWLEDGE TO PREDICT CONTENT

1 👥 👥👥 Learners discuss the questions in pairs or small groups. Allow 3 minutes for discussion and then elicit suggestions from the class. Avoid commenting on any of the ideas at this stage, as the learners will read the text to find the answers for themselves in Exercise 2.

2 👤 Give the learners 1 or 2 minutes (depending on the strength of the group) to quickly scan the text for the answers to the questions in Exercise 1. Then go through the answers with the class.

> **Answers**
>
> 1 a fruit and vegetables 35% b carbohydrates 35%
>   c dairy products 15% d proteins 10%
> 2 Answers will vary.

WHILE READING

READING FOR MAIN IDEAS

3 👤 👥👥 Learners complete the exercise individually and check their answers with a partner. Set a time limit of 90 seconds (1 minute for a stronger group). Go through the answers with the class.

> **Answers**
>
> 1 D 2 F 3 B 4 C 5 A 6 E

4 👤 👥👥 Allow 5–10 minutes for the learners to complete the exercise individually. Ask them to check their answers with a partner. You could also ask the learners in their pairs to think of one or two more ways to tackle obesity, along with reasons. Go through the answers with the class. Encourage further discussion by asking questions such as *Can you think of any other reasons why education campaigns might work? Why might they not work? What other ways are there to tackle obesity? Is obesity related to class? Is obesity related to a lack of education?*

> **Answers**
>
> 1 to maintain a healthy weight
> 2 to show more clearly how good or bad a particular food product is
> 3 to make junk food too expensive for people to buy in large quantities
> 4 to better protect children from the influence of junk food advertising
> 5 to encourage people to eat five portions of fruit and vegetables per day, to exercise and to discourage them from eating fats and sugars.

> **Reading for detail**
>
> Ask the learners to read the box and to discuss in pairs how they can get the most from a text. Allow a short time for discussion and then elicit from the class ways that readers can best understand the detail in a text.
>
> Explain that there are three styles of reading, which are used in different situations:
>
> 1 scanning for a specific focus
> 2 skimming to get the gist of something
> 3 reading for detail when you need to extract important information accurately.
>
> Tell learners that reading for detail involves a more careful reading of every word, and may also involve further work to help them learn from the text. Before reading a text for detail, it is often helpful to skim it first to get a general idea. This will help focus their

attention, and in turn help them to get more out of a more detailed reading. When reading for detail, tell them that active reading techniques may help them gain more from a text. Such techniques include underlining or highlighting the most important parts of a text, noting the key words (and looking them up in a good dictionary where necessary), asking themselves questions they hope to be answered by the text and writing short summaries (or summarizing the text orally). Remind them that will find it easier to get the detail from a text if they look for signalling language used by the writer. For example, paragraph E of the text contains the phrase *On the other hand*. This tells the reader that what follows contrasts with what has just been said.

READING FOR DETAIL

5 Learners complete the exercise individually and check their answers with a partner. Set a time limit of 5 minutes to encourage the learners to scan the text efficiently and find the information quickly. With a stronger group, set a shorter time limit (e.g. 3 minutes).

Answers

carbohydrates bread, rice, potatoes, pasta, other starchy food
dairy products milk, cheese
proteins meat, fish, eggs, beans
sweet foods cakes, biscuits
high-fat foods pizza, potato chips/crisps
sugary foods chocolate/s, sweets

READING BETWEEN THE LINES

MAKING INFERENCES FROM THE TEXT

6 Learners discuss the questions in pairs or small groups. Allow 5 minutes for discussion. Then invite feedback from the pairs or groups. These questions may lead to some stimulating comment and debate, especially question 3.

Possible answers

1 Obese people become ill more often than other people and take time off work as a result. This affects the economy and means the government has to pay more for healthcare.
2 We should eat a variety of different food to get a balance of vitamins and minerals, otherwise we risk malnutrition.
3 Junk food and ready-made meals are often cheaper than healthy fruit and vegetables or home-made meals.

DISCUSSION

7 Learners discuss the 3 questions in pairs or small groups. Allow 5 minutes for discussion and then elicit ideas from the groups. Try to get at least one idea from each of the groups.

Answers will vary.

Optional activity

As with other exercises in this unit, you may need to approach this discussion sensitively.

As a follow up discussion exercise, and if your class is still interested in this topic, you could ask them whether society should show more understanding of the needs of obese people. You could begin the discussion by alerting the class to the *Fat Acceptance Movement* (also known as the *Size Acceptance, Fat Liberation, Fat Activism*, or *Fat Power* movements), an effort to change societal attitudes in the USA towards obese people. Among other things, the movements argue that obese people are the targets of hatred and discrimination, that obese women are subjected to more social pressure than obese men and that prejudice against obese people, together with aggressive diet promotion, has led to an increase in psychological and physiological problems among the obese. These views are not shared by *National Action Against Obesity*, which actively campaigns against America's increasing waistline. You can find out more by typing *fat acceptance movement* and *National Action Against Obesity* into your search engine.

⊙ LANGUAGE DEVELOPMENT

Academic verbs and nouns

Ask learners to read the box and ask you any questions they might have.

1 Learners complete the exercise individually and check their answers with a partner. Set a time limit of 2 minutes (90 seconds for a stronger group). Go through the answers with the class.

Answers

1 injury 2 provision 3 reduction 4 suffering
5 encouragement 6 solution 7 recognition
8 involvement

COLLOCATION 2

2 👤👥 Learners complete the exercise individually and check their answers with a partner. Set a time limit of 90 seconds (1 minute for a stronger group). Go through the answers with the class.

> **Answers**
>
> 1 serious illness 2 heart disease 3 educational programmes 4 advertising campaigns 5 junk food 6 balanced diet 7 nutritional value 8 regular exercise 9 physical activity

3 👤👥 Learners complete the exercise individually or in pairs. Allow 3–5 minutes and then go through the answers quickly with the class.

> **Answers**
>
> 2 nutritional value 3 educational programmes 4 heart disease 5 physical activity 6 advertising campaigns 7 serious illness 8 balanced diet 9 regular exercise 10 junk food

CRITICAL THINKING

> Give the learners a minute to read the Writing task they will do at the end of the unit (a problem-solution essay, *What can people do to live longer? What can a government do to increase the average life expectancy of its country's citizens?*) and keep it in mind as they do the next exercises.

> **Subdividing arguments**
>
> Ask the learners to read the box. You could point out that this will not only lead to better-organized essays, but also help them develop more specific arguments and avoid generalizations.

UNDERSTAND

1 👤👥 Elicit one example of an answer that is related to diet (e.g. f *cut your calorie intake*) and one that is related to exercise (e.g. b *investing in school sports*). Learners then complete the rest of the exercise individually or in pairs. Allow up to 3 minutes and then go through the answers quickly with the class.

> **Answers**
>
> Exercise: b, e, h, i, k, m
> Diet: c, d, f, g, j, l

APPLY

2 👤👥 Elicit one example of an argument that refers to individuals (e.g. f *cut your calorie intake*) and one that relates to governments (e.g. b *investing in school sports*). Learners then complete the rest of the exercise individually or in pairs. Set a time limit of 2 minutes and then go through the answers quickly with the class.

> **Answers**
>
> **Diet** Individuals: c, f, j; Governments: d, g, l
> **Exercise** Individuals: a, e, h, k; Governments: b, i, m

WRITING

GRAMMAR FOR WRITING

> **Giving reasons**
>
> Ask the learners to read the box and to compare the different sentences. Ask them to look again at the information given on *to/in order to*. You could ask them which sounds more formal (=*in order to*). Note that while *to* and *in order to* are synonymous, some people prefer *to*, arguing that *in order to* is usually not necessary as it adds nothing to the meaning of the sentence. You could tell the learners that *so as to* is also possible, and is also quite formal. Ask the learners to read the notes on *so/so that* again and tell them that *in order that* is also possible when giving reasons, although it is much more formal.

1 👤👥 Learners complete the sentences individually and then check their answers in pairs. Allow 3–5 minutes for the exercise and then quickly go through the answers with the learners.

> **Answers**
>
> 1 to / in order to 2 so / so that 3 so / so that 4 to / in order to 5 to / in order to 6 so / so that

> **Optional lead-in**
>
> Ask the learners to close their books, and elicit from the class why it is important to add detail to their writing, and how this can be done. Allow some time for class discussion, commenting where appropriate.

> **Giving examples**
>
> Ask the learners to read the box. Check that they have understood the importance of giving examples by eliciting the reasons from the class (=they give more information; they add strength to the argument). You can also point out that examples help the reader understand the argument being made.

2 👤👥 Ask the learners to quickly read the gapped text. Tell them not to worry about the missing words; they should still be able to get a general idea of what the text is about. Elicit brief summaries. Then give the learners up to 3 minutes to complete the exercise individually and to check their answers with a partner. Go through the answers with the class.

Background notes: Food and football

- *Pizza* In Britain and some other countries, it is common for people to eat cheaply produced frozen pizzas that have relatively low nutritional value. These are very different from traditionally made Italian pizzas, which use fresh ingredients and have a far thinner crust.

- *Chips* In the UK, chips are long, thin pieces of potato that are cooked in oil. They are similar to American French Fries, but are often a little thicker. In American English, as well as in many European languages, the word *chips* refers to what the British call *crisps*, very thin slices of potato that have been cooked in oil and are eaten cold, usually bought in a sealed plastic or paper bag.

- *Football* is a sport in which two teams of players kick a round ball and try to score goals. In the USA, this sport is called *soccer*. The term *football* in American English refers to what the British call *American football*.

Answers

1 pizza 2 chips 3 heart disease 4 cancer 5 fish
6 salad 7 football 8 basketball 9 gardening
10 education

---

3 👤👥 Ask the learners to close their books, and write up on the board *There are many ways to lose weight, such as … .* Elicit from the class ways of burning fat. Allow some time for class discussion. Then complete the sentence on the board with some of the ways suggested by the learners. Learners then complete the exercise individually or in pairs. Allow 3–5 minutes. Then elicit possible answers from the class, giving feedback as appropriate.

Possible answers

2 Regular physical activity has a range of benefits, such as improving mood and self-esteem.
3 Obesity can result in medical problems, such as heart disease.
4 Junk food can be found in many places, for instance in the street, in schools and hospitals.
5 Schools offer children the chance to do many sports, especially team sports, such as football.
6 There are a number of solutions to the problem of obesity, for example, a tax on junk food.

ACADEMIC WRITING SKILLS

WRITING SUPPORTING SENTENCES

1 👤 Learners work individually and read the table. Ask them to pay close attention to the different parts of a problem-solution essay. Then work with the class and elicit the role of a topic sentence in a paragraph. Make sure that the learners understand that a topic sentence should only contain one main idea, and that this idea should then be supported with further details (the reason behind the topic sentence, plus a supporting example or examples). Ask the learners to read through the topic sentence and supporting sentences.

When the learners have read the sentences, check that they have understood by asking some or all of these questions:

What is a great way to stay healthy (according to the topic sentence)? (=eating *a balanced diet*). You might want to remind them of the meaning of a balanced diet (=a healthy mixture of different kinds of foods) along with examples of what this might include.

What is one source of protein? (=meat)

What are two sources of carbohydrates? (=rice and bread)

What examples of junk food are given? (=fried chicken and cola drinks)

What problems can be caused by obesity? (=heart disease and diabetes)

You could point out that the table provides a good model for the planning stage of an essay, and that it is always a good idea to make notes of what you will include in each paragraph before you start writing. This is especially true in an exam, where a few minutes spent making notes before starting to write the essay can lead to a better grade.

2 👤👥 Either have the learners work on these 4 supporting sentences individually, or ask them to work in pairs. If working alone, they should swap their 4 sentences with a partner for review and comment once they have finished. They should then make any changes that may be necessary following the peer review. Allow 15 minutes for this exercise. Remind the learners that the reason sentences should be directly related to the topic sentence, and that the example sentences should help illustrate the reason sentences.

Possible answers

Keeping fit is a great way for individuals to stay healthy and too little exercise can lead to problems later in life. It is important that people do regular physical activity to strengthen their heart and burn calories. For example, doing sports or even gardening or doing housework are good ways to keep fit. However, people who do not keep fit may face health problems as a result. These people could have problems with their weight or suffer heart disease if they do not keep active.

WRITING TASK

PLAN

1 👤👥 Learners complete the sentences individually and then check their answers in pairs. Allow 2–3 minutes for the exercise and then quickly go through the answers with the class.

Answers

1 Obesity and poor fitness 2 Governments and individuals 3 diet 4 physical activity 5 life expectancy

WRITE A FIRST DRAFT

2 👤👥 Learners use their notes from the Critical thinking and Writing sections above to write a first draft of the essay *What can people do to live longer? What can a government do to increase the average life expectancy of its country's citizens?* Monitor and help with any problems. They could then swap their work with a partner and review each other's work. They should amend their work as necessary before going on to the next stage. The learners should be very well prepared by now, so allow no longer than 20 minutes for a first draft (15 minutes for a stronger group).

EDIT

3 & 4 👤👥 Learners work individually to check the content and structure of their work against the Task checklist and make any changes necessary. Monitor and help with any problems. Allow up to 10 minutes. If there is time and if you think it will be helpful, ask them to peer review their work.

5 & 6 👤 Learners do the same with the Language checklist and make any changes necessary. Again monitor and help with any problems. If there is time and if you think it will be helpful, ask them to peer review their work. Allow up to 10 minutes including the peer review. Have something ready for those learners who finish early.

Answers

Model answer: see page 138 of the Teacher's Book

OBJECTIVES REVIEW

See Introduction, page 9 for ideas about using the Objectives review with your learners.

WORDLIST

See Introduction, page 9 for ideas about how to make the most of the Wordlists with your learners.

REVIEW TEST

See page 115 for the photocopiable Review test for this unit and page 93 for ideas about when and how to administer the Review test.

RESEARCH PROJECT

Help people eat healthily.

Divide the class into groups and ask them to research different ways of eating healthily. Tell them about different areas of the topic they could research such as:

1 vegetarian lifestyles
2 extreme diets
3 healthy eating
4 super foods

Ask the learners to design an informative guide, posters, websites and dietary schemes to explore their findings. Learners could also create journals to record what foods they have eaten and activities they have taken part in and analyze this data to present to the class.

7 DISCOVERY AND INVENTION

Lead-in

You could ask the learners to each write down the first 5 words that come to mind when thinking about science and technology. Then ask them to work in small groups. Each group chooses one of the words from each group member's list as the basis of their discussion. For example, if a learner writes *smartphones* then that group could discuss how smartphones will change in the next ten years. This might lead to a more focused discussion than simply having the learners discuss the world of science and technology in general.

UNLOCK YOUR KNOWLEDGE

Learners discuss the questions in pairs or small groups. Allow 3 minutes for discussion and then elicit one or two ideas for question 1 from the pairs or groups. Encourage discussion, especially where there is some disagreement between ideas presented by different groups. Then quickly go through the answers to question 2 with the class.

> ### Answers
>
> 1 Answers will vary. 2 1c 2b 3a

WATCH AND LISTEN

Videoscript

ROBOTS

Robots are very different from the Hollywood version. They are widely used today in factories, in space, and deep under water for jobs which are too dirty, boring or dangerous for humans to do.

Meet ASIMO. In 1986, the Honda automotive company wanted to see if it could make a humanoid robot that could act like we do, to help in the home, play football, balance on one foot, and even dance. Over the years there were some problems but soon the researchers managed to get a robot that could

walk on uneven surfaces, and shift its centre of gravity like we do to climb stairs. More recently, ASIMO was improved so it could turn round and run at 6 kilometres per hour, using its upper body to control movement.

ASIMO is designed to be people-friendly. It is hoped that robots like this could be used to help elderly people in their home. Honda are also using this technology to create mobility aids for disabled people. It can also push a cart and open and close doors. ASIMO can even shake hands and recognize gestures. It stands 120 centimetres tall, so that it can look into adult faces when they are sitting down. It can hold 2 kilograms in its hands and carry a tray without dropping the contents. So, where next for this kind of robot? Well, while ASIMO is physically impressive, it is still controlled by a human. Researchers in the USA are working on robots that can learn about the world around them, and respond to human touch and voice. The robots are even learning to recognize objects, people and vocabulary.

Soon, the descendants of these robots may be serving you drinks or helping with jobs at home and at work.

PREPARING TO WATCH

Optional activity

Ask the learners to close their books, to work with a partner and write down a definition of the word *robot*. Give them a couple of minutes and then elicit a definition from the class. Continue eliciting ideas until the class has listed all the points covered by *The Cambridge Student's Dictionary: a machine controlled by a computer, which can move and do other things that people can do.* Ask the learners if anyone has a robot at home. If they seem surprised by the question, remind them that robots are not necessarily machine versions of humans. Robots are often small devices that undertake one specific task (e.g. vacuuming, feeding the family pet or mowing the grass). If possible, keep the discussion going for a few minutes as a class before going on to Exercise 1.

USING VISUALS TO PREDICT CONTENT

1 Learners answer the 2 questions in pairs or small groups. Allow 2–3 minutes for discussion and then elicit ideas from the class.

> ### Possible answers
>
> 1 Robots are used in many different ways: for surgery in hospitals, in mining, in car factories, for vacuuming carpets and by firefighters to search dangerous buildings.

2 Future uses of robots include pilotless planes and driverless cars, in the military, in the home, as help for the elderly and for people with disabilities and as pets.

UNDERSTANDING KEY VOCABULARY

2 👤 Learners complete the sentences individually and then check their answers in pairs. Allow 3–5 minutes for the exercise. Then quickly go through the answers with the class. Point out that *humanoid* can be used both as a noun (=a machine or creature with the appearance and qualities of a human) and as an adjective (e.g. *The robot had humanoid features*).

Answers
1 humanoid 2 uneven 3 centre of gravity 4 mobility aid 5 disability 6 gesture

WHILE WATCHING

UNDERSTANDING MAIN IDEAS

3 ▶ 👥 Before playing the video, you could ask the learners to work in pairs and guess the order in which the ideas will be presented. Allow a minute for the learners to discuss their ideas and then elicit the most likely order from the class. Avoid commenting on any of the ideas at this stage. Instead, play the video and ask the learners to see if they were right. Go through the answers with the class. Allow up to 10 minutes for this exercise.

Answers
d c e a b

UNDERSTANDING DETAIL

4 👥 Ask the learners to work in pairs and to try to remember the different things that ASIMO can do now. Allow a minute for the learners to discuss their ideas and tick the skills that ASIMO currently has. Go through the answers with the class.

Answers
1, 2, 4, 6, 7, 8

5 ▶ 👤 👥 Learners complete the sentences individually and then check their answers in pairs. Allow 2–3 minutes for the exercise. Then quickly go through the answers with the class.

Answers
1 robot 2 walk 3 six 4 120 5 two 6 voice

6 👥 Allow 3 minutes for discussion, then elicit ideas from the class.

Possible answers
1 ASIMO was designed as a humanoid to make people react to it as though it were human.
2 We might be afraid of robots which look more powerful than we are or might be able to hurt us. ASIMO's height was designed so that it can look into the eyes of seated adult.
3 Answers will vary.

DISCUSSION

7 👥 Ask the learners to discuss the 3 questions with a different partner. Allow 3 minutes for discussion and then elicit ideas from the class. Encourage discussion, particularly on points where there seems to be some disagreement in the class.

Possible answers
1 Advantages: robots can save us time, robots can ensure that our house is regularly cleaned, even when we are away (e.g. a robot vacuum cleaner). Disadvantages: housework is the only exercise some people get, take away this and we may become fatter and lazier; robots can be expensive; robots can break down.
2 Important inventions for the home include: the washing machine, the tumble dryer, the refrigerator (fridge), the freezer, central heating, the shower, the doorbell, the landline telephone (slowly becoming obsolete as more and more people have mobile phones), the radio, the television, the home computer, the rice cooker, electric/gas ovens and hobs.
3 A robot vacuum cleaner that does the stairs; a robot capable of soothing babies during the night; a robot capable of dealing with email; a computer able to do exactly what you need it to do when asked using normal human speech; a waterproof stereo capable of detecting the song you are singing when in the shower and then playing the original for you to sing along to; a toaster that gives you perfect toast every time.

Optional activity
Write the following quote on the board:
'Unless mankind redesigns itself by changing our DNA through altering our genetic makeup, computer-generated robots will take over our world.' Stephen Hawking
Ask the learners to discuss the quote in pairs. You could assign the pairs roles: As agreeing with the quote and Bs disagreeing. Allow 2–3 minutes for discussion and then elicit ideas from the class.

Background note: Stephen Hawking

Stephen Hawking (born 1942) is an English theoretical physicist. His main work has been on space–time, quantum mechanics and black holes. He is possibly best known for his book *A Brief History of Time* (1988). He has had a motor neurone disease since his early 20s and uses a machine to generate his speech.

READING 1

PREPARING TO READ

USING YOUR KNOWLEDGE TO PREDICT CONTENT

1 👤 👥 👪 Learners could work individually or in pairs or small groups. Allow 5 minutes for reading and discussion if they are working with others and then elicit ideas from the class or the groups.

Answers

1 Possible answers: biology, biography, biofuel, bionics, biodegradable
2 *Mimicry* means copying something. *Biomimicry* means copying something that is living.
3 Possible answer: The wing shape of early planes came from the study of bird wings and wings in flight.

WHILE READING

SKIMMING

2 👤 👥 Give the learners 3 minutes to read through the text and answer the questions. Ask them to check their answers in pairs. Then go through the answers with the class.

Answers

1 Velcro® fasteners, Speedo Fastskin® swimming suits, Eagle Eyes® sunglasses, Mercedes-Benz Bionic Cars
2 burdock seeds, the skin of sharks, eagles and falcons, tropical boxfish

READING FOR DETAIL

3 👤 👥 Learners complete the exercise individually and check their answers in pairs. Go through the answers with the class. Allow 10 minutes for the exercise.

Answers

1 Switzerland 2 hooks and loops 3 swim faster
4 it stops bacteria growing 5 astronauts 6 the yellow oil in their eyes 7 its strength and light weight
8 the smooth shape of the boxfish

READING BETWEEN THE LINES

MAKING INFERENCES FROM THE TEXT

4 👥 👪 Ask the learners to form new pairs or small groups, and to discuss the 3 questions. Ask them to answer the questions as far as possible without reading the text again, but to check the text where they are not sure of the answers. Allow 3–5 minutes for discussion and reading. Then elicit ideas from the class.

Possible answers

1 Small children often have difficulty doing up their clothes and can get frustrated. Velcro fastenings are quick and easy to do up and as children are fascinated by the space programme, they are happy that their clothes used the same technology. Velcro® proved practical and reliable on NASA space missions.
2 Speedo Fastskin® swimsuits were controversial because some people thought they gave swimmers who wore them an unfair advantage over swimmers who did not.
3 Some people prefer cars with a more traditional or attractive shape, while some like products that look unique like the Bionic Car.

DISCUSSION

5 👥 👪 Learners discuss the 2 questions in pairs or small groups. Allow 3 minutes for discussion and then elicit ideas from the groups. Try to get at least one idea from each of the groups.

Possible answers

1 As biomimicry has already lead to a number of important innovations, it seems likely that it will become increasingly common in the future.
2 As it has produced so many diverse examples of flora and fauna (plants and animals) adapted perfectly to their respective environments, we can save time and money in research and development by simply studying and adapting the designs found in nature.

READING 2

PREPARING TO READ

> ### Scanning to predict content
> 👤 Ask learners to read the box. Point out thatç this is something we often do without even thinking about it, for example when we scan the pages of a newspaper or website for articles that might be of interest to us.

SCANNING TO PREDICT CONTENT

1 👤 Give the learners 1 minute to scan the text individually and complete the exercise. Elicit the answers from the class.

> **Answers**
> 1D 2B 3C

WHILE READING

SKIMMING

2 👤👥 Learners complete the exercise individually and then check their answers in pairs. Allow 3–5 minutes for the exercise. Then quickly go through the answers with the class.

> **Answers**
> 1 bi 2 ciii 3 aii

READING FOR DETAIL

3 👤 Learners complete the exercise individually and then check their answers in pairs. Allow 3–5 minutes for the exercise. Then quickly go through the answers with the class. Ask them to find the part of the text which helped them (see the sentences in brackets). With a stronger group, ask the learners to first answer the questions in pairs without reading the text again, and then to check these against the text.

> **Answers**
> 1 T (*We could fly at 480 kph, avoiding traffic lights, busy roads and speeding tickets.*)
> 2 F (*Another big problem is mechanical failure.*)
> 3 T (*In the future we could make our own furniture, jewellery, cups, plates, shoes and toys.*)
> 4 DNS

> 5 F (*BMW and Volkswagen already use 3D printers to make life-size models of car parts.*)
> 6 DNS
> 7 T (*Batteries only last about 15 minutes at the moment.*)

READING BETWEEN THE LINES

MAKING INFERENCES FROM THE TEXT

4 👥 👥👥 Ask the class if they would like to own a flying car and if not, why not? Lead a short class discussion on the topic, eliciting some of the possible problems (e.g. if flying cars broke down they might fall out of the sky, endangering the driver and people on the ground). Then ask the learners to discuss questions 2–4 in pairs or small groups. Allow 2–3 minutes for discussion. Then elicit ideas from the groups once it looks as though most learners are ready.

> **Possible answers**
> 1 If flying cars break down they might fall out of the sky, endangering the driver, passengers and people on the ground.
> 2 Flying cars will cause congestion in the sky as well as on the ground.
> 3 Robot suits could help disabled people move about more easily. They could help people walk long distances and be stronger. They could also enable soldiers to carry heavy weapons and equipment.
> 4 A robot suit arm which bent the wrong way could injure the wearer or break his/her arm.

DISCUSSION

5 👥 👥👥 This exercise could be set up as a pyramid discussion. Start the learners off discussing the 3 questions in pairs. They should then join another pair after a couple of minutes' discussion time. Continue joining the groups every couple of minutes until finally the whole class is involved in one discussion. Alternatively, continue joining groups until you have groups of 6–8 learners. Allow each group a few minutes' discussion time and then ask each group to present their findings.

> **Answers will vary.**

⦿ LANGUAGE DEVELOPMENT

Language note

Making predictions: the future with *might, going to* + infinitive or Present continuous

Point out that *might* can also be used instead of *could possibly*. You could also tell the learners that when a future event has already been decided, and is therefore not a prediction as such, we often prefer to use *going to*, or the Present continuous form (e.g. *I'm going to the club on Friday; I'm having my hair cut this afternoon.*). This is also true of events that you can see coming e.g. *It's going to rain* (=all the available evidence tells me that it will very shortly start to rain).

Definitely is pronounced /defɪnətli/. As the /ə/ sound is similar to the /ɪ/ sound, this can lead to spelling errors. Although the standard pronunciation of *probably* is /prɒbəbli/, many native speakers contract the word so that it sounds like this: /prɒbli/. Again, this can lead to spelling errors.

Optional activity

Ask the learners to think of examples that relate to their own lives. For example, they might say *I will definitely be at school for another two years. I could possibly go to university. I probably won't ever learn to fly a plane.* Beginning with *will definitely* and quickly go around the class eliciting ideas as to what the learners *will definitely* do. Tell the learners that they are not allowed to give an example that has already been given. If a learner is unable to give a new example, switch to *will probably* and continue eliciting examples. Carry on like this until you have exhausted all of the *probably won't* possibilities.

1 👤👥 Learners complete the sentences individually and then check their answers in pairs. Allow 2–4 minutes for the exercise. Then quickly go through the answers with the class.

> **Possible answers**
>
> 1 will definitely 2 probably won't 3 could possibly
> 4 will probably 5 will probably

2 👤👥 Learners complete the exercise individually and then check the language they have identified in pairs. Allow 2–4 minutes for the exercise. Then quickly go through the answers with the class.

> **Answers**
>
> 1 in years to come 2 before the decade is out
> 3 in the near future 4 before too long 5 within the
> next ten years

Optional activity

You could elicit other phrases that refer to future time from the class. Ask learners to write down such phrases in pairs or ask them to research phrases used to refer to future time as a homework exercise. Whichever of these options you chose, make sure that the learners have the chance to share their phrases with the group. Give feedback as appropriate.

Understanding prefixes

👤 Ask the learners to read the box. You could ask them if there are similar prefixes in their language/s.

3 👤👥 Give the learners 5 minutes to write down their predictions. As they are writing, monitor and give feedback as appropriate. After 5 minutes, ask them to compare their ideas with a partner, making any amendments to the language that might be necessary. Finish off by eliciting 1 or 2 ideas from each pair. If the learners seem sufficiently motivated by the exercise, allow a class discussion to develop. Encourage discussion on the likelihood of the predictions, reminding the learners to practice the language presented in the Language note above.

> Answers will vary.

Optional activity

👥 As an alternative to getting the learners to do Exercise 3 from their books or if you feel they need more practice after they have done Exercise 3, you could prepare one set of 33 cards for each pair of learners (prefixes, meanings and examples) and ask them to match each prefix with its meaning and example. Once they have got as far as they can, ask them to compare their ideas with another pair and make any changes necessary. The pairs of learners should then check their ideas against the table in Exercise 3.

Language note

The prefixes *anti-, co-, ex-, mid-, non-, pre-, post-, pro-* and *self-* are often separated from what follows with a hyphen, e.g. *pre-intermediate*. Sometimes new words are hyphenated when they first enter the language, but are then later often written without the hyphen as they become more commonly used, e.g. *post-modern* is now often written as *postmodern*. Other prefixes are often separated by hyphens to avoid unusual or confusing combinations of letters, e.g. *re-evaluate*.

4 👤👥 Learners complete the exercise individually and then check their answers in pairs. Allow 3–5 minutes for the exercise. Then go through the answers with the learners.

CRITICAL THINKING

Give the learners a minute to read the Writing task
they will do at the end of the unit (an advantage-
disadvantage essay *Choose one new area of
technology or invention and outline its advantages
and disadvantages*) and keep it in mind as they do the
next exercises.

Listing

Ask the learners to read the box and think of times
outside class when they make lists. Highlight the use
of *make a list*.

REMEMBER

1 👥 👥👥 Ask the learners whether *mechanical
failure* is an advantage or disadvantage
(=disadvantage). Then ask them whether *traffic
control* is an advantage or a disadvantage
(=advantage). Then ask the learners to
complete the exercise in pairs or small groups.
Encourage them to discuss the reasons
behind their answers e.g. *Why is freedom of
movement an advantage?* Allow 5–10 minutes
for discussion. Then go through the answers
with the class. Invite comments and encourage
discussion where the class's ideas differ from
the suggested answers.

Answers

flying cars advantages: avoid traffic congestion,
freedom of movement; disadvantages: traffic control
problems, mechanical failure
3D printing advantages: make your own products, do
less shopping; disadvantages: low quality, slow
robot suits advantages: super strong, help people
with disability; disadvantages: very expensive,
possible injury

Reasoning

Ask the learners to read the box. Point out that it is
always useful to read around a topic before forming
your own opinions, otherwise your opinions are likely
to be based on prejudice and received ideas rather
than fact. Good writers base their theses on some
initial research, and then carry out further research to
help support and/or inform their ideas.

UNDERSTAND

2 👥👥 Ask the learners to complete the exercise
in groups of 4. Encourage discussion as the
groups complete their notes. Allow 5–10
minutes for the exercise.

Possible answers

Advantages: Computer schoolbooks are lighter and
hold more information. Work can be marked instantly
and the textbooks can be easily updated.
Disadvantages: Computer schoolbooks are fragile,
easy for learners to break and expensive to buy.

3 👥👥 Learners work in the same groups to
discuss an invention and complete 3 in the
table above.

Answers will vary.

WRITING

GRAMMAR FOR WRITING

Language note

Relative clauses identify or classify nouns. There are
two types of relative clauses: identifying and non-
identifying (also called defining and non-defining).
The example given in the Student's Book is of a
non-identifying/non-defining relative clause. It is non-
identifying/non-defining because it doesn't identify
a particular person or thing, it simply gives us more
information about a person that has already been
identified:

*Velcro® was invented in 1941 by George de Mestral,
who saw the seeds on his dog's fur.*

George de Mestral has already been identified. The
relative clause in the above sentence simply gives us
more information about him.

The following sentence is an example of an
identifying/defining relative clause. It is called an
identifying/defining relative clause because it tells
us which person or thing, or which sort of person or
thing, is meant:

*Do you have anything **which will get seeds out of a
dog's hair?***

Non-identifying/non-defining relative clauses tend to
be more formal, and have a high frequency in more
formal, academic texts. They are not as common in
informal speech.

As well as referring to people, relative clauses can also
refer to things:

*George de Mestral invented Velcro®, **which has many
applications where a temporary bond is required.***

That is used as a connecting word and has little real meaning other than showing that a clause forms part of a longer sentence. Some verbs, nouns and adjectives can be followed by *that*-clauses, but others cannot. There are no rules on which verbs, nouns and adjectives can be followed by *that*-clauses and which cannot, but a good dictionary may help. Alternatively, there are several free online corpora that can be used to find good examples of word usage.

1 🔹 Ask the learners to complete the exercise individually. Monitor the learners as they write, clearing up any difficulties. When most of the learners seem to have finished, ask them to finish off the sentence on which they are working and then go through the answers with the class. Allow up to 10 minutes for the exercise.

Answers

1 Scientists are developing new robots, which will be able to do dangerous work.
2 There is a great deal of research to help elderly people, who will benefit from this new technology.
3 There is a lot of new investment in biofuels, which are cleaner and more sustainable than fossil fuels.
4 This technology will save energy, which is good for the environment.
5 The concept car has a special design, which makes it more fuel efficient.
6 The research will be done by scientists at the University of Cambridge, who hope to publish it next year.

2 🔹🔹 Ask the learners to look at questions 5 and 6 and to find the word that can be replaced with *it*. Do this together as a class exercise.

Answers

concept car, the research

Advantages and diasdvantages

Ask the learners to read the box. Point out that signalling language such as prepositional phrases, often referred to as discourse markers or linking expressions, focus attention on what is going to be said. This helps prepare the reader for what ideas and opinions are about to be expressed by announcing the subject in advance, and are a good way of making writing clearer.

3 🔹🔹 Ask the learners to complete the exercise individually. They should then compare their ideas with a partner. Go through the answers quickly with the class. Allow 5 minutes for the exercise.

Answers

1 positive 2 negative 3 negative 4 positive
5 negative 6 positive 7 positive 8 negative

4 🔹🔹 Give the learners 3–5 minutes to complete the exercise individually and then check their answers in pairs. Tell them that more than one answer is possible. Go through the answers quickly with the class. With a stronger class, you could elicit alternative phrases as a follow-up class or pairwork activity.

Possible answers

1 One good thing 2 One point 3 The main advantage / A real benefit / The main argument in favour
4 Perhaps the biggest concern / The problem
5 The main worry

ACADEMIC WRITING SKILLS

Common errors

Ask the learners to read the box. Point out that while writers often mistakenly omit small words, it is sometimes acceptable for words to be left out in both spoken and written English – usually to avoid repetition or when meaning can be understood without them, e.g. *Are you at home on Saturday morning? No – football training*. This is often more natural than a full sentence, and is referred to as ellipsis. However, in academic writing it is usually better to write in full sentences, and omitting small words can confuse the reader. You could give some of the following examples of where omitting small words can confuse or have a negative impact on the reader.

- ~~They are building new digital library.~~ (=They are building a new digital library.)
- ~~Parliament debate the use of tablet PCs in education.~~ (=Parliament *will* debate the use of tablet PCs in education.)
- ~~Robots are expected become much more common over the next decade.~~ (=Robots are expected *to* become much more common over the next decade.)

1 🔹🔹 Ask the learners to complete the exercise individually and then compare their answers with a partner. Go through the answers quickly with the class. Allow 5–10 minutes for the exercise.

Answers

1 to 2 of 3 the 4 as 5 to 6 be 7 in 8 is 9 to 10 will
11 like 12 are

2 🔹🔹 Learners complete the exercise individually and check their answers with a partner. Go through the answers with the class. If you are including regular short spelling quizzes in your teaching, remind your learners to note down any words they find difficult and to include these in their end of unit Objectives review. Note down any words that are causing difficulty and include them in a future quiz.

Answers

1 studying 2 tried 3 money 4 true 5 really 6 which 7 different 8 people 9 with 10 believe

WRITING TASK

WRITE A FIRST DRAFT

1 👤 Learners use their notes from the Critical thinking and Writing sections above to write a first draft of the essay *Choose one new area of technology or invention and outline its advantages and disadvantages.* The learners should be very well prepared by now, so allow no longer than 20 minutes for a first draft (15 minutes for a stronger group).

EDIT

2 & 3 👤👥 Learners work individually to check the content and structure of their work against the Task checklist and make any changes necessary. Monitor and help with any problems. Allow up to 10 minutes. If there is time and if you think it will be helpful, ask them to peer review their work.

4 & 5 👤 Learners do the same with the Language checklist and make any changes necessary. Again monitor and help with any problems. If there is time and if you think it will be helpful, ask them to peer review their work. Allow up to 10 minutes including the peer review. Have something ready for those learners who finish early.

Answers

Model answer: see page 139 of the Teacher's Book

OBJECTIVES REVIEW

See Introduction, page 9 for ideas about using the Objectives review with your learners.

WORDLIST

See Introduction, page 9 for ideas about how to make the most of the Wordlists with your learners.

REVIEW TEST

See page 119 for the photocopiable Review test for this unit and page 93 for ideas about when and how to administer the Review test.

RESEARCH PROJECT

Invent a robot concept.

Divide the class into groups and ask them to think about how they could use robots in these areas:

1 food production

2 the household

3 in the care of elderly people

4 companionship

5 construction

6 helping in dangerous places.

Tell them that they have to produce a brochure and presentation which sells a robot concept to a particular group of people. They have to think about design, the target audience, specifications, features, marketing and the user experience.

Learners should present their projects to the rest of the class and decide on the best idea.

8 FASHION

Learning objectives

Before you start the Unlock your knowledge section, ask the learners to read the Learning objectives box so that they have a clear idea of what they are going to learn in this unit. Tell them that you will come back to these objectives at the end of the unit when they review what they have learned. Give them the opportunity to ask you any questions they might have.

Lead-in

Write the names of two or three well-known brands of clothing on the board. Then ask the learners individually to write down as many other brands as they can think of in 2 minutes on the left hand side of a piece of paper. After 2 minutes, tell them to stop and then give them another 2 minutes to go round the class and find as many people wearing the brands on their list as possible. They should do this as a fast-paced mingling activity, asking their fellow learners which of the brands on their own list they are wearing. They should write the name of a learner wearing that brand on the right hand side of the paper next to the brand name. After 2 minutes ask the learners to stop and count up the number of brands found. The winner is the learner with the most brands found in the class.

UNLOCK YOUR KNOWLEDGE

1 👥 👥 Learners discuss the questions in pairs or small groups. There is much scope for an interesting exchange of ideas here, so it would be worth allowing time for a either a pyramid discussion (see Unit 6, page 54) or following up the initial discussion with a more extended class discussion. Class discussions are useful as they give learners the opportunity to present their ideas to the whole class, and they give the teacher the chance to focus on individual learners' English. However, they can become dull for learners not actively involved so keep them as lively as possible. Allow 5 minutes for the initial discussion of the questions in the Student's Book and up to 10 more minutes for a follow-up pyramid or whole class discussion. If possible, try to have a mix of male and female in each group for this exercise. You can then ask the groups if there were any differences of opinion between the sexes.

> Answers will vary.

WATCH AND LISTEN

Videoscript

MISSONI FASHION

Milan is in the Lombardy region in the north of Italy. It is Italy's second biggest city and one of the great fashion capitals of the world. Like London, Paris and New York, twice a year Milan has Fashion Week.

The fashion industry is worth six billion dollars a year. Angela Missoni is a fashion designer. Her label, Missoni, is one of the most famous, but it has not been easy to be a successful fashion label. The Missoni label was started in 1953 in a one-bedroom flat by Angela's parents, Ottavio and Rosita. Angela runs the business with her brothers, Vittorio and Luca.

Eight hundred people work in Missoni's factories, helping to produce the label's popular collections.

Their company now makes more than $250 million dollars a year.

Angela is busy preparing for Milan Fashion Week.

Milan Fashion Week has started. Critics, journalists and buyers come to the city from around the world. Angela is making last-minute preparations. She has to choose which dresses to include in the show.

Finally, the show starts. Fashion Week is a great success.

PREPARING TO WATCH

USING VISUALS TO PREDICT CONTENT

1 👥 👥 Put the learners into pairs or groups of 3 and ask them to discuss the answers to the 2 questions. Allow 3–5 minutes for the exercise. Then quickly go through the answers with the class.

> #### Answers
>
> 1a the city of Milan in Italy b the Italian fashion designer, Angela Missoni c the Missoni factory d models on the catwalk during Milan Fashion Week
> 2 the fashion industry

Optional activity

You could ask the learners to choose one or two of the photos to discuss in greater detail. What else can they say about the photos? What do they know about the subjects? What would they like to know?

2 ▶ 👤👥 Learners watch the video and check their answers in pairs. Then quickly go through the answers with the class.

> **Answers**
> 1c 2d 3a 4e 5b

WHILE WATCHING

UNDERSTANDING MAIN IDEAS

3 ▶ 👤👥 Play the video. Then check the answers with the class.

> **Answer** d

4 ▶ 👥👥 Play the video again as the learners listen for the answers. Then elicit the answers from the class. With a stronger group you could ask the learners to circle the correct answers before you play the video a second time. They then check their answers against the video.

> **Answers**
> 1 second 2 parents 3 brothers 4 800 5 dresses

LISTENING FOR DETAIL

5 👤👥 Learners work individually and then check their answers with a partner. Quickly go through the answers with the class. Allow 5 minutes for this.

> **Answers**
> 1 800 2 1953   3 6 billion dollars   4 $250 million
> 5 twice a year 6 one-bedroom

DISCUSSION

6 👥👥 Learners work in pairs or small groups and discuss the 3 questions. Allow 3–5 minutes for discussion, and encourage the learners to explore some of the ideas behind their opinions. The *Why/Why not?* extra questions are especially important here, so be sure to explore these during a follow-up class discussion. Allow 5–10 minutes, including time for a class discussion.

> **Answers will vary.**

READING 1

PREPARING TO READ

USING YOUR KNOWLEDGE TO PREDICT CONTENT

1 👥 Learners briefly discuss the 3 questions in pairs or small groups. Allow no more than 1 minute, as the learners may well not know the answers, although they might be able to guess. Elicit suggestions from the groups, but avoid too much comment as the answers are provided in the next exercise.

2 👤👥 Ask the learners to read the web article and check their answers in pairs. Go through the answers with the class. This exercise is intended to train learners to find specific information quickly so set a time limit of 60–90 seconds, depending on the level of the group.

> **Answers**
> 1 Fast fashion implies cheap clothes.
> 2 Traditionally there were 4 changes each year, one for
>   each season, but fast fashion is changing all that.
> 3 If fashion designers changed fashions every month,
>   a lot more clothes would be produced.

WHILE READING

READING FOR MAIN IDEAS

3 👤 Learners complete the task individually. Point out that not all the ideas listed are mentioned in the text. Allow 2–4 minutes for the learners to complete the exercise and then go through the answers with the class.

> **Answers**
> 1d 2c 3b 4f 5a (e is not mentioned)

READING FOR DETAIL

4 👤👥 Ask the learners to complete the exercise individually and then check their answers in pairs. Go through the answers with the class.

> **Optional activity**
>
> You could encourage a little competition here, if appropriate, by asking learners to do the task as quickly as possible and to raise their hands as soon as they have all the answers. The person with their hand up first should be called on to provide the answers. Encourage feedback from the rest of the class. If the answering learner got any of the questions wrong, try to elicit the correct answer/s from the class.

Answers

2 ~~month~~ week
3 ~~customer~~ manufacturer / retailer
4 ~~the theft of ideas~~ impact on the environment
5 ~~water~~ pesticides / chemicals
6 ~~designer clothing~~ fast fashion
7 ~~economy~~ environment

READING BETWEEN THE LINES

MAKING INFERENCES FROM THE TEXT

5 Learners complete the exercise individually. Allow 10 minutes, and when most learners are ready, ask them to form new pairs or small groups to compare their answers. Allow 5 minutes for discussion and encourage the learners to read the text carefully to find the reasons behind any differences in their answers. Go through the answers with the class. For question 4 you could ask the class to speculate why Fatima has the most likes, and for question 5 ask why Jasmine has the fewest likes. Encourage the learners to support their suggestions, and invite discussion from the class. There are many possible reasons so encourage the learners to explore the most likely ones.

Answers

1 Ahmet 2 Carmen and Fatima 3 Sara 4 Fatima probably because she has an ethical approach to fashion and cares about the planet. 5 Jasmine probably because she seems selfish and uncaring

DISCUSSION

6 Learners discuss the questions in pairs or small groups. Allow 2 minutes for discussion and then quickly elicit ideas from the groups.

Answers will vary.

Optional activity

Who buys fashion?

While the obvious answer to question 3 might seem to be younger people, the adult fashion sector is extremely important in many countries, and seniors often have more disposable income than younger people. In the UK this phenomenon is called the *grey pound* (=the money spent by older people as a group), referred to in the USA as the *gray dollar*.

You could ask the learners to discuss the implications of older people becoming more fashion conscious and having a higher disposable income than younger

people. What are the consequences for the fashion industry? As a follow up Internet research task, learners could find out the differences in the amount of disposable income available to some or all of the following age groups in their own country, and see if they can find out what percentage of annual earnings are spent on clothing: 13–19, 20–35, 36–50, 50–65, 66+.

READING 2

PREPARING TO READ

USING YOUR KNOWLEDGE TO PREDICT CONTENT

1 Learners discuss the questions in pairs or small groups. Allow 3–5 minutes for discussion. When the discussions seem to be trailing off, put the pairs/groups together with another pair/group and ask them to share their ideas and to be ready to present them in 2 minutes. Ask the first group to present their ideas. Then ask the second group if they have anything to add. Continue like this until all ideas have been exhausted. Avoid commenting on any of the ideas at this stage, as the learners will read the text to find the answers for themselves in Exercise 2.

2 Ask learners to read the article and check their answers. Then go through the answers with the class.

Possible answers

1 Companies move their production overseas to save money. Labour, tax and raw material costs can be lower overseas.
2 When a multinational company moves its production to a less economically developed country, it creates jobs and provides training for the workers.
3 The main disadvantage for workers in the country where the company is based may be job losses.

UNDERSTANDING KEY VOCABULARY

3 Ask the learners to complete the exercise individually and then check their answers in pairs. Challenge the class to complete the exercise in under 1 minute. Go through the answers with the class.

Answers

1g 2e 3b 4h 5f 6c 7a 8d

WHILE READING

SKIMMING

4 👤👥 Look at the ideas found in paragraph A together with the class. Then ask the learners to complete the exercise individually and to check their answers in pairs. Allow 5 minutes for the exercise.

> **Answers**
>
> B minimum wage, low pay C local laws, dangerous conditions D child labour, education E increased investment, lost jobs

READING FOR DETAIL

5 👤👥 Learners complete the sentences individually and check their answers with a partner. Allow 3–5 minutes and then go through the answers with the class.

> **Answers**
>
> 1 sweatshop 2 media 3 minimum 4 employment

READING BETWEEN THE LINES

> ### Distinguishing fact from opinion
>
> 👤 Ask the learners to read the box and to ask any questions they might have. Point out that it is important to read texts carefully and to be able to distinguish fact from opinion. They must also be clear about which is the author's opinion and which are opinions held by people other than the author.

6 👤👥 Learners complete the task individually or in pairs. Allow 3–5 minutes and then go through the answers with the class.

> **Answers**
>
> 1 fact 2 other opinion 3 other opinion 4 other opinion
> 5 author opinion 6 author opinion

DISCUSSION

7 👥👥 Learners discuss the questions in pairs or small groups. Allow 3–5 minutes for discussion and then ask the pairs or groups to tell the class about their ideas.

> **Possible answers**
>
> 1 Overseas production makes sense for company shareholders if it returns a higher profit. Such outsourcing of production can also benefit local economies, as long as a fair wage is provided and that the workers are well treated (this is also true of domestic production).

2 This depends on the multinational and particular situation in question. The media have highlighted poor practices employed by multinationals in low wage economies, and it is likely that multinationals will respond to such criticisms by emphasizing and improving the work they do in such regions.

> ### Optional activity
>
> If Internet access is available, you could ask the learners to follow up question 2 by researching what multinationals are currently doing to support the local communities in which they invest. Begin by asking the learners to brainstorm what keywords they would need to use to conduct a search, and what websites they could use to find information. Point out that simply going to a search engine and typing in some keywords is not always the best option when trying to find specific information; they could start by going to a multinational's website and seeing if they can find any information on local initiatives.
>
> This could also be done as a preparatory task before the learners discuss question 2. This would lead to a more informed discussion. It would also be useful for the learners to know what multinationals are currently doing for the local communities before deciding whether or not more should be done.

⊙ LANGUAGE DEVELOPMENT

> ### Hyponyms
>
> Ask the learners to read the box and to pay close attention to the example. Elicit other examples of hyponyms from the class to check that they have understood (e.g. *fork* as a hyponym of *cutlery*, *orange* as a hyponym of *colour* and *drama* as a hyponym of *film*). If the learners are struggling, remind them that a hyponym is a word with a more specific meaning than a more general term (e.g. *orange* is more specific than *colour*, and *drama* is more specific than *film*).

1 👤👥 Give the learners 2–3 minutes to complete the flow chart individually or in pairs. Go through the answers with the class.

> **Answers**
>
> 1 beauty products 2 high-heeled shoes 3 natural fibres
> 4 wool 5 nylon 6 casual clothes 7 jeans 8 T-shirts

2 👤👥 Give the learners 3–5 minutes to complete the task. Elicit ideas from the class. You could write the suggestions on the board and challenge the class to come up with 10, 15 or 20 different types of clothing.

Homonyms

Ask the learners to read the box, to look at the Wordlist on page 157 and to find 3 examples of homonyms. Give them 5 minutes and then elicit words from the class.

3 👤 Ask learners to complete the task individually. Allow 5 minutes for the exercise and then go through the answers with the class.

Answers

1B 2B 3B 4B 5B 6B 7B 8A

CRITICAL THINKING

Give the learners a minute to read the Writing task they will do at the end of the unit (a balanced opinion essay *Fashion is harmful. Discuss*.) and keep it in mind as they do the next exercises.

Identifying arguments and counter-arguments

👤 Ask the learners to read the box and to ask any questions they might have. This might be a good opportunity to carry out some revision by eliciting the structure of a typical argumentative essay. Remind the learners that a typical argumentative essay has an introduction, a body and a conclusion. Then elicit the purpose and structure of these three main parts of the essay.

Language note: the structure of an argumentative essay

- *The introduction* gives the background to the topic and includes a statement of the writer's position on the topic (=the thesis statement). It might also briefly outline some of the different views on the topic, and how the essay is to be organized.
- *The body* makes arguments for or against one or more views, to which the writer then responds with counter-arguments, and provides evidence in support of these counter-arguments.
- *The conclusion* summarizes the different views and reinforces the writer's original thesis statement by saying which side of the argument is stronger and why. It should not introduce any new information.

EVALUATE

👤👥 Ask the learners to look at the two examples in the table and to complete the exercise individually. Give them 3 minutes to complete the exercise. Then ask them to check their answers with a partner. Quickly go through the answers with the class.

Answers

A Arguments in favour of fashion: 1, 5, 6, 7, 9, 12, 14
B Arguments against fashion: 2, 3, 4, 8, 10, 11, 13

WRITING

GRAMMAR FOR WRITING

Prepositional phrases

Ask the learners to read the box. Point out that these prepositional phrases must be learned as single items as otherwise it is difficult to know which preposition to use after a particular word to form a prepositional phrase. Lists of some of the most common prepositional phrases, as well as frequent noun/verb/adjective + preposition combinations, can be found online.

Pay close attention to the kind of problems that your learners have with prepositions in both their speaking and writing, and provide support accordingly. For example, one common error at B1 is the incorrect use of prepositions before the conjunction *that*:

*I wasn't **aware of** the deadline.*

*I wasn't **aware that** there was a deadline.*

(NOT ~~I wasn't aware of that there was a deadline~~).

1 👤👥 Ask the learners to complete the exercise individually or in pairs. Elicit the answers from the class. Allow 5 minutes for this exercise.

Answers

1 instead of, rather than 2 except for, apart from
3 in addition to, along with

2 👤👥 Ask the learners to complete the exercise individually and then check their answers in pairs. Point out that more than one answer is possible in each case. Go through the answers with the class. Allow 2–4 minutes for this exercise, depending on the level.

Answers

1 instead of/rather than 2 apart from/except for
3 rather than/instead of 4 apart from/except for
5 Along with/In addition to 6 except for/apart from

Counter-arguments

Ask the learners to look at the tables and read the examples of counter-arguments. Point out that counter-arguments are important in an argumentative essay, as they give the writing a sense of balance and show that the writer has considered a range of opinions.

3 Ask the learners to read the 3 questions, and remind them that they can find arguments and counter-arguments in Readings 1 and 2 on page 145 and page 147. Give them 5 minutes to discuss their answers to the questions in pairs or small groups. Go through the answers with the class.

Possible answers

1 Supporters of fast fashion say it increases the volume of sales and customers can keep up with fast-changing fashion trends (fashions change monthly rather than 4 times a year). Critics say the quality of the clothes is poor, that there is a negative impact on the environment when people throw their clothes away to keep up with the trends. The environment is also badly affected by the amount of pesticides and chemicals that are needed to grow more cotton.

2 Supporters of designer labels say that the clothes last longer and are more environmentally friendly because people keep them longer. Critics say they are too expensive and they don't like being walking advertisements for the designers.

3 Supporters of fashion magazines argue that they are a useful means for customers and industry insiders to keep up to date with the world of fashion. Critics of fashion magazines claim that they encourage a shallow, consumerist view of life.

ACADEMIC WRITING SKILLS

Cohesion

Ask the learners to read the box. You could summarize the language notes in the Student's Book by telling the learners that taken together, coherence and cohesion refer to how well a piece of writing connects together or flows. If any of your learners will be taking the IELTS exam, you could point out that *coherence and cohesion* is one of four major aspects of the essay that IELTS examiners consider when marking the writing papers. With a stronger group, you could go into more detail. The term *cohesion* refers to the formal, stylistic aspects of a piece of writing at the paragraph and sentence level. A text is cohesive if it demonstrates a good use of grammar and vocabulary to bind the paragraphs and sentences in it. While it is common in speech and informal writing to leave out words that are superfluous or able to be understood from contextual clues, such ellipsis can make a formal text difficult to follow and leave a bad impression on the reader.

1 Ask the learners to complete the exercise individually. Elicit the answers from the class.

Answers

2 ones 3 they 4 fashion 5 style 6 This 7 that 8 and 9 these 10 clothing

Coherence

Ask the learners to read the box. Elicit from the class the kinds of things that can go wrong when using spelling tools on a computer (e.g. if you use a correctly spelled word, which is incorrect in the context, the computer may not highlight this as an error). As with the cohesion box above you might want to go into more detail with a stronger group and explain that the term *coherence* relates to the overall content of a piece of writing. An essay is coherent if it presents its arguments in a clear, convincing and logical order, with no holes in its reasoning. A coherent essay also avoids irrelevant facts, arguments or opinions.

2 Give the learners 3 minutes to complete the exercise. Then elicit the answers from the class.

Answers

1 ~~then~~ than 2 ~~thought~~ though 3 ~~bed~~ bad 4 ~~two~~ too
5 ~~thing~~ think 6 ~~bye~~ buy 7 ~~health~~ healthy 8 ~~quiet~~ quite

WRITING TASK

PLAN

1 Ask the learners to read the title of the Writing task again (*Fashion is harmful. Discuss.*) and in pairs or small groups ask them to review the advantages and disadvantages of fashion they discussed during the Critical thinking and Writing sections above. They should then work individually and complete the plan for their essay. Point out how important it is to plan an essay before starting to write. This is especially true in an exam where you are under pressure and it is more difficult to make changes to your writing. Allow 10–15 minutes for the exercise, monitor the class and help where necessary. When most learners seem to be coming to the end of the task, ask them to finish the part of the plan on which they are working and to be ready to discuss their ideas. Elicit ideas that could go into the different sections from the learners and encourage comment and discussion from the class.

WRITE A FIRST DRAFT

2 Learners write the essay individually. Allow 20–30 minutes, depending on the strength of the group.

EDIT

3 & 4 👤👥 Learners work individually to check the content and structure of their work against the Task checklist and make any changes necessary. Monitor and help with any problems. Allow up to 10 minutes. If there is time and if you think it will be helpful, ask them to peer review their work.

5 & 6 👤 Learners do the same with the Language checklist and make any changes necessary. Again monitor and help with any problems. If there is time and if you think it will be helpful, ask them to peer review their work. Allow up to 10 minutes including the peer review. Have something ready for those learners who finish early.

> **Answers**
> Model answer: see page 140 of the Teacher's Book

OBJECTIVES REVIEW

See Introduction, page 9 for ideas about using the Objectives review with your learners.

WORDLIST

See Introduction, page 9 for ideas about how to make the most of the Wordlists with your learners.

REVIEW TEST

See page 123 for the photocopiable Review test for this unit and page 93 for ideas about when and how to administer the Review test.

RESEARCH PROJECT

Find out how ethical your brands are.

After dividing the class into groups, ask learners to list as many different brands as they know. Tell them that they have to pick five from their list and find out how ethical they are. They have to look at:

1 how each company affects the environment

2 how sustainable the clothing is

3 where the clothing is made and the conditions of the workers

4 what the company's ethical and environmental policies are.

Learners can create an awareness campaign to educate people on the most ethical brands. They should write about how different fabrics are made and the lives of people who make their clothes.

9 ECONOMICS

Lead-in

If your learners are interested in economics and would like to know the terms economists use, write the following on the board: *primary industry, secondary industry, _____ industry*. Elicit *tertiary*. If the learners do not know the word, write it on the board and then elicit examples of each type of industry from the class (see Background note below). If the learners are not familiar with the terms, explain what they mean and give one example for each, then elicit further examples. You could further personalize the task by asking for examples from the learners' own countries (only elicit a few of these as learners will go into this in more detail during Exercise 1).

Background note

In economics, industry is traditionally divided into three sectors: primary, secondary and tertiary. The primary sector includes farms, which produce crops and raw materials, and mines, which extract raw materials like metals. Secondary industries are manufacturing industries, which make things from the raw materials. The tertiary sector covers service industries, such as education, banking and finance.

UNLOCK YOUR KNOWLEDGE

1 👥 👥👥 Learners answer the questions in pairs or small groups. Allow 5–10 minutes for discussion and then elicit ideas from the class. Try to get answers from each pair or group. Encourage discussion in case of either disagreement in the class or alternative answers being offered by other learners.

> Answers will vary.

WATCH AND LISTEN

Videoscript

EMERGING ECONOMY

When the Soviet Union fell in 1991, Russia's economy suffered major difficulties. For the next decade, the country went from financial crisis to financial crisis. Foreign investors stayed away, and there was a rapid decline in the value of the Russian currency, the ruble.

Since then, the Russian economy has grown at an average of seven per cent a year, and the country has one of the strongest stock markets in the world. Global investment banks describe Russia's economic performance as 'remarkable'.

So how did Russia turn a failing economy into a financial powerhouse? The oil wealth created a lot of very rich people. These people invested in industries after the fall of the Soviet Union, and now Russia has over one hundred billionaires and Moscow has more than any other world city in the world. But it's not only the rich in Russia who are benefitting from the oil. Retail sales are growing, and multinational companies are now competing to invest in Russia. New shopping malls are now spreading beyond Moscow to the rest of Russia.

However, there is a problem with relying on natural resources for economic growth. The oil is running out fast. It is predicted that the oil will only last for another 30 to 40 years. However, Russian oil has restarted an economy which was in crisis and brought wealth and economic stability to the country.

PREPARING TO WATCH

USING YOUR KNOWLEDGE TO PREDICT CONTENT

1 👥 Learners discuss the questions in pairs. Allow a very brief time for discussion and then elicit the answers from the class.

> ### Answers
>
> 1 tourism, taxation, trade agreements, natural resources, exports, government owned companies.
> 2 d (Russia produced 12% of the world's oil in 2011, compared with 10% for Saudi Arabia.)

Optional activity

As an alternative approach to the above exercise, set this up as a class activity and simply elicit the answers without the learners first discussing them. If anyone in the class is likely to have some understanding of economics, you could elicit the two main measurements of a country's income, namely gross domestic product (GDP) and the gross national product (GNP).

Background note

A country's gross domestic product (GDP) is the total value of goods and services it produces in a year. The gross national product (GNP) is the value of the GDP plus income from foreign investments. The revenue raised through taxation goes to the state, and can be considered as a percentage of a country's GNP. It is not included a country's GNP as to do so would be to count the same money twice.

2 👥 👥👥 Learners discuss the questions in pairs or small groups. Allow up to 5 minutes for discussion and then elicit ideas from the class. Encourage learners to support their suggestions with evidence. Where do they get their ideas from? Again, encourage discussion between class members where there are differences of opinion.

| Answers will vary.

Background note

• The popular view of Russian weather is that it is cold and wintry. This is true but only of the winters. July and August are warm months, which is when most tourists travel to the country. However, these are also the wettest months, with rainfall on one in three days. As with other very large countries such as the USA and Canada, the climate can vary dramatically from region to region.

• Following the collapse of the Soviet Union in 1991, some well-placed Russian businesspeople took advantage of their new freedoms and the general confusion brought about by the fall of the communist regime. Some invested in industry, others sold off unclaimed state assets and properties and used the proceeds as their capital. In a relatively short period of time, many people became very rich very quickly. Russia has its share of super-rich, but there is little evidence that this is disproportionate compared with other major world economies.

• According to a World Bank report published in 2012, in 2011 the Russian economy was the ninth largest in the world. As with other countries across the world, at the time of writing Russia continues to be affected by the consequences of the 2008 financial crisis.

UNDERSTANDING KEY VOCABULARY

3 👤 👥👥 Learners complete the sentences individually and check their answers with a partner. Allow 3–5 minutes and then go through the answers with the class.

Answers

1 economic stability 2 investment bank 3 standard of living 4 natural resources 5 economic growth 6 retailing

WHILE WATCHING

UNDERSTANDING MAIN IDEAS

4 ▶ 👤 👥👥 Learners complete the exercise individually and check their answers in pairs. Go through the answers with the class. Allow 5 minutes for this activity.

Answers

1b 2a 3d 4e 5c

Optional activity

👥 As an alternative approach to the exercise above, put the learners into pairs and give them 2 minutes to put the main ideas into the most likely order before playing the video. Then play the video and ask them to check their answers. Go through the answers with the class.

5 ▶ 👤 👥👥 Play the video again. Ask the learners to complete the exercise individually and then check their answers in pairs. With stronger groups, you could ask them to first complete the lecture notes in pairs from what they remember from the first showing. Then play the video and ask them to check their answers. Go through the answers with the class.

Answers

1 very rich people 2 industries 3 billionaires 4 growing 5 running out 6 30 to 40 years

6 👥 👥👥 Ask the learners to form new pairs or small groups, and to discuss the 3 questions. Allow 2–3 minutes for brief discussion and then elicit ideas from the class.

Answers

1 The oil made some people very rich. These people invested in industry, which in turn strengthened the stock market.
2 Because more people in Russia are now richer and can buy more products and services.

DISCUSSION

7 👥 👥👥 Learners discuss the 3 questions in pairs or small groups. Allow 3–5 minutes for discussion and then elicit answers from the class. Encourage the learners to justify and support their ideas about questions 1 and 2.

Possible answers

1 The source of income (in Russia's case, the oil) may decrease or stop.
2 Answers will vary. The UK , for example exports music, films, video games, fish, car parts, aeroplanes, medicine, minerals like tin and chalk, and weapons. The UK imports cars, fruit and vegetables, oil, gas, clothes, toys and computer equipment.
3 Answers will vary. The UK economy, for example is strong in the service sector. Research and development will probably play a greater role in the UK economy in the future.

Optional activity

As a follow-up task, you could ask learners to carry out some Internet research and to see how accurate their suggestions for all 3 questions were.

READING 1

PREPARING TO READ

UNDERSTANDING KEY VOCABULARY

1 👤 👥👥 Challenge the learners to complete the exercise individually in under 2 minutes, and then check their answers in pairs. Go through the answers with the class. Allow 2–4 minutes.

Answers
1e 2d 3g 4f 5a 6b 7h 8c

2 Quickly elicit possible answers from the class.

Possible answers

1 stocks and shares, art, wine, cars, property, a business, gold, government bonds, land, antiques, a savings account at a bank
2 classic cars

WHILE READING

READING FOR MAIN IDEAS

3 👤 Learners read the text and answer the question. Elicit the answer from the class.

Answer
Stocks and shares are probably best.

SKIMMING

4 👤 👥👥 Ask the learners to complete the exercise individually and then check their answers in pairs. Remind them that they should use no more than 2 words in each gap. With a stronger group, ask them to first complete the summary in pairs without referring back to the text. They should then read the text again, check their answers and complete any empty gaps. Go through the answers with the class. Allow 3–5 minutes for the activity.

Answers

1 investing 2 classic cars 3 prices 4 enjoy 5 return
6 investment 7 risky 8 fashion

READING FOR DETAIL

5 👤 👥👥 Ask the learners to complete the exercise individually or in pairs. Allow 3–5 minutes and then go through the answers with the class.

Answers

1 £200 2 £400 3 £1,200 4 £3,500 5 £9,000
6 £500,000 7 3,000% 8 over £1.5m

READING BETWEEN THE LINES

MAKING INFERENCES FROM THE TEXT

6 👥👥 👥👥👥 Learners discuss the questions in pairs or small groups. Allow 5 minutes for discussion and then elicit ideas from the groups. During the class feedback, ask the learners whether or not they agree with the article.

Answers

1 He says stocks and shares are a better long-term investment than gold because since 1965 the total return on gold was 4.455% while the total return on stocks and shares was 6.072%. He also thinks it is better for society to invest in stocks and shares than in gold.
2 Investing in businesses, i.e. in stocks and shares, increases employment and helps the economy.
3 You can buy the wrong car or fashions can change and it can be expensive to keep cars in the best condition.

Optional activity

You could ask half the class to research sources that disagree with the advice given in the article, and half the class to find sources that agree. The learners could then compare their ideas in small groups ('agree' groups and 'disagree' groups) and report back to the class. This would be useful reading practice, and would help the learners see that it is important to check sources before relying on them. For example, good journalists often check a 'fact' against at least two authoritative sources before relying on it in an article. The same is true of other professional writers, as their reputations rest on both the accuracy of their work and the way in which they interpret the facts about which they write.

DISCUSSION

7 Learners discuss the questions in pairs or small groups. These questions could lead to a lot of very useful discussion, so allow 5–10 minutes for the learners to discuss all 3, depending on whether you set this up as a pair work or group work activity. Alternatively, you could ask the learners to choose the question that most interests them, or allocate different questions to different groups. Once the discussions seem to be coming to an end, ask the learners to finish and then elicit summaries of the discussions from the different groups.

Answers will vary.

READING 2

PREPARING TO READ

USING YOUR KNOWLEDGE TO PREDICT CONTENT

1 Elicit answers to question 1 from the class but do not comment on the answer. Ask the learners to discuss question 2 in pairs. Allow a short time for discussion and then elicit ideas from the class. Avoid commenting on any of the ideas at this stage, as the learners will read the text to find the answers for themselves in Exercise 2.

2 Give the learners 3–5 minutes to read the text individually and check their answers. Then check the answers with the class.

Answers

1 It stayed the same.
2 a There has been no real increase in the economy.
  b Unemployment is higher now than it was in the 1950s.
  c Life expectancy has grown but more slowly than in some European countries.
  d People have more money but have to work longer and harder.

WHILE READING

SKIMMING

3 You could do this exercise straight or you could elicit the best summary from the class, based on their first reading of the text. Avoid commenting on their answers, and ask them to quickly skim through the text again to check whether the answer given was correct. Set a time limit of 90 seconds and then elicit the correct answer from the class.

Answer   c

Skimming

Ask learners to read the box. Elicit suggestions as to specific situations when it might be useful to be able to skim a text effectively. Answers might include skimming through an article in a magazine or website to see if it is interesting, skimming through a text in a test before starting to answer the questions and skimming through academic journals to find arguments and ideas to include in an essay.

READING FOR DETAIL

4 With a strong class you could ask the learners to choose the correct statements without first reading the text again. Then ask them to read the text to check their answers. Allow 3–5 minutes for learners to complete the exercise, before going through the answers with the class.

Answers

1a 2a 3b 4a 5b

READING BETWEEN THE LINES

MAKING INFERENCES FROM THE TEXT

5 Learners discuss the questions in pairs or small groups. Alternatively, elicit possible answers from the class.

Answers

1 A healthy diet/good food, good medical care and a healthy lifestyle (taking exercise, not smoking etc.) can improve life expectancy.
2 Obesity reduces life expectancy.

DISCUSSION

6 Learners discuss the questions in pairs or small groups. Allow up to 5 minutes for discussion, then elicit suggestions from the class and encourage further discussion between the learners. As a financial crisis can have devastating effects on families, be sensitive when leading the class discussion.

Answers will vary

● LANGUAGE DEVELOPMENT

ACADEMIC VOCABULARY

1 Ask the learners to read the lists of nouns and adjectives individually and to tick (✔) the ones that they think they can define. Then ask them to work in pairs or small groups and to take it in turns to choose words to define. They should give a definition for their partner(s) to guess. Ask them to do this for all of the words the group has ticked, and then to look up any words about which they are unsure in the Glossary on page 197.

Optional activity

This would be a good time to introduce online dictionaries if you have not already done so, and if the technology is available in the classroom. If so, learners could find definitions of the words online rather than using printed dictionaries. You can find the online version of the *Cambridge Student's Dictionary*. Remember that your learners may have their own devices, such as smart phones or tablets that they can use for exercises such as these. Such devices can be very useful if used correctly, appropriately and efficiently.

2 Give the learners 2–3 minutes to fill in the gaps individually and to check their answers with a partner. Go through the answers with the class. If appropriate, try to elicit the answers from learners who have not participated very much so far during the class.

Answers

1 economy 2 financial 3 wealthy 4 Poverty
5 manufacturing 6 Employment 7 Professional
8 industry

SYNONYMS

3 Ask the learners to complete the exercise individually and then check their answers in pairs. Then quickly go through the answers with the class. With a stronger group, do this as a class activity and elicit the answers directly from the class.

Answers

1d 2f 3e 4b 5c 6a

4 Go through the two example sentences with the class. Then ask the learners to complete the exercise individually. Quickly go through the answers with the class.

Answers

3 pay for 4 salaries 5 employee 6 buyers 7 fund
8 income 9 consumers 10 workers

5 Ask the learners to complete the exercise individually and then check their answers in pairs. Quickly go through the answers with the class.

Answers

1 and 2 3 and 7 4 and 8 5 and 10 6 and 9

CRITICAL THINKING

Give the learners a minute to read the Writing task they will do at the end of the unit (a description of 2 graphs, *The graphs show the retail price and annual sales of two different types of television. Describe both graphs and explain the data.*) and keep it in mind as they do the next exercises.

Lead-in

You could ask the class whether they think more CRT TVs or more LCD TVs (see Exercise 1 below for an explanation of CRT and LCD TVs) were sold over the past ten years. Avoid commenting, as the answer will be provided during the work which follows. You could also ask the learners if they know of any other types of TV set (the other common type of TV set is the plasma TV), or on what devices they mostly watch video clips, TV shows and films (many people now watch such content on tablet PCs, laptops, desktop computers and mobile phones).

UNDERSTAND

1 👥 Before the learners start work, explain that CRT means Cathode Ray Tube and LCD means Liquid Crystal Display. Give the learners 3–5 minutes to complete the exercise in pairs. Go through the answers with the class.

> **Answers**
>
> 1 a £1,000 b £850 c £850 d £350
> 2 a £400 b £400 c £150 d £150
> 3 a 2,000,000 b 4,000,000
> 4 a 5,000,000 b 2,500,000
> 5 2010
> 6 2010

ANALYZE

2 👥 Give the learners 5 minutes to answer the questions in pairs. Go through the answers with the class.

> **Answers**
>
> 1 When LCD TVs were first introduced they were much more expensive than CRT TVs because the technology was new and new technology is always expensive.
> 2 Prices of both types of TV probably went down as the technology and parts required became cheaper.
>
> 3 CRT TVs came on to the market first. We know this because as established products they were cheaper at the beginning of the period. As sales of LCD TVs went up, sales of CRT TVs went down, which suggests that people stopped buying CRT TVs because they were old-fashioned.
> 4 Yes. As more people bought LCD TVs, the number of people who bought CRT TVs decreased.
> 5 Based on the data given, sales of LCD TVs in 2011 were probably around 11m.

WRITING

GRAMMAR FOR WRITING

1 👤 Learners complete the exercise individually and check their answers with a partner. Allow 2–3 minutes and then go through the answers

with the class. You could do the first one with the class as an example.

> **Answers**
>
> 1a 2f 3d 4c 5b 6e

2 👤👥 Ask the learners to do the exercise individually and then to check their answers with a partner. Allow 2–3 minutes and then go through the answers with the class. If the class is mixed ability, try to pair stronger learners with weaker learners.

> **Answers**
>
> 2 a dramatic fall 3 a slight decrease 4 a gradual increase 5 a considerable (=large, or of notable importance) fluctuation

3 👤👥 Give the learners 3 minutes to complete the exercise individually or in pairs. Then quickly check the answers with the class.

> **Answers**
>
> 1 of, from, to 2 from, to, of 3 Between, and, from, to
> 4 between, and / from, to 5 from, to

APPROXIMATIONS

4 Do this as a class exercise.

> **Answers**
>
> 1 roughly, about, approximately, around
> 2 over, more than
> 3 almost, nearly, less than, under

5 👤 Give the learners 2 minutes to complete the task individually. Then quickly go through the answers with the class.

> **Answers**
>
> 1g 2d 3e 4a 5c 6b 7f

ACADEMIC WRITING SKILLS

WRITING A DESCRIPTION OF A GRAPH

1 🧍👥 Give the learners 3–5 minutes to complete the exercise individually or in pairs. Tell them to pay special attention to the descriptions of the different parts of the paragraph, and point out that not all of the headings (a–f) are used.

> **Answers**
> 1b 2c 3e

WRITING TASK

WRITE A FIRST DRAFT

1 🧍👥 Learners use their notes from the Critical thinking and Writing sections above to write a first draft of the description of the two graphs (*The graphs show the retail price and annual sales of two different types of television. Describe both graphs and explain the data.*). They could then swap their work with a partner and review each other's work. They should amend their work as necessary before going on to the next stage. Monitor and help with any problems. Allow 20–30 minutes including the peer review, depending on the level.

EDIT

2 & 3 🧍👥 Learners work individually to check the content and structure of their work against the Task checklist and make any changes necessary. Monitor and help with any problems. Allow up to 10 minutes. If there is time and if you think it will be helpful, ask them to peer review their work.

4 & 5 🧍 Learners do the same with the Language checklist and make any changes necessary. Again monitor and help with any problems. If there is time and if you think it will be helpful, ask them to peer review their work. Allow up to 10 minutes including the peer review. Have something ready for those learners who finish early.

> **Answers**
> Model answer: see page 141 of the Teacher's Book

OBJECTIVES REVIEW

See Introduction, page 9 for ideas about using the Objectives review with your learners.

WORDLIST

See Introduction, page 9 for ideas about how to make the most of the Wordlists with your learners.

REVIEW TEST

See page 127 for the photocopiable Review test for this unit and page 93 for ideas about when and how to administer the Review test.

RESEARCH PROJECT

Advise your government on how to grow a sustainable economy.

Explain to your class that they are going to research different ways to make their country's economy more sustainable. Ask them to look at these different areas of the economy: manufacturing, fishing (if relevant), small business, technology, farming. Ask them to research how to make these areas more sustainable. Some direction you could offer may be to look at areas like, local produce, minimizing environmental impact from manufacturing, local economies, technology and health and overfishing.

They could produce a report to present to local government representatives.

Learning objectives

Before you start the Unlock your knowledge section ask the learners to read the Learning objectives box so that they have a clear idea of what they are going to learn in this unit. Tell them that you will come back to these objectives at the end of the unit when they review what they have learned. Give them the opportunity to ask you any questions they might have.

Lead-in

This might be a good place to do a freewrite, which is a simple pre-exercise activity that gets learners thinking about and discussing a particular topic. The topic here is *the brain*, but the procedure can be adapted for any topic.

1 Tell the learners that you are going to give them a word related to today's lesson. Their task is to write about this topic non-stop for 2 minutes. They will not be handing in their writing, and don't need to be too concerned with the accuracy of their language. If they need time to think, they must continue writing the words 'nothing, nothing, nothing ...' until some more ideas come to mind.

2 Tell them to write about the brain. They have 2 minutes, and should start immediately. Remind them that if they can't think of anything, they should write 'nothing, nothing, nothing…'. You could model this by writing 'nothing, nothing, nothing…' on the board. This usually generates a few laughs, and can help get the session off to a lighthearted start.

3 After two minutes, say, 'Come to the end of your thought, and stop writing'. Learners then share some of the ideas they wrote about in pairs, small groups or with the class.

This is a great way of getting learners to seize their thoughts as they occur. The texts that this activity produces can be used as the basis of a number of possible follow-up activities.

UNLOCK YOUR KNOWLEDGE

1 👥 Do this either with learners working in pairs or as a class activity. If pairwork, allow 3–5 minutes for discussion and then give the answers to the class. As a class activity, elicit ideas from the class for each question, encourage discussion and then ask the learners to write down T or F next to each question. Then go through the answers with the class.

Answers

1 T However, this is a generalization. Recent research suggests that both sides have some logical and some creative characteristics.
2 T
3 F Every part of the brain is known to have a function.
4 T
5 F The brain is made up of about 75% water.
6 T However, humans have larger brains relative to their body size.
7 T
8 F The brain stops growing at 18 years old.

WATCH AND LISTEN

Video script

THE BRAIN

This organ – one and a half kilos of fat, the size of a grapefruit – holds all the secrets of what makes us human. It is the most complicated object in the known universe.

Young Jody Miller is living proof of the brain's amazing abilities. She has a normal life as a nine-year-old schoolgirl. You would never guess that she only has half a brain.

Jody's first three years were normal but a few weeks after her third birthday, something started to go wrong. Epilepsy took control of her brain.

They found that she was suffering from storms of electricity in her right brain. Seizures happened all the time, and she lost control of the left side of her body. Doctors became worried that the epileptic seizures might kill Jody. The doctors and Jody's parents were left with one choice: to take out the damaged side of her brain.

Our brains are made of two different sides, each split into four parts. Parts on both sides control thinking, movement and feeling. The right side controls the left side of the body, and the left side controls the right. Jody would lose all of the right side of her brain. The space would then fill up with liquid.

The operation was slow and careful but it was a success. Doctors hoped that Jody's brain would change shape, and the left side of the brain would learn to do everything for Jody. Her brain started to change very quickly and she was able to walk out of the hospital. Jody's recovery is proof of the amazing power of the brain.

PREPARING TO WATCH

USING YOUR KNOWLEDGE TO PREDICT CONTENT

1 Do question 1 with the class. It should only take a few seconds. You could then tell the learners to take out a piece of paper and a pen. Ask them to write the answers to question 2 on their own, as quickly as possible. They should put their hand up as soon as they have finished. When the first three learners have finished, tell the rest of the class to stop writing and take the first three papers in. Read out the first list of answers to see if the learner was correct. If not, go on to the next set of answers. Then do questions 3 and 4 with the class. Encourage discussion, and ask the learners to give examples where possible. Allow 3–5 minutes, or as long as the exercise is generating useful language and is engaging the learners.

Answers

1 yellow, blue, black, red, orange, green, brown
2 pink, red, brown, purple, blue, red, green, black
3 Question 2 was probably more difficult. This is because in adults the left side of the brain deals with sensitivity to colour differences and it is the left side of your brain where most language functions are. So this part of your brain is trying to do two similar things at once, which is why it seems more difficult.
4 You might become brain damaged. However, in some cases, people who lose part of their brain experience brain plasticity, which means that their brain grows new connections to allow it to work correctly.

UNDERSTANDING KEY VOCABULARY

2 🧍🧑‍🤝‍🧑 Learners complete the sentences individually and check their answers with a partner. Allow 2–3 minutes and then go through the answers with the class.

Answers

1 Epilepsy 2 seizures 3 liquid 4 Proof 5 operation, recovery 6 organ

Optional activity

🧑‍🤝‍🧑 You could ask learners in pairs to draft 1 or 2 short paragraphs that include all of the vocabulary in the box. You could take these in for correction or ask one or more of the pairs to read them out and invite comment from the class.

WHILE WATCHING

LISTENING FOR KEY INFORMATION

3 ▶ 🧑‍🤝‍🧑 Ask the learners to read through the notes before they watch the video. Tell them not to worry about the gaps or about any new words. They should just get a general idea of what the text is about, together with as many facts as possible. Give them a minute or so to read the text, then elicit the following from the class: *The notes are about a girl who has some kind of problem with her brain, which possibly took a turn for the worse some time after her third birthday. She was perhaps affected by seizures, and these threatened to kill her. She had an operation, which was successful.*

Ask the learners to read the text again and with a partner try to work out what word, or what kind of word (noun, verb, adjective etc.), is missing. Do the first gap with the class as an example (=the missing word is probably a number). Elicit possible ideas from the class, but avoid commenting too much. Then play the video and ask the learners to complete the notes. Go through the answers quickly with the class.

Answers

1 nine 2 half 3 epilepsy 4 right 5 left 6 take 7 slow 8 everything 9 quickly 10 walk

Language note

When we read or hear something, we usually have some idea of the context. In reading, this might be a newspaper headline or the chapter title of a book. When we listen, what we hear may be part of a conversation that we are having, or part of a podcast we're listening to. It is rare that we are exposed to completely decontextualized language. This is why we teachers usually do a pre-reading or pre-listening exercise before presenting new texts. By going through the above procedure with your learners, you will help them notice that they can get a lot out of a text before reading or hearing it in full. By encouraging your learners to think carefully about the missing words, you will prepare them better for the exercise and help improve their confidence in dealing with more complex language. This is also a useful preparatory task for learners taking listening exams that involve completing a set of notes with words from a monologue, such as a lecture or a presentation. Cambridge English Language Assessment (formally Cambridge ESOL) provides free examples of listening papers (as well as reading, writing and speaking papers) online. These can be extremely useful when preparing learners for Cambridge exams. The accompanying Teacher's Handbooks also provide useful teaching ideas for exam classes.

UNDERSTANDING DETAIL

4 ▶ 👤👥 Play the video again while learners complete the exercise individually and then check their answers in pairs. With a stronger group, you could ask them to first choose the correct words in pairs from what they remember from the first showing. Then play the video a second time and ask them to check their answers. Go through the answers with the class.

> **Answers**
> 1 one and a half kilos, grapefruit 2 right, controls
> 3 four, feeling

MAKING INFERENCES

5 👥👥 Ask the learners to form new pairs or small groups, and to discuss the 4 questions. Allow up to 5 minutes for discussion and then elicit ideas from the class. Encourage the learners to justify and support their ideas during the class feedback session.

> **Possible answers**
> 1 Because she is able to function normally even though she only has half a brain.
> 2 They probably felt worried and scared that their daughter would become brain damaged.
> 3 Because Jody was so young and her brain was still growing, when the epileptic side of her brain was removed, the left side of the brain quickly learned to do everything for her, i.e. to compensate for the lack of a right brain.
> 4 It showed how well and how quickly she had recovered.

DISCUSSION

6 👥👥 Learners discuss the questions in pairs or small groups. Allow 3–5 minutes for discussion and then elicit ideas from the class.

> **Possible answers**
> 1 The risks were that the operation might not stop the seizures and Jody might be brain damaged after the operation. She might not recover her speech, her ability to move or her personality might be changed.
> 2 Reading, conversation and playing music are all proven to help build more connections in the brain.

READING 1

PREPARING TO READ

PREVIEWING

1 👥👥 Learners complete the exercise in pairs or small groups. Allow 3–5 minutes for discussion. Then elicit the answers from the class. You could ask the learners if they noticed the gorilla in the first set of photos!

> **Answers**
> 1 Three.
> 2 They are asking for and giving directions.
> 3 No, the man asking for directions in the third photograph is not the same man as the one asking for directions in the first photograph.
> 4 No, he hasn't.

> **Previewing**
>
> Ask the learners to read the box. Point out that this is something that we often do without thinking about it. For example when we scan a website, newspaper or magazine for articles that we might find interesting, the photographs and headlines help focus us on the subject of the texts, preparing us for the kind of information we might expect if/when we read a particular article in full.

WHILE READING

SKIMMING

2 👤 Remind the learners of the procedure you adopted for Exercise 3 on page 179 (where the learners had to complete the notes). Give them 2 minutes to skim read the text and to answer the 2 questions. Elicit the answers from the class.

> **Answers**
> 1 They wanted to investigate 'change blindness'.
> 2 They wanted to investigate whether people noticed when the person they were talking to changed.
> 3 The results showed that we sometimes do not see what is in front of our eyes, because we are concentrating on something else.

READING FOR DETAIL

3 👤👥 Give the learners 5–10 minutes to complete the exercise individually. Then ask them to check their answers with a partner and remind them that there should be no more than 2 words per gap. Go through the answers with the class.

> ### Answers
> 1 Invisible gorilla 2 count 3 ball 4 gorilla 5 50%/half 6 Door study 7 directions 8 door 9 stranger 10 half/50% 11 different

READING BETWEEN THE LINES

MAKING INFERENCES FROM THE TEXT

4 👥👥👥 Ask the learners to form new pairs or small groups, and to discuss the 2 questions. Allow 2 minutes for discussion and then elicit ideas from the class.

> ### Answers
> 1 The people involved in an experiment.
> 2 Because they were concentrating on giving correct directions.

DISCUSSION

5 👥👥👥 Learners stay in the same pairs or small groups, and discuss the 2 questions. Allow up to 2–4 minutes for discussion. Then elicit ideas from the class. Encourage the learners to justify and support their ideas during their discussions.

> ### Answers
> 1 It might be a way for the human brain to control the amount of information it receives at one time.
> 2 Answers will vary.

READING 2

PREPARING TO READ

SCANNING TO PREDICT CONTENT

1 👤 Give the learners a strict time limit of 90 seconds to complete the exercise individually. With a stronger group, give them one minute. There is no need to go through the answers with the class.

2 👤 Learners complete the exercise individually and quickly check their answers in pairs. Elicit the answers from the class.

> ### Answers
> 1 A, B, C 2 A, C 3 A, B, C 4 D is about research

WHILE READING

READING FOR DETAIL

3 👤👥 Learners complete the exercise individually and then check their answers in pairs. Remind them that there should be no more than 3 words per gap. Allow up to 5 minutes.

> ### Answers
> 1 Professor John Donoghue (and his research team)
> 2 controls movement 3 (computer) chip 4 a robotic arm 5 challenges 6 interested

4 👤👥 Learners complete the exercise individually and then check their answers in pairs. They should be quite familiar with the text by now, so set a time limit of 2 minutes. With a stronger group, ask the learners to first complete the exercise without reading the text again. They should then check their answers against the text.

> ### Answers
> 1 T 2 T 3 DNS 4 F (thousands of dollars) 5 F (they are planning a mini wireless version) 6 DNS

READING BETWEEN THE LINES

MAKING INFERENCES FROM THE TEXT

5 👥 Learners work in pairs to discuss the questions. Allow them 2 minutes and then elicit ideas from the class.

> ### Answers
> 1 To control robot planes (*drones*) or tanks.
> 2 Scientists may not want their technology to be used in weapons.

DISCUSSION

6 👥👥👥 Learners discuss the questions in pairs or small groups. Allow 2 minutes for discussion and then open this up as a class discussion. Encourage a deeper exploration of ideas in case of disagreement in the class.

> ### Answers will vary.

Optional activity

You could also do Exercise 6 as a mini-debate, or series of mini debates depending on the size of the class.

- Divide the class into small groups of about three learners. There should be an even number of groups, and for every two groups there should be one chair. For example, if you have a class of 21, then you would have 6 groups of 3 and 3 chairs. If possible, give the learners with the strongest language skills the position of chair.

- Give half of the groups the following statement to discuss: *We believe that the potential benefits of BrainGate outweigh the risk that people might abuse the technology.* The other groups should discuss the statement: *The risk that people might abuse BrainGate outweighs the potential benefits.*

- Each group should prepare arguments that support their statement and think about how the other groups will support their own statement. The groups should also prepare counter arguments for all of the ideas they discuss. The 3 chairs should brainstorm all of the possible arguments for and against BrainGate.

- Give the groups and chairs 10 minutes to prepare their arguments. Then put each group together with an opposing group and a chair. The chair should introduce the topic, and invite the first group to put forward their main arguments. The opposing group should then put forward their main arguments. Each group should then put forward any arguments that oppose the other group's position. Finally, the chair should invite any further comment from both groups. At this stage, the groups should only put forward any new arguments. The chair should manage the debate throughout, preventing people from interrupting, and making sure that each side is able to put forward their arguments.

- During the debate, the chair should take notes on each side's performance, focusing on the following: arguments put forward, language used, professionalism during the debate, e.g. did they let the other side speak, or did they constantly try to interrupt?

- Set a strict time limit of 10 minutes for the debate, then invite each chair to summarize the debate and comment on which side put forward the best case.

- To finish off, you could either ask the chair to declare the winner based on the quality of the debate, or you could ask all participants to vote, with the chair having the casting vote in case of a tie.

⊙ LANGUAGE DEVELOPMENT

MEDICAL LANGUAGE

1 👤👥 Give the learners 2 minutes to complete the exercise individually and then check their answers in pairs. Quickly go through the answers with the class.

> **Answers**
> 1i 2d 3h 4g 5a 6c 7j 8f 9e 10b

2 👤 Give the learners 3–5 minutes to complete the exercise individually and then check their answers in pairs. Go through the answers with the class. You could point out that *cure* and *transplant* are both nouns and verbs.

> **Answers**
> 1 disorder 2 surgery 3 infectious disease 4 treatment
> 5 side-effect 6 limb 7 cure 8 vaccination 9 medication
> 10 transplant

3 👥👥 Ask the learners to discuss the 4 questions in pairs or small groups. Alternatively, divide the class into 4 groups and assign one question to each. Allow adequate time for discussion and then elicit suggestions from the class. Go through any answers below that have not already been covered by the learners.

> **Answers**
> 1 The heart, brain, lungs, kidneys, liver, skin, stomach, intestines, glands, bones and nerves.
> 2 Infectious diseases can be controlled by good hygiene (washing hands, keeping surfaces clean and ensuring that water is clean) and by vaccination. Putting people with an infectious disease into quarantine (=keeping them away from healthy people) can also prevent the disease spreading.
> 3 A cure makes you healthy again. A treatment tries to make you healthy again but may not always be successful.
> 4 It is very expensive. An average heart transplant costs $750,000 in the first year alone. People who receive new organs have to take medication for life in order to stop rejection (=when the body does not accept the transplanted organ).

Academic verbs

Ask learners to read the box and ask them whether in their first language people use different words in academic writing from those they would use in less formal contexts. If possible, try to elicit some examples. You could point out that most people use language in different ways depending on the occasion, both in speaking and in writing. English, in common with many other languages, has certain words and phrases that are used mainly in formal situations. However, most words and phrases are neutral, rather than being either formal or informal.

4 Elicit the meanings of the verbs in the box from the class. Where the learners do not know the verb, write it on the board. Ask the learners to check the verbs on the board in the Glossary on page 194 at the back of their books and elicit the answers once they have had time to check. If learners have laptops, tablets or smartphones, remind them that they may have a dictionary integrated into the operating system, or as an app.

5 👥 Give the learners 3 minutes to complete the exercise in pairs. Go through the answers with the class. Where the learners offer an alternative order, ask them to find reasons to support that order. This may not be possible, but it can be a useful exercise for learners to find reasons against the most likely order or the usual way of doing things.

Answers
The correct order is: d, h, e, g, f, b, c, a

CRITICAL THINKING

Give the learners a minute to read the Writing task they will do at the end of the unit (4 process paragraphs *Write a four-paragraph description of this flow chart, explaining how the body responds to changes in temperature.*) and keep it in mind as they do the next exercises.

ANALYZE

1 👤 Ask the learners to complete the exercise individually. Then elicit the answers from the class.

Answers
1f 2a 3d 4c 5e 6b

2 👥 Elicit the answers from the class.

Answers
1 In the (centre of the) brain.
2 Heat sensors in the skin send signals to the hypothalamus.
3 So that it can adjust the temperature of the body and maintain it as near to 37 degrees as possible.
4 Hyperthermia results if the body gets too hot and hypothermia results if the body gets too cold. Both can lead to seizures, unconsciousness and even death.

WRITING

GRAMMAR FOR WRITING

Language note

Ask the learners to read the box and to discuss the differences between the two example sentences (A and B) in pairs. Elicit from the class the change in emphasis when sentence A is made passive (=sentence B). Point out that the focus shifts to BrainGate, rather than the Brown Institute. Point out that in some texts it is better not to use the passive, as it can encourage vague writing. For example, a lawyer writing a letter to a client will use the active so that the client is clear about who does what. When discussing the passive, the *who* is referred to as the *agent*. However, in some situations, the passive can be perfectly acceptable and even preferred. Give the learners one or two examples from the Language note below, and then elicit further situations from the class where we might want to use the passive.

If you feel your learners would benefit from more information about the use of the passive you could go through the following with the class:

All sentences written in English are in either the active or the passive voice:

• active: *Krois-Lindner wrote the book in 2006.*

• passive: *The book was written by Krois-Lindner in 2006.*

However, in a passive sentence we often leave out the agent completely:

The book was written in 2006.

In academic writing, it is acceptable to use the passive in the following cases:

• The agent is unknown.

• The agent is irrelevant.

• The agent is obvious from the context.

- To connect ideas in different clauses more clearly *The information was given by an unnamed relative, who has since been given a new identity.*
- The writer wants or needs to be deliberately vague about who is responsible *These illegal practices were revealed by a member of staff.*
- The writer is making a general statement, announcement or explanation.
- The writer wants to emphasize the person or thing acted on.
- The writer is writing in an academic genre that usually relies on the passive voice, for example in a scientific research paper *When 15.3 g of sodium nitrate was dissolved in water in a calorimeter the temperature fell from 25 to 21.56 degrees Celsius.*

However, writers should be careful when using the passive. The passive can encourage vague writing, which can be problematic when it is important to show who or what is responsible for the particular action being described.

To find more examples of the use of the passive in academic writing type *the passive in academic writing* into your search engine.

1 Give the learners 3–5 minutes to complete questions 1–3 individually and then check their answers in pairs. Go through the answers with the class.

Answers
1b 2 BrainGate 3 Both sentences are in the present tense but the verb in sentence B has the past participle with *-ed* because of the passive.

2 Give the learners up to 5 minutes to complete the exercise individually and then ask them to check their answers in pairs. If you have time, ask them to copy out the examples of the passive in full sentences. Alternatively, ask them to highlight these sentences in Reading 2, and to consider incorporating some extra study of the use of the passive into their end of unit Objectives review. Go through the answers with the class.

Answers
are put, are (then) connected, are picked up, are created, are sent, (can already) be used

3 Give the learners 3 minutes to complete the exercise individually and then check their answers in pairs. Go through the answers with the class.

Answers
1 was invented 2 be damaged 3 is produced
4 be trained 5 are released 6 is increased

4 Ask the learners to complete the exercise individually or in pairs. Allow 3–5 minutes and then go through the answers with the class.

Answers
1 The brain can be fooled with/by simple tricks.
2 The brain can be trained to relearn skills after an injury.
3 The brain is made up of forty billion nerve cells.
4 The working of the brain is interrupted by epilepsy.
5 The brain can be damaged in an accident or through disease.
6 Brain development can be promoted by playing music.

ACADEMIC WRITING SKILLS

Writing a description of a process
Give the learners 2 minutes to read the box. You could give an example of a process, for example writing an essay, dealing with a complaint or passing a new law.

Optional activity
Ask the learners in pairs to each describe one process with which they are familiar, using as much of the vocabulary in the box as possible.

1 Give the learners 3–5 minutes to complete the exercise individually and then check their answers in pairs. Go through the answers with the class.

Answers
1 shows 2 First 3 After 4 Next 5 step 6 However
7 begin 8 then 9 finally 10 Overall

WRITING TASK

WRITE A FIRST DRAFT

1 Ask the learners to read the title of the Writing Task again (*Write a four-paragraph description of this flow chart, explaining how the body responds to changes in temperature.*) and write a first draft of the 4 paragraphs using their notes from the Critical thinking and Writing sections above. Suggest a word limit of 150–175 words. Monitor and help with any problems. Allow 15–20 minutes, depending on the strength of the group. They could then swap their work with a partner and review each other's work. They should amend their work as necessary before going on to the next stage.

EDIT

2 & 3 👤👥 Learners work individually to check the content and structure of their work against the Task checklist and make any changes necessary. Monitor and help with any problems. Allow up to 10 minutes. If there is time and if you think it will be helpful, ask them to peer review their work.

4 & 5 👤 Learners do the same with the Language checklist and make any changes necessary. Again monitor and help with any problems. If there is time and if you think it will be helpful, ask them to peer review their work. Allow up to 10 minutes including the peer review. Have something ready for those learners who finish early.

Answers

Model answer: see page 142 of the Teacher's Book

OBJECTIVES REVIEW

See Introduction, page 9 for ideas about using the Objectives review with your learners.

WORDLIST

See Introduction, page 9 for ideas about how to make the most of the Wordlists with your learners.

REVIEW TEST

See page 130 for the photocopiable Review test for this unit and page 93 for ideas about when and how to administer the Review test.

RESEARCH PROJECT

Plan an exhibition called, 'The beautiful brain'.

As a class, explain that the learners will be setting up an exhibition. They should brainstorm what the different parts of the exhibition will be and allocate these to different groups. Learners could research:

1 the anatomy of the brain

2 amazing tasks done by the brain

3 how to improve mental health

4 IQ tests and whether they are accurate.

They should also think about who the visitors will be, the location, marketing, the date and if they are going to charge (and give the money to charity). They should also think about activities in the exhibition, producing videos and perhaps inviting specialists to talk about maintaining a healthy brain.

REVIEW TESTS

The review tests are designed to be used after the learners have completed each unit of the Student's book. Each Review test checks learners' knowledge of the key language areas taught in the unit and practices the reading skills from the unit. The Review tests take 50 minutes to complete but you may wish to adjust this time depending on your class or how much of the Student's book unit you covered. Review tests can be given as homework as general revision. Photocopy one test for each learner. Learners should do the tests on their own. You can check the answers by giving learners their peers' papers to mark or correct the papers yourself. Keep a record of the results to help monitor individual learner progress.

REVIEW TEST 1 ANSWERS

Reading
1 A4 B2 C3 D1
2 A3 B3 C1 D4 E2 F1

Vocabulary
3 1a 2b 3b 4a 5b

Language development
4 Possible answers
 a Tiger sharks are more dangerous than whale sharks.
 b The tiger shark is more common than the whale shark.
 c Tiger sharks are stronger than whale sharks.
 d The grey squirrel is larger than red squirrel.
 e Grey squirrels are heavier than red squirrels.

Grammar for writing
5 Suggested answers
 1 The grey squirrel is thriving, whereas the red squirrel is under threat.
 2 Red squirrels are much loved in the UK, but they have been known to attack humans.
 3 Both the red and the grey squirrel have long tails.
 4 Neither the red nor the grey squirrel lives on the Isle of Man.
 5 There are many reasons why animals become endangered.
6 *but* (B) 1, 3; *but* and *whereas* (BW) 2, 4, 5
7 1 both 2 neither 3 neither 4 neither 5 both

Academic writing skills
8 Possible answers. These are the most likely ways of punctuating the sentences but accept other correct ways.
 1 An animal is a living organism that eats organic matter, and is typically able to respond quickly to its environment.

2 A bird has feathers, wings and a beak and is usually able to fly. OR A bird has feathers, wings, and a beak, and is usually able to fly.
3 Fish have no limbs and are cold-blooded. They live only in water. OR Fish have no limbs, and are cold-blooded. They live only in water.
4 Insects are small animals with six legs, usually with one or two pairs of wings.
5 Arachnids are arthropods, such as scorpion or spiders.
9 d, c, f, a, e (b and g are not relevant)

REVIEW TEST 2 ANSWERS

Reading
1 1e 2b 3g 4f 5c
2 1 (The fact that) most morris dances are performed by groups of men.
 2 The document dated 1448.
 3 (The fact that) it is not certain that the name 'morris' comes from the Moors of North Africa.
 4 The Thaxted Morris Dancing Festival.
 5 The Great Bustard.

Vocabulary
3 1e 2c 3a 4b 5d
4 1a 2a 3b 4a 5b

Language development
5 Possible answers
 1 Many people in England love football.
 2 Americans often dress casually.
 3 German speakers tend to be more direct than English speakers, who sometimes misinterpret this as rudeness.
 4 Many Indians do not like to say 'no'.
 5 The Japanese can be quite formal.
6 1 major 2 brief 3 separate 4 common 5 certain
7 1 In a business meeting, Japanese people often like to know what your position is in your company before they talk to you.
 2 Traditions are respected in the rural areas where little has changed for generations.
 3 When the couple leave the church, guests throw paper confetti and take a lot of photographs of them.
 4 I told my florist I wanted the flowers to look very natural, as if the bouquet had just been cut.
 5 Susan told me that Muriel wanted a pink iced cake for her wedding in May.

Academic writing skills
8 1b 2d 3a 4e 5c

REVIEW TEST 3 ANSWERS

Reading

1 A2 B5 C1 D3 E4

2 1 ~~Felix~~ Gunther

2 ~~The professor~~ The professor's secretary

3 ~~Athens~~ Heraklion, Crete

4 ~~Officials~~ Cretan labourers

5 ~~The state archaeologist~~ The Greek government

Vocabulary

3 1b 2e 3d 4a 5c

4 1 exhibit 2 knight 3 tuition 4 hieroglyphics 5 fossil

Language development

5 1 research 2 financial 3 period 4 display 5 tuition
6 document

6 Possible answers

1 Visiting museums is a good idea.

2 We should learn from the past.

3 Exhibiting artefacts found during digs is a good
idea.

4 Children should be encouraged to visit museums.

Grammar for writing

7 Possible answers (the most likely answer is provided
first, but all are correct).

1 **Although** the results appear to be valid, further
testing is required. / The results appear to be valid,
although further testing is required.

2 **Although** Higgins makes some interesting points,
I disagree with many of his conclusions. / Higgins
makes some interesting points, **although** I disagree
with many of his conclusions.

3 **Although** this book is written mainly for those
working in education, the ideas can be used in
other fields. / This book is written mainly for those
working in education, **although** the ideas can be
used in other fields.

4 This is a practical manual of paper chromatography,
although theoretical aspects are considered in the
introduction. / **Although** this is a practical manual
of paper chromatography, theoretical aspects are
considered in the introduction.

5 **Although** Professor Bird retired officially from
his university position nine years ago, he remains
very active in research. / Professor Bird retired
officially from his university position nine years ago,
although he remains very active in research.

8 1 The results appear to be valid. **However**, further
testing is required.

2 Higgins makes some interesting points. **However**, I
disagree with many of his conclusions.

3 This book is written mainly for those working in
education. **However**, the ideas can be used in other
fields.

4 This is a practical manual of paper chromatography.
However, theoretical aspects are considered in the
introduction.

5 Professor Bird retired officially from his university
position nine years ago. **However**, he remains very
active in research.

Academic writing skills

9 1S 2S 3T 4B 5S 6T 7B 8S 9T 10B

REVIEW TEST 4 ANSWERS

Reading

1 C

2 1 ox carts 2 a bicycle/bicycles 3 ox carts/slow moving
vehicles/ox carts and other slow moving vehicles 4
traffic problems 5 Public 6 1951 7 traffic jam 8 1853 9
2.8 million tonnes

Vocabulary

3 1f 2h 3g 4i 5c 6a 7d 8k 9l 10e

Language development

4 1 traffic congestion 2 cycle lane 3 public transport 4
parking restrictions 5 road rage

5 1 convince 2 realize 3 prevent 4 require 5 attempt

Grammar for writing

6 a not b unless c If d unless e not f if g not h Unless i
unless j if

Academic writing skills

7 a sum b main c caused d lack e Overall f would g
solution h only i also j friendly

REVIEW TEST 5 ANSWERS

Reading

1 f, b, e, c, a, d

2 1 biodiversity 2 climate change 3 submerged (*flooded*
is also possible but *flooding* is usually associated with
a sudden rush of water) 4 account for

Vocabulary

3 a deforestation b subsistence c effects d aridity e
climate change f logging g graze h consequences i
leads to j erosion

Language development

4 1 challenge 2 predict 3 trend 4 annual 5 issue

5 1 renewable energy 2 greenhouse gasses 3 climate
change 4 subsistence farming 5 environmental
disasters

Grammar for writing

6 1 because 2 result 3 because of 4 leads to 5 due 6
result 7 caused 8 because of 9 because 10 due

Academic writing skills

7 1 causing, number of 2 changing, three main 3 cause
of, because of 4 loss, results 5 effect, cause

REVIEW TEST 6 ANSWERS

Reading

1   1 100 kilometres 2 35 litres 3 75% of the energy 4 2,700 (4,000-1,300) 5 21 days (=23 days minus 2 rest days)

2   1F 2C 3E 4B 5D

Vocabulary

3   a physical activity b realize c exercise d reduce e serious illness f self-esteem g obesity h heart disease
i life expectancy j junk food

Language development

4   1 provision 2 reduction 3 suffering 4 encouragement 5 solution

5   1 nutritional value 2 serious illness 3 regular exercise 4 balanced diet 5 advertizing campaign

Grammar for writing

6   1 such as 2 so that 3 to 4 so that 5 to 6 For example 7 such as (for example is not an option here as there would need to be a comma before and after it) 8 so that 9 To 10 so that

Academic writing skills

7   1b 2c 3a 4e 5d

REVIEW TEST 7 ANSWERS

Reading

1   1F 2C 3E 4A 5D

2   1F 2F 3T 4F 5T

Vocabulary

3   1 centre of gravity 2 humanoid 3 gestures 4 mobility aid 5 uneven

4   1 definitely 2 probably 3 advantage 4 concern 5 benefit

Language development

5   1 will definitely 2 will probably 3 could possibly 4 probably won't 5 definitely won't

6   1 auto- 2 bio- 3 mis- 4 sub- 5 pre-

Grammar for writing

7   1   One case study involved a 10-year-old girl, who had been given a robot doll for several weeks.

    2   The head of design has a favourite question, which he puts to those unsure about using robots in caring situations.

    3   Most people choose the elevator, which is a kind of robot.

    4   I'm sending you an email I received from Max Mustermann, who attended your webinar about robots.

    5   You must also provide a short biography, which should include qualifications and teaching experience.

8   1c 2e 3d 4b 5a

Academic writing skills

9   1 correct 2 carry 3 possibly 4 correct 5 innovation 6 Changing 7 successful 8 correct 9 larger 10 should

REVIEW TEST 8 ANSWERS

Reading

1   1d 2h 3j 4b 5i 6e

2   1 ~~Panama~~ San Francisco 2 ~~denim~~ canvas 3 ~~rivets~~ marks
    4 ~~early~~ the end of

Vocabulary

3   1 ~~accomodate~~ accommodate 2 ~~beuty~~ beauty 3 ~~aproximately~~ approximately 4 ~~bay~~ pay 5 ~~abart~~ apart

4   1 ~~fibres~~ textiles 2 ~~areas~~ plants 3 ~~artificial~~ casual 4 ~~payments~~ costs 5 ~~in addition to~~ instead of

Language development

5   1 labour costs 2 consumption 3 textiles 4 artificial fibres
    5 natural fibres

6   1A 2B 3A 4B 5B

Grammar for writing

7   1 apart 2 rather 3 except 4 along 5 except 6 in addition 7 instead 8 rather 9 along 10 apart

Academic writing skills

8   1 that 2 them 3 out 4 in 5 on 6 of 7 for 8 such 9 to 10 this (such would also be possible, but should already have been used for 8)

REVIEW TEST 9 ANSWERS

Reading

1   1 democratically elected governments 2 economy/ economic growth 3 (natural) resources 4 (a) recession 5 (outside) investment 6 retail sales 7 interest 8 (shopping) malls
9 standard of living 10 manufacturing

Vocabulary

2   1 poverty 2 decrease 3 retail sales 4 investment 5 economy 6 wealth 7 investors 8 market value 9 recession 10 increase

Language development

3   1 financial 2 manufactured 3 value 4 economy 5 profession

4   1 financial system 2 occupation 3 stability 4 return 5 development

Grammar for writing

7   1 rise sharply 2 fall dramatically 3 decrease slightly 4 increase gradually 5 fluctuate considerably

6   1 of 2 in/for 3 for 4 by/from 5 to

Academic writing skills

7 *The term 'widget' is used in economics to describe an imagined small product made by a company. In general English, it is also used to refer to any small device whose name you have forgotten or do not know.*

1D 2A 3E 4B 5F

REVIEW TEST 10 ANSWERS

Reading

1 1D 2D 3B 4C 5A

2 1 disorders 2 proof 3 organ 4 seizures 5 carry out

Vocabulary

3 1 recovery 2 complain 3 organ (*the sentence describes the appendix*) 4 treatment 5 surgery 6 operation 7 seizure
8 care 9 disorder 10 recover

Language development

4 1 appear 2 complain 3 advise 4 confirm 5 recover

5 1 infectious diseases 2 medication 3 vaccinations 4 transplant 5 cure

Grammar for writing

6 1 be trained 2 was advised 3 are produced
4 be cured 5 are released 6 is increased 7 were transplanted 8 were damaged 9 was confirmed 10 was invented

Academic writing skills

7 1 To begin with 2 then 3 When 4 Following this 5 is then

NAME: .... Date: ....

READING (10 marks)

1 Read the factsheet and match the main ideas (A–D) to the paragraphs where they were mentioned (1–4). 1 mark for each correct answer.

A What to do if you are hurt by a man-of-war. _____

B Portuguese men-of-war mainly swim in warm water. _____

C Touching these creatures can be very upsetting. _____

D Portuguese men-of-war stay together in large groups. _____

---

1 If you should ever go swimming in one of the world's warmer oceans, it might be a good idea to first check that there are no Portuguese men-of-war in the area. These creatures look like jellyfish, but are in fact colonies of tiny creatures working together. They are usually found in groups, each of which can contain over a 1,000 men-of-war.

2 Men-of-war prefer warm waters such as the tropical and subtropical parts of the Pacific and Indian oceans, which are rich sources of food. They float wherever the wind or the currents in the sea take them. Because of this, men-of-war have also been found in colder areas, such as the coasts of Scotland, Wales and Ireland.

3 So, why would you want to avoid swimming near these creatures? Their tentacles. Although men-of-war float on the surface, their tentacles can find prey 10 metres under the water and in some cases they can reach up to 50 metres. Each of these tentacles is covered with poisonous venom that the carnivorous man-of-war uses to paralyze fish and other small sea creatures. The sting is rarely fatal for humans, but it is extremely painful. Imagine the worst pain you have ever experienced and multiply that by ten. You are not even close. And even when they are dead, these creatures can still give you a nasty sting.

4 If you should be unlucky enough to be stung by one of these creatures, vinegar should never be used. It could cause severe bleeding. The best thing to do is to remove any parts of the tentacles that may be stuck to your skin, being careful not to touch them with your fingers. You should then apply salt water (not fresh water, as this will make the sting worse). You can further ease the pain by soaking the affected area in hot water for 15–20 minutes.

---

2 Look at the words in bold in the questions below. Which paragraph (1–4) of the factsheet should you look at to find the answer? 1 mark for each correct answer.

A Can men-of-war **kill** people? _____

B How far can a man-of-war reach when **attacking** a creature? _____

C What type of **life-form** is the man-of-war? _____

D What could cause loss of **blood**? _____

E Do men-of-war **live** only in warm water? _____

F What is the usual **habitat** of the man-of-war? _____

VOCABULARY (5 marks)

3 Choose the one word (a or b) that fits both sentences. 1 mark for each correct answer.

1   It's quite _____ to see grey squirrels in the UK.

The surname 'Martin' is very _____ in France.

a   common   b   familiar

2   It's not surprising you feel _____ if you haven't slept for days.

Cats often prey on _____ animals such as small mice and birds that have fallen out of their nests.

a   endangered   b   weak

3   If I am late home, he gets _____ and starts shouting.

These _____ marketing tactics are effective but unethical.

a   cruel   b   aggressive

4   I prefer animals to be in their natural _____.

Almost 65% of the original forest _____ was destroyed by fire.

a   habitat   b   sanctuary

5   This rare illness is _____ in almost all cases.

He made the _____ error of accepting bad advice.

a   dangerous   b   fatal

LANGUAGE DEVELOPMENT (10 marks)

4 Use the information in sentences 1–5 to complete sentences a–e. Use comparative forms of the adjectives in the box to complete the sentences. 2 marks for each correct answer.

strong   common   dangerous   heavy   large

1   Whale sharks do not attack humans, whereas tiger sharks have attacked 119 humans since 2009.

a   Tiger sharks are _____ whale sharks.

2   The tiger shark is not at risk of extinction, whereas the whale shark is endangered.

b   The tiger shark is _____ the whale shark.

3   Whale sharks do not have sharp teeth or a powerful bite, unlike tiger sharks.

c   Tiger sharks are _____ whale sharks.

4   The red squirrel has a typical head-and-body length of 19 to 23 centimetres, whereas the grey squirrel has a typical head-and-body length of 23 to 30 centimetres,

d   The grey squirrel _____ the red squirrel.

5   Grey squirrels weigh more than red squirrels.

e   Grey squirrels are _____ red squirrels.

GRAMMAR FOR WRITING (15 marks)

5 Put the words in the correct order to make sentences. The first word for each sentence has been written for you. 1 mark for each correct answer.

1 The grey squirrel / whereas / thriving / under threat / the red squirrel / is / is

The _____

2 Red squirrels / humans / but / much loved in the UK / have been known / are / they / to attack

Red _____

3 Both / tails / the red squirrel / have / the grey squirrel / and / long

Both _____

4 Neither / the Isle of Man / nor / the red squirrel / live / the grey squirrel / on

Neither _____

5 There / animals / endangered / why / are / many reasons / become

There _____

6 Each of these sentences can be completed with *but*. Some of them can also be completed with *whereas*. For each sentence, write B (for *but* only) or BW (for both *but* and *whereas*). 1 mark for each correct answer.

1 I like romance films, _____ not comedies.

2 The climate is quite mild in the south of the country, _____ in the north it is often cold and rainy.

3 The book was badly written, _____ I still enjoyed it.

4 Some couples now live separately, _____ before they would only have one home.

5 Austria has many mountains, _____ Denmark is a very flat country.

7 Complete the sentences using *neither* or *both*. 1 mark for each correct answer.

1 _____ the red squirrel and the grey squirrel have a nasty bite and can attack humans when they are angry.

2 _____ my aunt nor my uncle live on the Isle of Man.

3 _____ of my parents eat red meat, although they do eat chicken.

4 _____ species of shark pose a danger to swimmers.

5 _____ the lynx and the lion are wild cats, but they are much larger than domestic ones.

ACADEMIC WRITING SKILLS (10 marks)

8 Correct the punctuation of the sentences below (sometimes there are two sentences to punctuate). 1 mark for each correct answer.

1 an animal is a living organism that eats organic matter and is typically able to respond quickly to its environment

_____

2 a bird has feathers wings and a beak and is usually able to fly

_____

3 fish have no limbs and are cold-blooded they live only in water

_____

4 insects are small animals with six legs usually with one or two pairs of wings

_____

5 arachnids are arthropods such as scorpion or spiders

_____

9 Put the sentences in the best order to make a 5-sentence paragraph that starts with a topic sentence, then has supporting sentences and ends with a concluding sentence. You will not need to use two of the sentences. 1 mark for each correct answer.

a Although this skill is useful in keeping it out of danger, the lynx is a protected animal in many countries. _____

b It lends its name to a constellation of stars between Ursa Major and Gemini. _____

c It is possibly best known for its excellent hearing. _____

d The lynx is a medium-sized wild cat with yellowish-brown fur, a short tail and pointed ears. _____

e For example, the Alpenzoo in Innsbruck provides a safe environment from which young lynx cubs can be reintroduced into the wild. _____

f Indeed, in some countries people are described as having the hearing of a lynx. _____

g It should not be confused with the sphinx, which was a winged monster with a woman's head and a lion's body. _____

TOTAL ___/50

REVIEW TEST 2

NAME: .... **Date:** ....

READING (10 marks)

1 Read the article about a traditional English folk dance. Choose the best sentence (a–g) to fill each of the gaps. You will not need to use all of the sentences. 1 mark for each correct answer.

a The side's founder said, 'We try to raise awareness of the Bustards every time we dance.'

b One such example is the Thaxted Morris Dancing Festival which is held in June.

c More recently, morris sides have attempted new dances based on contemporary themes.

d Their green and gold costumes reflect the country's flag.

e It is performed outside, usually by groups of men.

f Some morris sides can trace their roots back over 150 years.

g Whatever their particular costume, Morris Men usually wear white shirts, with coloured bands around their chests.

A Morris dancing, also known simply as 'morris' is a type of English folk dance, traditionally associated with the month of May.
1_____. Despite this, some morris 'sides' do allow women, and there are also some all women sides. The exact origins of the dance are unclear, although one document dated 1448 makes reference to the morris men. This details the payment of seven shillings (about 30p in today's money) to morris dancers by the Goldsmiths' Company in London. Some people believe that the name 'morris' comes from the Moors of North Africa, although this is not certain.

B Although the dance is closely linked with spring festivals such as May Day, some towns hold morris gatherings throughout the summer months. 2_____. This celebrated gathering attracts sides from all over England. Indeed, Thaxted has been described as the spiritual home of the morris. The town has played a major role in the current popularity enjoyed by the morris and its traditions and helped revive the morris tradition at the start of the 20th century.

C Morris dancing is very lively and is usually accompanied by an accordion player or violinist. The dancers often have bells on their knees that ring loudly as they dance. The dancers are usually arranged either in two lines, or in a circle facing each other. They wear different clothes, depending on which part of England they are from. 3 _____. They often wave white handkerchiefs, or carry short sticks that they bang together as they dance.

D 4_____. The Britannia Coco-nut Dancers from Bacup have staged the annual Easter Boundary Dance since the mid-nineteenth century. The dancers blacken their faces to reflect the coal mining traditions of the group. 5 _____. In April 2012, a Wiltshire morris dancing troupe created a series of dances that mimic the world's heaviest flying bird, the Great Bustard. This was hunted to extinction in the UK in 1832, but reintroduced to Wiltshire in 2004. The new dances were invented to raise awareness of the Bustard.

---

2 What does the word *this* refer to in the following phrases? 1 mark for each correct answer.

1 Despite this (paragraph A) _____

2 This details the payment (paragraph A) _____

3 this is not certain (paragraph A) _____

4 This celebrated gathering (paragraph B) _____

5 This was hunted to extinction (paragraph D) _____

VOCABULARY (10 marks)

3 Match the words (1–5) with the definitions (a–e). 1 mark for each correct answer.

1 engagement _____	a the area immediately surrounding someone
2 registry office _____	b a friendly sign of welcome
3 personal space _____	c a local government building where civil marriages are held
4 greeting _____	d arriving or happening at the correct time
5 punctual _____	e an agreement to marry someone

4 Choose the one word (a or b) that fits both sentences. 1 mark for each correct answer.

1 The _____ looked beautiful in her long, white dress.

In some cultures, the father 'gives away' the _____ at the wedding.

a bride   b groom

2 They gave us a very warm _____.

The wedding _____ must have been very expensive. There were over 150 guests!

a reception   b greeting

3 The _____ is proof that you have passed the course.

We were given a marriage _____ at the registry office.

a requirement   b certificate

4 We plan to have a very traditional wedding _____.

The _____ will be held at St Paul's Cathedral in London next Wednesday.

a ceremony   b engagement

5 Are there any _____ that must be met before you are allowed to marry?

What are the _____ for establishing a company in your country?

a personal spaces   b legal requirements

LANGUAGE DEVELOPMENT (10 marks)

5 Rewrite the sentences using the words in the brackets to avoid generalizations. You may also need to make some other changes for the sentences to be correct. 1 mark for each correct answer.

1 Everyone in England loves football. (many people)

_____

2 Americans always dress casually. (often)

_____

3 German speakers are always more direct than English speakers, who sometimes misinterpret this as rudeness. (tend)

_____

4 Indians do not like to say 'no'. (many)

_____

5 The Japanese are quite formal. (can)

_____

6 Replace the words in bold in the sentences (1–5) below with the academic adjectives in the box. You will not need to use all the words. 1 mark for each correct answer.

| obvious   separate   serious   brief   major   common   certain |

1 The ruling will have a **big** _____ impact on the way schools are run.
2 During her **short** _____ time in office, Ms Pillar became a much-respected leader.
3 These are **different** _____ issues, and should not be discussed together.
4 In this country, it is not **usual** _____ for people to walk barefoot in the streets.
5 Should children be allowed to use study materials in **some** _____ exams?

GRAMMAR FOR WRITING (10 marks)

7 Rewrite each sentence, using the words in the boxes to add interest. 2 marks for each correct answer.

1 Japanese people often like to know what your position is.

| in your company   in a business meeting   before they talk to you |

_____

_____

2 Traditions are respected in the areas where little has changed.

| generations   for   rural |

_____

_____

3 When the couple leave the church, guests throw confetti and take photographs.

| paper   a lot of   of them |

_____

_____

4 I told my florist I wanted the flowers to look as if just cut.

| been   the bouquet had   very natural |

_____

_____

5 Muriel wanted a cake for her wedding.

| iced | that | in May | pink | Susan told me |

_____

_____

ACADEMIC WRITING SKILLS (10 marks)

8 Put the paragraphs (a–e) in the correct order to form a complete essay. 2 marks for each correct answer.

a The couple may serve tea to the bride's parents before the wedding ceremony. The ceremony itself is quite simple and the most important event is the wedding reception and dinner. The wedding dinner may have ten courses. At the end of the reception, the guests line up and the bride and groom say goodbye to them all individually.

b Weddings are one of the most important occasions in Chinese life. There are many traditions in a Chinese wedding, some of which are still common today.

c Weddings are special in most cultures and Chinese weddings are also very important events for the families involved.

d Before the wedding, the bride spends some time with her close friends and sometimes she has a special person who helps her to do her hair on the day of the wedding. The groom's parents dress him on the day of the wedding and then there is a procession from his house to the bride's house to collect her and take her back to his parents' house or to the wedding venue. For fun, the bridesmaids may try to block the way for the groom and ask him lots of questions about the bride.

e In the past, marriages were arranged between the parents. The groom's family would take presents to the bride's family before the wedding. Then, three days before the wedding, the bride's family would take gifts to the groom's house. The groom would also buy a marriage bed for his new wife. The gifts would be wrapped in red paper as a symbol of joy. It is still normal to exchange gifts but arranged marriages are much less common and not everyone can afford to buy a new bed, so they may just buy new bed linen instead.

1 _____ 2 _____ 3 _____ 4 _____ 5 _____

TOTAL ___/50

REVIEW TEST 3

NAME: ....   Date: ....

READING (10 marks)

1 Read the article about voluntary work on Greek archaeological sites and match the main ideas (A–E) to the paragraphs where they are mentioned (1–5). 1 mark for each correct answer.

A An important message arrives _____

B An exciting discovery _____

C A great opportunity for those interested in ancient history _____

D Felix's first day in Greece _____

E Getting ready for the dig _____

1 Students of archaeology can now experience the thrill of an archaeological dig by signing up to a new voluntary scheme. If you can get there, and if you are willing to put in some hard work, this opportunity could be extremely rewarding. In the following article, Felix Nowell tells us about his experience of life on a dig.

2 'In the autumn of 2012 I received an email from an old school friend who had studied archaeology at university. In his email, Gunther mentioned that he was going to volunteer as an excavator in Greece the following summer, searching the earth for clues about how the ancient Greeks might have lived. I was immediately taken by the idea of travelling down to Greece for the summer, and contacted the professor who was directing the dig. Her secretary got back to me saying that although I had little practical experience of such work, the professor would be happy to take me on.

3 'The dig began in June 2013, when a small number of volunteer archaeologists met in Athens for the initial training. We spent a day in the archaeological museum, some hours on the Acropolis, and then prepared for the next stage of our adventure. The next day we went to Piraeus, the port of Athens, and took a ferry to Heraklion, Crete, where the dig was happening.

4 'The first week was spent on preparatory work before the start of the actual excavation. This involved cleaning and preparing the site for inspection by an official appointed by the Greek government. It was tough work, although we had help from some Cretan labourers hired by the organizers. The next day we began the task that had attracted me to Greece–the excavation itself. And it was on that day that I made my first discovery.

5 'I was moving a pile of earth covering some Late Minoan pottery, which I then had to take down a ramp to a deep pit in a wheelbarrow. The earth had been searched for possible artefacts, and was being used to fill the holes left by the large rocks we had moved on the first day. And that was when I realized, to my amazement and delight, that someone had missed something. It might be extremely important and it might change our view about the ancient Minoan civilization! Unfortunately I have been sworn to secrecy by the Greek government while the state archaeologist conducts her own research in the area so I can't tell you any more – yet!'

2 Look at the article again and correct the factual mistakes in the sentences below. The first one has been done for you as an example. 1 mark for each correct answer.

Example: Under a new ~~compulsory~~ scheme, learners of archaeology are being given the opportunity to take part in an archaeological dig. ___voluntary___

1 The writer received an email from his friend, Felix, in autumn 2012. _____

2 The professor replied to the writer's email immediately. _____

3 The dig began in Athens in June 2013. _____

4 Officials were hired to help prepare the dig. _____

5 The state archaeologist has told the writer not to publish his findings. _____

VOCABULARY (10 marks)

3 Match the definitions (1–5) with the words (a–h). You will not need to use all the words. 1 mark for each correct answer.

1 to show objects such as paintings to the public _____	a ancient
2 part of an animal or plant from thousands of years ago, preserved in rock _____	b exhibit
3 a site where people dig in the ground to look for objects from the past _____	c artefact
4 from a long time ago _____	d excavation
5 an object, especially something very old, of historical interest _____	e fossil
	f document
	g natural history
	h archaeology

4 In each of the sentences below there is one spelling mistake. Find and correct the spelling mistakes. 1 mark for each correct answer.

1 The museum was full of interesting exibits, although I understand that many more artefacts are stored away in boxes.

2 He was a brave night, although I doubt that he actually killed any dragons.

3 The tuision fees are set to rise by almost 100% next semester.

4 I used to be able to read and understand hieroglyfics, but I no longer study the ancient Egyptians.

5 My work has little to do with uncovering fosils. I find ancient pots, walls and other examples of civilization much more interesting.

LANGUAGE DEVELOPMENT (10 marks)

5 Complete the sentences 1–6 with the words from the box. You will not need to use all the words. 1 mark for each correct answer.

financial   research   display   economic   period   tuition   compulsory   document   exhibition

1 This book is a useful introduction to the two main approaches in educational _____.

2 More advanced statistical tools are needed to understand today's _____ markets.

3 This important _____ of ancient Egyptian history is best known for the building of the Step Pyramid.

4 The idea behind the three-dimensional _____ is to present the user with an image which changes as he or she moves.

5 The study highlights the relationship between rising _____ fees and falling numbers of undergraduate students.

6 The full text of the _____ will be published in the Journal of Contemporary Egyptology.

6 Rewrite the sentences below using the correct form of the verb in brackets. The first one has been done for you as an example. 1 mark for each correct answer.

Example: We should pay to visit museums. (pay) _Paying to visit museums_ is a good idea.

1 We should visit museums. (visit)

_____ is a good idea.

2 It is important to learn from the past. (should)

We _____.

3 We should display artefacts found during digs. (exhibit)

_____ is a good idea.

4 It is important to encourage children to visit museums. (should)

Children _____ encouraged _____.

GRAMMAR FOR WRITING (10 marks)

7 Rewrite the sentences below using *although*. More than one answer may be possible. 1 mark for each correct answer.

1 The results appear to be valid, but further testing is required.

_____

2 Higgins makes some interesting points, but I disagree with many of his conclusions.

_____

3 This book is written mainly for those working in education, but the ideas can be used in other fields.

_____

4 This is a practical manual of paper chromatography, but theoretical aspects are considered in the introduction.

_____

5 Professor Bird retired officially from his university position nine years ago, but he remains very active in research.

_____

8 Rewrite the sentences in 7 again, this time using *however*. 1 mark for each correct answer.

1 _____

2 _____

3 _____

4 _____

5 _____

ACADEMIC WRITING SKILLS (10 marks)

9 Read these sentences from introductions to essays. Decide whether each sentence provides background information (B), is a structuring sentence (S) or a thesis statement (T). Write B, S or T next to each sentence. 1 mark for each correct answer.

1 This essay will suggest that despite the various reforms to the laws on marriage, many traditional aspects of Chinese weddings still prevail. _____

2 This essay will show that smoking, drinking alcohol and overeating can cause numerous health problems. _____

3 I will argue that while the Cultural Revolution introduced some fundamental changes to the nature of modern Chinese marriages, many aspects of traditional Chinese weddings are still common today. _____

4 Human activity is having a major effect on the environment, which will cause many problems for human and animal life in the future. _____

5 This essay will set out the main causes of climate change and the effects of human activity on the environment. _____

6 I will argue that by making changes to their lifestyle, individuals can increase their chances of a longer, (healthier) life. _____

7 Marriage reform was a priority of the People's Republic of China following its establishment in 1949. _____

8 This essay will show that the smartphone has been one of most important inventions in recent years. _____

9 This essay will argue that the advantages of smartphones outweigh the disadvantages, but that smartphone owners must treat their devices with caution. _____

10 Laws were designed to put an end to forced marriages and the sale of women to landowners. _____

TOTAL ___/50

REVIEW TEST 4

NAME: .... Date: ....

READING (10 marks)

1 Read the article and choose the best title (A–D). 1 mark

   A India's developing transport system _____

   B The nationalization of India's railways _____

   C Private and public transport in India _____

   D India's traffic problems _____

There are only 13 million cars in India, although the country has a population of 1.2 billion. Some forms of private transport have been in use in India for centuries, and the public transport system is slowly improving.

One form of traditional transport is the water taxi. These carry thousands of passengers along the river Ganges every day. Another means of travel is by ox cart, traditionally used in rural India. In recent years, some cities have banned ox carts and other slow moving vehicles on the main roads because of traffic problems. Bicycles are also a common mode of travel in much of India, and more than 40% of households own one. While such private means of transport are useful, India's public transport systems are among the most heavily used in the world.

The public transport system is essential for city life, and is the main means of transport in urban India. The main forms of public transport are small motor vehicles, buses and railways. Cycle rickshaws (a type of small, cycle-powered taxi) are also common in smaller cities. Although 25 of India's main cities with a population of over one million have some form of bus system, 80% of public transport is by smaller road vehicles.

The railways were first introduced to India in 1853. In 1951 the many different systems were nationalized into one system, becoming one of the largest networks in the world. Indian trains carry over 30 million passengers and 2.8 million tonnes of freight daily. Indian Railways are the world's biggest employer, with over 1.4 million staff. Indian trains are safe and generally very efficient, but they do often run late. However, they are preferable to spending hours in a traffic jam.

2 Complete the table using words from the article. 1 mark for each correct word or phrase

Traditional transport	5 _____ transport.
1 _____ are used in the countryside.	6 India's train system was privately owned until _____.
2 Fewer than half of all Indian homes own _____.	7 Being stuck in a _____ is worse than being delayed on a train.
3 _____ may not be used in certain areas.	8 There have been railways in India since _____.
4 Some vehicles can cause _____.	9 _____ of goods are transported by rail every day.

VOCABULARY (10 marks)

3 Match the definitions (1-10) with the words (a-l). You will not need to use all the words. 1 mark for each correct answer.

1 the crime of damaging property _____	a route
2 areas on the edge of a town or city _____	b road rage
3 to need something or make something necessary _____	c issue
4 to persuade someone or make them certain _____	d restriction
5 a subject or problem that people are thinking and talking about _____	e commuting time
6 a way or road between places _____	f vandalism
7 an official limit on something _____	g require
8 where there is too much traffic and movement is made difficult _____	h outskirts
9 to stop something from happening _____	i convince
10 how long it takes to get to work from home or from work home again _____	j distance
	k congestion
	l prevent

LANGUAGE DEVELOPMENT (10 marks)

4 Complete each sentence using two words, one from each box (A and B), to make noun noun collocations. You will not need to use all the words. 1 mark for each correct answer.

A cycle traffic public road rush parking car	
B restrictions congestion transport rage hour lane share	

1 The new railway will transport 310,000 passengers daily, decreasing _____ and air pollution.
2 I go to work by bike and use the _____ that runs along the edge of the river.
3 The _____ system here is very unreliable. The trains and buses are always late.
4 There are _____ in place between 8am-6pm, so you mustn't leave your car in the road during the day.
5 The man deliberately drove into the car in front of him in an apparent _____ incident.

5 Replace the words in bold with the academic synonyms in the box. You will not need to use all the words. 1 mark for each correct answer.

prevent run select attempt consider convince realize require

1 You can't **tell** me that you'd prefer to travel by bus than to drive your own car. _____
2 The Government must **understand** that better roads are safer roads. _____
3 This will not **stop** further accidents. In fact, it may make things more dangerous. _____
4 We do not **need** any further investment in public transport. The system functions perfectly well. _____
5 It would be stupid to **try** to force people off the roads and onto the railways. _____

GRAMMAR FOR WRITING (10 marks)

6 Fill in the gaps (a-j) using *if*, *not* or *unless*. 1 mark for each correct answer.

The railway system will ᵃ _____ improve ᵇ_____ we build better trains.
ᶜ _____ we use cleaner transport, then pollution will be reduced. However, ᵈ _____
we act now, we may as well do nothing. It will be too late.
We will ᵉ _____ solve the traffic problem ᶠ _____ we do ᵍ _____ build houses
closer to the business areas.
ʰ _____ the Government is prepared to increase taxation, there will be no money for the
necessary improvements.
People will continue to experience these delays ⁱ _____ we build a new road.
ʲ _____ this project goes on much longer, we will run out of funds.

ACADEMIC WRITING SKILLS (10 marks)

7 Fill in the gaps (a-j) with the words in the box to complete the conclusion. You will not need to use all
the words. 1 mark for each correct answer.

conclusion friendly should also caused lack Overall solution main happy sum would is Finally only

To ᵃ _____ up, the ᵇ_____ problem in this city is the bottleneck ᶜ _____ by the single
road, the ᵈ _____ of bridges and the congestion and pollution this causes. ᵉ _____, a
Personal Rapid Transit system ᶠ _____ be the best ᵍ _____ to this problem. It would not
ʰ _____ reduce congestion, but would ⁱ _____ be the most environmentally ʲ _____
choice.

TOTAL ___/50

NAME: .... Date: ....

READING (10 marks)

1 Read the article and number the main ideas (a–f) in the order that they are mentioned. 1 mark for each correct answer.

  a the glaciers are melting faster than ever before _____

  b the speed at which glaciers travel _____

  c what happens when there is not enough snow _____

  d the glacial melt is causing the earth's oceans to grow _____

  e efforts to understand what is happening to the glaciers _____

  f the development and life of a glacier _____

Until recently, the world's frozen glaciers remained unchanged for millions of years. These ice sheets start life as snow, turn to glaciers and eventually crash into the sea. They are essential to the world's biodiversity. However, across the globe these huge masses of snow and ice are melting. The impact on our environment is already evident.

A single glacier can move up to a metre every hour. For example, an astonishing 20,000 trillion tonnes of ice move across the state of Alaska every day. And this has been the case for over three million years. However, Alaska's 100,000 glaciers are now under threat of disappearing because they are very sensitive to the effects of climate change. To better understand how and why this is having such an impact on Alaska's glaciers, in recent years parties of scientists have followed the melt streams that run through these slowly disappearing mountains of ice and snow.

These fast rivers of freezing water are formed as glaciers melt, and are an important measure of glacial health. Every glacier is in balance. The amount of snow falling in winter must equal the amount that melts in the summer. If that balance changes, and there is less snow than the amount that melts in the summer, the glacier will disappear. Right now, that is what is happening. These glaciers are melting faster than they are growing. And when a glacier disappears, it is gone for good. It tumbles off the mountains and into the sea, never to return.

Alaska's glaciers are retreating at an increasing rate. Every year 19 trillion tonnes of melt water are pouring into the sea and not being replenished. As the glaciers melt, it is the rest of the world that is affected. Alaskan glaciers are melting so fast they currently account for ten per cent of the world's rising sea levels. This is the most dramatic transformation the area has undergone since the last ice age and shows how global warming is changing our environment. Already, many of the world's island nations are under risk of flooding. Very soon, these small, defenceless countries could be completely submerged.

2 Read the article again and find the words or phrases that mean the same as the words in bold below. 1 mark for each correct answer.

  1 Maintaining **the variety of plant and animal life** across the globe is essential for the future of the planet. _____

  2 Scientists first began measuring **the differences in global weather patterns** during the 20th century. _____

  3 Many coastal regions are in danger of being **covered with water** as a result of glacial melting. _____

  4 The melting glaciers **make up** a large proportion of the world's rising sea levels. _____

VOCABULARY (10 marks)

3 Complete the text using the words and phrases in the box. You will not need to use all the words. 1 mark for each correct word.

> climate change emission deforestation decade biodiversity aridity drought
> consequences effects logging subsistence graze erosion leads to environment

The main causes of [a]_____ are the need for commercial agriculture by big businesses and for [b]_____ farming by local people. It can have many adverse [c]_____. These include [d]_____, where the land becomes very dry and there is not enough rain for plants, damage to animal habitats and [e]_____, which is related to global warming. An example of big business agricultural development is industrial [f]_____ where areas are cleared of trees for the large-scale production of, for example, palm oil or beef cattle. Subsistence farmers also clear areas of trees to [g]_____ their cattle and to grow the crops they and their families need to live on. The [h]_____ of this can be disastrous. Clearing land by cutting down trees and burning them [i]_____ the destruction of the land through soil [j]_____. This happens when the layer of soil that protects the ground is removed during the crop growing process.

LANGUAGE DEVELOPMENT (10 marks)

4 Complete the sentences using the academic vocabulary in the box. You will not need to use all the words. 1 mark for each correct answer.

> issue area trend cause predict decade annual environment challenge

1 The greatest _____ facing scientists today is finding a solution to the problems caused by climate change.
2 It is not possible to accurately _____ exactly when the last glacier on earth will melt.
3 There has been an upward _____ in people looking for alternatives to fossil fuels to heat their homes.
4 The Institute is publishing its _____ report on the effects of climate change next week. It is expected to be more detailed than last year's report.
5 Our politicians must address this serious _____ immediately.

5 Complete the collocations related to the environment by adding the missing vowels. 1 mark for each correct collocation.

1 We can reduce CO_2 in the atmosphere by switching from fossil fuels to r__n__w__bl__ __n__rgy.
2 The increase in gr__ __nh__ __s__g__ss__s in the atmosphere is one of the main causes of global warming.
3 Human activity is a major cause of cl__m__t__ ch__ng__.
4 S__bs__st__nc__ f__rm__ng leads to soil erosion, destroying vast areas of farmland.
5 Further __nv__r__nm__nt__l d__s__st__rs are inevitable, so we must be prepared to deal with them when they happen.

GRAMMAR FOR WRITING (10 marks)

6 Complete the sentences using *leads to, result, due, caused, because of,* or *because*. You will need to use some of these words and phrases more than once. 1 mark for each sentence.

   1 A loss of biodiversity is dangerous to the planet _____ it will limit new sources of food and medicine.

   2 Moving from cattle farming to producing crops may _____ in lower greenhouse gas emissions.

   3 Island nations may be submerged _____ rising sea levels.

   4 Burning fossil fuels _____ an increase in carbon emissions.

   5 Demand for food and energy are expected to rise _____ to the increase in the population.

   6 Dry conditions following periods of drought may _____ in forest fires.

   7 The damage _____ by environmental change grows every year.

   8 The climate is changing _____ human activity.

   9 Carbon emissions are rising _____ humans are burning fossil fuels.

   10 Flooding is a potential problem _____ to rising sea levels.

ACADEMIC WRITING SKILLS (10 marks)

7 Complete the topic sentences using the words in the box. You will not need to use all the words. 1 mark for each correctly completed gap.

cause of	changing	effect	number of	causing	devastating	leading
three main	due	because	because of	loss	results	cause	change

   1 Human activity is _____ the environment to change in a _____ ways.

   2 The environment is _____ in _____ ways.

   3 Humans are the _____ climate change _____ deforestation and burning fossil fuels.

   4 Rising temperatures, _____ of biodiversity and rising sea levels are the main _____ of climate change.

   5 Human activity is having a major _____ on the environment, which will _____ many problems for human and animal life in the future.

TOTAL ___/50

NAME: .... Date: ....

READING (10 marks)

1 Read the article and answer the questions. 1 mark for each correct answer.

1 On average, how far do people in training for a race cycle per day?

_____

2 How much blood goes to a cyclist's muscles every sixty seconds?

_____

3 How much of the energy that would normally be needed does a team leader use when he is protected by his team?

_____

4 During a race, how many more calories from carbohydrates do cyclists eat a day compared with non-cyclists?

_____

5 How many days do cyclists actually ride during the Tour de France?

_____

A The best of the world's road cyclists ride in races which take them over three and a half thousand kilometres at an average speed of forty kilometres per hour. How is this amazing physical achievement possible?

B Teams who compete in the world's toughest road cycle races put their success down to training. The riders set goals for each day's training, much as we might set targets at work. They also take regular breaks. This means that even though cyclists in training average about seven hundred kilometres a week, they do not train so hard that they get injured before their race.

C Cyclists are much fitter than normal people. The best riders extract twice as much oxygen from each breath as an average healthy person, so they are able to generate twice as much energy. Riders like this train their hearts to pump thirty-five litres of blood to their muscles per minute, whereas most people's hearts can only manage twenty.

D Each team of riders is built entirely around helping the team leader win the race. The team works together to make sure that the leader is fresh to cycle fastest at the end of the race. The team's job is to block the wind that the leader rides into. They ride in a V-shape so that the leader only needs to use seventy-five per cent of the energy that would normally be spent riding into the wind.

E The team prepares using only the most advanced equipment and the most suitable food. Modern bicycles use space technology, and weigh 1.3 kilograms. A wind tunnel is used to analyze a rider's position on the bike and reduce drag. Cyclists train their body to burn fat by not eating too many carbohydrates. However, as they start to race they need more fuel, and eat a lot more. During a long distance race, a cyclist can consume up to four thousand calories per day in carbohydrates alone. The average person's recommended daily intake is just two thousand calories a day, of which only one thousand three hundred calories should come from carbohydrates.

F This kind of preparation is the key to winning a race, and it is especially true of long distance races such as the Tour de France. This famous race takes twenty-three days, which includes two rest days. Even the smallest aspect of a rider's performance could make the difference between winning and losing.

2 Which paragraph (A–F) contains these themes? 1 mark for each correct answer.

Example: Elite cyclists race over very long distances   <u>A</u>

1 A well-known race.   _____

2 How does a cyclist's health compare with that of non-cyclists?   _____

3 The role of technology.   _____

4 How do cyclists become so good at racing?   _____

5 The role of the team members.   _____

VOCABULARY (10 marks)

3 Complete the text using the words in the box. You will not need to use all the words. 1 mark for each correct word or phrase.

| heart disease   evidence   self-esteem   suffer   serious illness   exercise   realize |
| injure   physical activity   reduce   obesity   life expectancy   calories   junk food   provide |

How much ª_____ do you do in a week? Are you getting enough? Did you ᵇ_____ that adults who ᶜ_____ for just 150 minutes a week can ᵈ_____ their risk of ᵉ_____ by 50%? It also improves your mood and sleep quality, and makes you feel better about yourself through increased ᶠ_____. Finally, you will find it easier to maintain a healthy weight, meaning that the risk of ᵍ_____, one of the main factors leading to ʰ_____, will be significantly lower. All of this could lead to an increase in your ⁱ_____, especially if you also cut out ʲ_____ and eat healthily instead.

LANGUAGE DEVELOPMENT (15 marks)

4 Complete the table with the noun forms of the verbs on the left. The first one has been done for you as an example. 1 mark for each correct answer.

verb	noun
injure	*Example:* __injury__
provide	1 _____
reduce	2 _____
suffer	3 _____
encourage	4 _____
solve	5 _____

5 Complete table with the collocations next to their definitions. The first one has been done for you as an example. 2 marks for each correct answer.

collocation	definition
Example: ___life expectancy___	how long a person can expect to live
1 __ __ __ __ itional val __ __	how good a particular kind of food is for you
2 se__ __ __ __ __ __ __ __ __ess	a very bad medical problem
3 r__ __ __ __ ar e__ __ __ __ __ __e	sport or physical activity which people do at the same time each day, week, month, etc.
4 bal__ __ __ __ __ d__ __ __	a mixture of the correct types and amounts of food
5 advert__ __ __ __ __ __ __ __ __ __gn	paid publicity to convince people to buy a product

GRAMMAR FOR WRITING (10 marks)

6 Complete the sentences using *for example, to, such as,* or *so that.* You will need to use some of these words and phrases more than once. 1 mark for each correct answer.

1 There are many ways to burn fat, _____ gardening and running.

2 Local councils should build more sports centres _____ people can do more sports.

3 School canteens should help promote healthy eating _____ increase life expectancy.

4 Nutritional information should be clearly written on the packaging _____ people can see how healthy their food is.

5 Governments can discourage people from eating junk food _____ improve their diets.

6 _____, we need a good balance of proteins, carbohydrates and fats in order to stay healthy.

7 Governments should increase the tax on junk food _____ burgers and chips.

8 Schools should provide free access to their sports facilities at weekends _____ people from poorer backgrounds can do sports.

9 _____ really make a difference, the government needs to fund a massive educational campaign.

10 It might be a good idea to ban smoking in public places _____ people find it more difficult to smoke.

ACADEMIC WRITING SKILLS (5 marks)

7 Put the five sentences (a–e) in the best order (1–5) to form a complete paragraph with a topic sentence and supporting sentences. 1 mark for each correct answer.

a For example, we need protein from meat and carbohydrates from rice and bread, as well as vitamins from fruit and vegetables, in order to stay healthy.	
b Eating a balanced diet is a great way for individuals to stay healthy.	
c In fact, nutritionists and doctors are agreed that we need a good mix of carbohydrates, proteins and healthy fats such as omega 3s and 6s.	
d Obesity can lead to heart disease or diabetes.	
e However, consuming too much sugar and fat in junk food such as fried chicken or cola drinks causes health risks.	

TOTAL ___/50

REVIEW TEST 7

NAME: ……………………………………………………………………………………………………… Date: ……………

READING (10 marks)

1 Read the article and fill in the gaps (1–5) with the sentences (A–F). There is one sentence that you will not need to use. 1 mark for each correct answer.

A It can push a cart and open and close doors.

B Over the years there were some problems developing a machine to move like humans do.

C ASIMO is the most advanced humanoid robot in the world.

D These robots are even learning to recognize objects, people and vocabulary.

E The first version of ASIMO was able to move its limbs naturally, imitating human actions.

F They are also increasingly common in the home.

Robots are widely used today in factories, in space and deep under water for jobs which are too dirty, boring or dangerous for humans to do. [1]_____. Robot vacuum cleaners, lawn mowers and other such devices have become very popular in some countries. However, while these robot devices have their uses, they are nothing compared with the potential offered by ASIMO, which has been in development by Honda since 1986.

[2]_____. It has been available to consumers since 2000, when the first version of a humanoid robot was introduced to the market. Honda wanted to see if it was possible to build a robot that could act like a human, help out in the home, play sports, balance on one foot and even dance. [3]_____. However, researchers soon had a robot that could walk on uneven surfaces and climb stairs. The technology has since been improved so that the robot can turn around and reach speeds of up to six kilometres per hour, using its upper body to control movement.

The machine is designed to be people-friendly. It is hoped that robots like this could be used to help elderly people in their homes. Honda are also using this technology to create mobility aids for people with disabilities. [4]_____. It can even shake hands and recognize gestures. Standing at 120 centimetres tall, the ASIMO looks like a child wearing a spacesuit. Like a child, it can look into the faces of adults when they are sitting down. It can hold two kilograms in its hands and carry a tray without dropping the contents.

The most recent version of ASIMO is autonomous, which means it can continue moving without being controlled by an operator. Researchers are now working on robots that can learn about the world around them and respond to human touch and voice. [5]_____. Although robots seem to be becoming more human in their appearance and abilities, it is unlikely that in the future they will look any more like us than they currently do. This is because in general people feel uncomfortable with robots that resemble humans too closely.

---

2 Read the article again and write true (T) or false (F) next to the statements below. 1 mark for each correct answer.

1 The ASIMO has been on the market since 1986. _____

2 The ASIMO was built with the ability to make friends with people. _____

3 The most recent version of ASIMO can move without a human operator. _____

4 You can now buy a robot that is able to develop according to its immediate environment. _____

5 Consumers do not like robots that look too much like real people. _____

VOCABULARY (10 marks)

3 Use the words and phrases in the box to complete the sentences below. You will not need to use all the words. 1 mark for each correct answer.

centre of gravity   humanoid   gestures   uneven   robotics   mechanical failure   mobility aid   biomimicry

1 Small children can learn to ski quickly because their _____ is very low, and so they don't fall down.
2 In the future, _____ robots that look, move and talk like people will help us perform many boring tasks.
3 The robots can perform a number of simple hand _____, such as waving and clapping.
4 Since 1986, Honda have been working on a robot that can act as a _____ for people with disabilities.
5 Robots can find it difficult to walk on _____ surfaces, preferring flat roads, pathways and floors.

4 Use the words and phrases in the box to complete the sentences below. You will not need to use all the words. 1 mark for each correct answer.

probably   definitely   advantage   disadvantage   concern   possibly   benefit   scientific   discovery   innovation

1 We will _____ all die one day.
2 The research will _____ lead to some interesting innovations, but it is too early to be certain.
3 The main _____ of the new system is that it makes online payment much more secure.
4 My only _____ about humanoid robots is that they might one day take over the planet.
5 I am too old to _____ from these discoveries, but I know that they will make life easier for my grandchildren.

LANGUAGE DEVELOPMENT (10 marks)

5 Complete the table using *will*, *could* or *won't* together with *definitely*, *probably* and *possibly*. 1 mark for each correct answer.

level of certainty	prediction
100% yes	1 Computers _____ be more powerful in the future.
70% yes	2 People who don't smoke _____ live longer than those who do.
50% yes	3 The directors _____ hire new staff later in the year, but the decision could go either way.
30% yes	4 I _____ get the job because I couldn't answer all their questions. I'll know for certain next week.
0% yes (=no)	5 We _____ be able to breathe in space without special equipment.

6 Complete the table with the prefixes from the box. You will not need to use all the prefixes. 1 mark for each correct answer.

pre- mis- auto- dis- post- sub- bio- re- un-

prefix	meaning
1 _____	self
2 _____	life
3 _____	badly
4 _____	under
5 _____	before

GRAMMAR FOR WRITING (10 marks)

7 Link the pairs of sentences using *who* or *which*. You may also need to make some other changes for the sentences to be correct. 1 mark for each correct sentence.

1 One case study involved a 10-year-old girl. She had been given a robot doll for several weeks.

_____

2 The head of design has a favourite question. He puts this question to those unsure about using robots in caring situations.

_____

3 Most people choose the elevator. An elevator is a kind of robot.

_____

4 I'm sending you an email I received from Max Mustermann. Max Mustermann attended your webinar about robots.

_____

5 You must also provide a short biography. The biography should include details of all relevant qualifications and experience.

_____

8 Match the sentence halves (1–5 and a–e) to form sentences outlining the advantages and disadvantages of a subject. 1 mark for each correct sentence.

1 That said, there could be some _____	a be aware of the potential problems.
2 Although they offer a range of advantages, _____	b have some unintended consequences.
3 Also, there may be _____	c disadvantages of using computer schoolbooks in the future.
4 However, changing biology like this may _____	d health problems associated with eating these new crops.
5 Overall, while these technologies have clear advantages, we should _____	e there are some problems with using these new technologies.

ACADEMIC WRITING SKILLS (10 marks)

9 Most of the lines in these extracts from an essay contain a spelling mistake. Underline the spelling mistakes and write the correct spelling next to the sentence. Where there is no spelling mistake, write 'correct'. The first two lines have been done for you as examples. 1 mark for each correct answer.

Example: There many technologies <u>wich</u> will be important in the coming years.	___which___
Example: Perhaps the most important are computer schoolbooks.	___correct___
1 Before the end of the decade, students will all have tablet computers.	_____
2 These will cary all of the books they need for the entire school year.	_____
3 One problem is that they could posibly get broken easily in school bags.	_____
4 These tablet computers will also be expensive to buy and replace.	_____
5 Genetic modification is another area of inovation.	_____
6 Changeing biology like this may have some unintended consequences.	_____
7 Tablet PCs are unlikely to be sucessful unless they are tough and cheap.	_____
8 Genetically modified food will help starving people if properly controlled.	_____
9 However, lager crops may mean more insects and weeds.	_____
10 We shoud be aware of the potential problems.	_____

TOTAL ___/50

NAME: .... Date: ....

READING (10 marks)

1 Read the article about Levi's Jeans and number the main ideas (a–j) in the order that they are mentioned. Not all the ideas are mentioned. 1 mark for each correct answer.

> Many inventions have shaped American culture in the minds of people around the world. One was created many years ago but is still popular today: Levi's jeans.
>
> Levi Strauss was born in 1829 in Bavaria, which is part of present day Germany. As a young man he moved to the USA and settled in New York. In 1853, the young immigrant decided that he wanted to start his own business. He moved from New York to San Francisco, where the gold rush was well underway. He travelled across Panama and began trading on 14 March that year.
>
> Unlike many other hopeful travellers, Strauss did not go to California to mine for gold. He sold tents and covers for wagons to the miners. One day a man asked Strauss if he sold trousers. Looking for gold was hard work and miners needed clothes that would last. This conversation inspired Strauss to make strong trousers suitable for workers.
>
> In 1866 he started selling canvas trousers called Levi's and the miners bought them faster than Strauss could make them. Strauss soon received a lot of advice on ways to improve his jeans. In 1873 Jacob Davis gave him an idea to make the jeans even stronger by adding metal rivets to the pockets so that they would not tear. Strauss liked the idea and decided to use it. However, many people complained that the canvas was uncomfortable, so Strauss changed from canvas to a heavy denim material. It was dyed indigo blue and miners liked the new material because dirty marks did not show on the dark colour.
>
> In 1873 the jeans sold for 22 cents a pair. By the end of that year, demand for the product had increased dramatically. Strauss opened a factory in San Francisco and hired hundreds of workers to keep up with demand. When he died in 1902, the company kept going.
>
> By the 1920s, the miners had left California and instead cowboys and steel workers were buying Levi's. It became the leading brand in men's work clothing. In the 1950s, after movie stars Marlon Brando and James Dean were seen wearing them, jeans became a common item of clothing for all Americans. Today Levi's jeans are still one of the most popular products of American culture.

a Levi's jeans are the most important of all American inventions. _____

b Levi's went through several changes before the best design was found. _____

c Levi's were first bought by cowboys and steel workers. _____

d Levi's are still well-liked today even though the brand is very old. _____

e The market for jeans has extended beyond its original target group. _____

f Bavaria is next to Germany. _____

g Marlon Brando and James Dean were major film stars. _____

h Levi Strauss moved from Europe to the USA, where he started his own company. _____

i The company expanded rapidly during its first 30 years. _____

j Strauss got the idea for Levi's after speaking to a miner. _____

2 Look at the article again and correct the factual mistakes in the sentences below. The first one has been done for you as an example. 1 mark for each correct answer.

Example: Levi Strauss ~~moved to~~ Bavaria in 1829. was born in

1 Strauss set up his business in Panama in 1853. He began by selling products needed by the miners. _____

2 The first Levi's jeans were made from denim. _____

3   The dark blue colour was very popular because it hid the rivets on the miners' trousers. _____

4   By early 1873, many more people were buying Levi's jeans. _____

VOCABULARY (10 marks)

3 In each of the sentences below there is one spelling mistake. Find and correct the spelling mistake. 1 mark for each correct answer.

1   I'm sorry, but we can only acommodate you for one night. Would you like the number of another hotel?

2   I spend very little money on beuty products.

3   Approximately how many employes are working for you now?

4   When we inspected the firm last year we criticized the low bay and poor working conditions.

5   Abart from those able to spend money on expensive fashion, do you have many other customers?

4 In each of the sentences below there is one wrong word or phrase. Find and correct the mistakes using the words and phrases in the box. You will not need to use all the words. 1 mark for each correct answer.

| relax   casual   brief   textiles   plants   costs   goal   instead of |

1   All of our fibres are produced from the best quality wool and cotton. _____

2   The company has manufacturing areas in Canterbury, Prague and Little Waldingfield. _____

3   I like to wear artificial clothes when I'm not at work. I can't relax in a suit. _____

4   Labour payments are our biggest expense. We hope to move some of our production offshore to save money. _____

5   From next year we will need to source locally in addition to offshore, as the government has announced an import ban. _____

LANGUAGE DEVELOPMENT (10 marks)

5 Add the hyponyms in the boxes to the charts below. 1 mark for each correct hyponym.

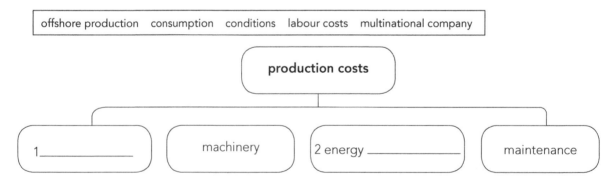

| offshore production   consumption   conditions   labour costs   multinational company |

production costs

1_____   machinery   2 energy _____   maintenance

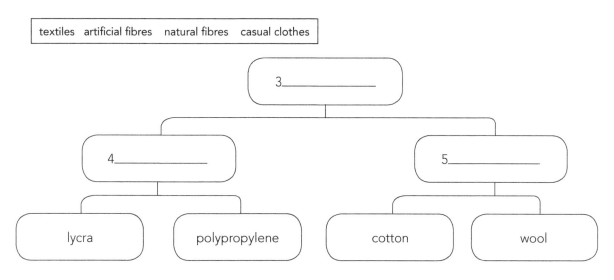

textiles   artificial fibres   natural fibres   casual clothes

3 _____

4 _____   5 _____

lycra   polypropylene   cotton   wool

6 Read sentences 1–5. Then look at the table below and decide whether the word in bold in each sentence is being used with its general meaning (A) or its academic meaning (B).

1 Unfortunately, we can only **accommodate** you for one night. _____

2 I've been working in this **area** for almost five years. When I began, it was a relatively new field. _____

3 We are now **approaching** Gatwick airport. _____

4 I had a quick look at the **brief** this morning, and would be keen to examine it in more detail before making a decision. _____

5 Young Hargreaves must find some **goal** in life other than playing football. _____

	A general meaning	B academic meaning
goal	a point scored in a ball game	an aim
brief	short	instructions
approach	coming nearer	a method
to accommodate	to give someone a place to stay	to give someone what is needed
area	a piece of land	an academic subject

GRAMMAR FOR WRITING (10 marks)

7 Complete the sentences using the words in the box. You will need to use some words more than once. 1 mark for each correct answer.

rather   in addition   instead   apart   except   along

1 Quite _____ from the longer hours, the promotion will also mean extra responsibilities.

2 When possible, I prefer to take public transport _____ than going by car.

3 _____ for my gold watch, I don't own any precious metals.

4 _____ with swimming, running is my favourite sport.

5 I don't eat any meat, _____ for fish. And chicken. Oh, and the occasional burger!

6 _____ to your interpersonal skills and good timekeeping, what else can you offer our company?

7 I'd like to see a younger woman on the board of directors _____ of just another old man in a grey suit.

8 He seemed disappointed _____ than angry.

9   They interviewed fifty of us in one day! Five of us were called for a second interview the next week. I was so pleased to have been chosen _____ with another four young fashion designers.

10   I had no proof of identification _____ from my gym membership card.

ACADEMIC WRITING SKILLS (10 marks)

8 Complete the paragraph using the words in the box. Do not use any of the words more than once. You will not need to use all the words. 1 mark for each correct answer.

them   when   in   up   on   from   such   out   how   this   because   to   for   of   that

Another point [1]_____ should be considered is that developing countries encourage developed countries to invest in [2]_____ to provide jobs. Supporters of overseas production point [3]_____ that increased investment has positive effects [4]_____ the long term. Growth in manufacturing has an impact [5]_____ the rest of the economy, because it reduces the number [6]_____ people needing to work in agriculture and increases competition [7]_____ labour. This leads to higher wages, which then leads to other improvements, [8]_____ as the ability to send children [9]_____ school. However, the disadvantage of [10]_____ foreign investment is the fact that it can have a negative impact on the economy of developed countries, because people lose their jobs when production is outsourced to other countries.

TOTAL ___/50

NAME: .... Date: ....

READING (10 marks)

1 Read the article and complete the summary below using no more than three words in each gap. Use only words that best summarize the content of the article. 1 mark for each correct answer.

The citizens of countries ruled by democratic governments are used to regular elections being held. Governments change, but often this has little immediate effect on a country's economic growth. However, the situation can be different in countries ruled by unelected regimes, such as those of the former Soviet Union.

When the government of an undemocratic regime falls, the country's economy can experience major difficulties. Interest rates often rise, natural resources may not be properly protected and economic stability can suffer. This loss of wealth can lead to poverty and to recession. One reason for this is a reduction in investment from abroad. A typical pattern is as follows: a country's leader falls, foreign investors leave, there is a rapid decrease in the market value of the currency, unemployment increases and retail sales decline.

Many investors would rather put their money into overseas economies, which offer higher returns. However, they must be aware of the risks involved. Businesspeople benefitted from the high interest rates offered by banks based in Cyprus. However, this model could not be sustained and wealthy businesspeople lost huge amounts of money in Cyprus in 2013. Some say that these losses are unfair, but others say that the investors got what they deserved.

Investors looking for a safer, long-term return can invest in the real economy of a country rather than simply saving their money in banks. Such investments can fund jobs, develop new businesses, restaurants and shopping malls such as those found in the USA. Outside wealth can turn a failing economy around. Russia is an example of what can happen. It was once dismissed as a country without hope, but it is now a financial powerhouse. High returns offered to wealthy businesspeople by offshore banks are becoming increasingly rare, and there is now a chance that Russia might be able to raise more money in taxes. This would lead to more investment in the Russian economy, leading to a better standard of living for all.

If businesses invest in long-term projects such as factories, mining and resources needed for manufacturing, and if governments can establish effective means of redistributing income through spending and taxation, their countries' economies will become more stable and their societies fairer.

States run by [1]_____ hold regular elections. However, when a non-democratic government falls, a country's [2]_____ can suffer. 3. When important [3]_____ such as coal, wood and cotton are wasted, the economy can decline dramatically. When an economy suffers badly, the country can experience negative growth. This is known as [4]_____, typified by loss of jobs and increased poverty. This can happen when there is a sudden loss of [5]_____ coming from other countries. A drastic fall in the value of a currency can lead to a reduction in [6]_____, as people are no longer able to afford the prices charged by shops. Some financial institutions offer very high [7]_____ rates, although investors risk losing a lot of money if the market fails. When people have more money to spend, there is an increased demand for shops, sometimes built together within large American-style [8]_____. Greater investment in an economy can lead to a better [9]_____ for a country's citizens. Economies will become more stable if businesses invest in large projects such as those needed for the [10]_____ industry.

VOCABULARY (10 marks)

2 Read the extract from the article. Find synonyms for the words and phrases in bold in sentences 1–10. 1 mark for each correct answer.

> When the government of an undemocratic regime falls, the country's economy can experience major difficulties. Interest rates often rise, natural resources may not be properly protected and economic stability can suffer. This loss of wealth can lead to poverty, and to recession. One reason for this is a reduction in investment from abroad. A typical pattern is as follows: a country's leader falls, foreign investors leave, there is a rapid decrease in the market value of the currency, unemployment increases and retail sales decline.

1   She lived in **extremely poor conditions**. _____

2   There has been a **fall** in the number of jobs available. _____

3   Building larger shops will lead to a rise in **goods being bought by consumers**. _____

4   New businesses need to find reliable sources of **money to help them develop**. _____

5   This country's **system of trade and industry** needs to be made more competitive. _____

6   During her career she gained **a large amount of money and valuable possessions**. _____

7   It is not easy to find **people who will put their money into new businesses**. _____

8   He is selling it for $100, but the **usual price** is closer to $120. _____

9   Our country is going through a **period when the economy is doing very badly and many people are losing their jobs**. _____

10 The number of jobs available is predicted to **go up** next year. _____

LANGUAGE DEVELOPMENT (10 marks)

3 In each of the sentences below, one word has been written using the wrong part of speech. Either a noun has been written where there should be an adjective, or an adjective has been written instead of a noun. Correct the sentences. 1 mark for each correct answer.

1   The country has been in a very poor finance state ever since the decline of the steel industry.
_____

2   We need to encourage consumers to buy goods manufacture at home, rather than spending money on foreign goods. _____

3   Houses have fallen in valuable over the past few years. _____

4   This is exactly the kind of investment our economic needs to avoid recession. _____

5   She could not find work as an accountant so considered training for a new professional.
_____

4 For each of the sentences (1-5) below, choose the word or phrase from the box that can replace the word in bold without changing the overall meaning. You will not need to use all the words and phrases.1 mark for each correct answer.

balance   investment   development   market   return   occupation   stability   financial system   decrease

1   The **economy** is going through a very difficult period at the moment. _____

2   Please complete the form, including your name, address and **profession**. _____

3   One of the benefits of our political system is its **strength**. In contrast, some countries are sometimes forced to hold elections almost every year. _____

4   My financial adviser was certain that my investment would soon lead to a healthy **profit**.
_____

5   There has been little **growth** in the industrial sector since the 1980s. _____

GRAMMAR FOR WRITING (10 marks)

5 Complete the table by writing the noun phrases (1–5) as verb phrases. 1 mark for each correct answer.

1 a sharp rise	_____
2 a dramatic fall	_____
3 a slight decrease	_____
4 a gradual increase	_____
5 a considerable fluctuation	_____

6 Complete the description of the data with the correct prepositions. 1 mark for each correct answer.

Members [1]_____ the Westland Trade Block have reported an average contraction of 0.2% [2]_____ the last quarter of 2012. However, [3]_____ some individual members the figures are more promising. In the Republic of Voeslauer, output rose [4]_____ 0.2% in December 2012 [5]_____ 0.3% in January 2013.

ACADEMIC WRITING SKILLS (10 marks)

7 Read the description of a graph presenting data on the sale of widgets. Complete gaps 1–5 with the best sentence (A–F). You will not need one of the sentences. 2 marks for each correct answer.

The data shows the retail price of Widgets in 2012-2013. [1]_____.

The first graph shows how the price of both the older model 'Widget One' and the more modern 'Widget Plus' fell dramatically over the course of that year following the introduction of the widget's only rival so far, the 'Wedglet'.

The Widget One retailed at approximately €800 during the first quarter of 2012. However, most retailers dropped the price to around €500 in the second quarter. [2]_____. This newer model retailed at €850 when it was first introduced, a small increase in price when compared with the initial retail price of the Widget One. [3]_____.

The retail price of the Widget One continued to drop throughout the third and fourth quarters, and the product was eventually withdrawn from the market. Sales of the Widget Plus continued to be fairly healthy during the third quarter of 2012. [4]_____.

Sales of the Widget Plus picked up following the January sales, but by the end of February sales had once again levelled out. [5]_____. Although the price of the Widget Plus was reduced following the news of its replacement model, sales fell to almost zero. It was withdrawn from sale in the last quarter of 2013, by which time the Widget Plus One had established itself as the market leader.

A This followed the introduction of the newer Widget Plus.
B The dramatic drop in the final quarter can be explained by the anticipated introduction of the Widget Plus One in early January 2013.
C This dramatic increase is difficult to explain.
D It also shows how many widgets were sold during that period.
E However, the difference is quite significant when compared with the price reductions on offer for the older model following the introduction of the Widget Plus.
F The Widget Plus One was officially announced in March 2013.

TOTAL ___/50

REVIEW TEST 10

NAME: ....   Date: ....

READING (10 marks)

1 Read the article about the brain. Which paragraphs (A–D) do the ideas (1–5) refer to? You will need to use some of the letters more than once. 1 mark for each correct answer.

1   The parts of the brain not mainly concerned with thought _____

2   A description of the smaller parts of the brain _____

3   An amusing observation about the brain's mass _____

4   A reference to research into the brain _____

5   A general description of the brain _____

A The brain is an organ made of soft tissue, and can be seen as a kind of control centre for the body. It takes care of all the essential processes the body needs to perform in order to survive. When we are awake we are only aware of some of these processes. In contrast, the brain remains alert both day and night.

B Your brain has five main parts that work together. In order of size, they are the cerebrum, the cerebellum, the brain stem, the pituitary and the hypothalamus. The average adult human brain weighs approximately 1,300 to 1,400 grams. A newborn baby's brain weighs between 350 and 400 grams. Men's brains weigh a little more than women's, but there is no relationship between the size of a person's brain and their intelligence. However, some people have joked that the fact that a man's brain weighs more than a woman's is proof that heavier brains are less effective! In fact, Albert Einstein's brain weighed 1,230 grams, far less than the average brain.

C The largest part of the brain is the cerebrum, accounting for about 85% of the brain's weight. It is the part of the brain that controls the voluntary muscles, such as those you might need when writing an email, eating or playing sports. There have been many papers published on the cerebrum, in particular on the exact role played by its two halves. Neuroscientists believe that the right half is mainly responsible for abstract thought about music, colours, and shapes. The available evidence suggests that the left half is more analytical, and is involved in activities such as maths, logic, and speech.

D While the cerebrum is perhaps the key to the brain's secrets, the other four main parts are also essential. The cerebellum is much smaller than the cerebrum. It is situated at the back of the brain, and controls balance, movement and coordination. Problems with the cerebellum can lead to neurological disorders such as epilepsy or more minor seizures. The brain stem sits between the cerebrum and the cerebellum, connecting the brain to the spinal cord. It helps the body carry out the functions needed to keep us alive, such as breathing, digesting and blood circulation. Finally, the pituitary gland controls growth through the release of hormones, and the hypothalamus controls temperature.

---

2 Look at the extracts from the article and find the terms used to express the words and phrases in bold in sentences 1–5. 1 mark for each correct answer.

The brain is an organ made of soft tissue, and can be seen as a kind of control centre for the body. It takes care of all the essential processes the body needs to perform in order to survive. When we are awake we are only aware of some of these processes. In contrast, the brain remains alert both day and night.

....there is no relationship between the size of a person's brain and their intelligence. However, some people have joked that the fact that a man's brain weighs more than a woman's is proof that heavier brains are less effective! In fact, Albert Einstein's brain weighed 1,230 grams, far less than the average brain.

Problems with the cerebellum can lead to neurological disorders such as epilepsy or more minor seizures. The brain stem sits between the cerebrum and the cerebellum, connecting the brain to the spinal cord. It helps the body carry out the functions needed to keep us alive, such as breathing, digesting and blood circulation. Finally, the pituitary gland controls growth through the release of hormones, and the hypothalamus controls temperature.

---

1 Liquid on the brain can lead to very serious **difficulties**. _____

2 There is no **evidence** of extra-sensory powers such as telepathy. _____

3 The skin is the largest **self-contained part of the body performing a specific, vital function**. _____

4 Peanut allergies can lead to **sudden attacks of illness, or fits.** _____

5 After the accident he could no longer **perform** a number of major tasks. _____

VOCABULARY (10 marks)

3 Which word from the box can be used to complete both sentences in each pair? You will not need to use all the words. 1 mark for each correct answer.

> operation recover advise organ liquid appear proof epilepsy care seizure recovery complain medication infectious disease vaccination surgery transplant disorder cure treatment side-effect

1 a The Eurozone will not experience a _____ while the markets remains so nervous.

  b _____ can be slow following serious operations such as a hand transplant.

2 a Why don't you _____ to the manager?

  b She began to _____ of frequent headaches.

3 a An _____ is a self-contained part of the body that has a particular and important function.

  b This particular _____ is of no actual benefit to humans, but is essential for the survival of rabbits and other grass eating animals.

4 a She's receiving _____ for a leg injury.

  b He had to undergo months of _____ following the diagnosis.

5 a Do you know the doctor who will be performing the _____?

  b The _____ will be expensive, with little chance of success.

6 a The police had been planning the _____ for weeks.

  b The _____ will last several hours and involve several doctors and nurses.

7 a The _____ of the illegal goods took place in the early hours of Tuesday morning.

  b He experienced a massive _____, which indicated that he could be suffering from epilepsy.

8 a At this point, I really don't _____ any more. Do what you want!

  b He spent all of his money on _____ for his elderly relatives.

9 a We know little about this particular mental _____.

  b The amount of coffee you drink has made your sleep _____ even worse.

10 a I do not expect your husband to _____. His injuries are too severe.

  b All attempts to _____ the stolen goods have so far been unsuccessful.

LANGUAGE DEVELOPMENT (10 marks)

4 Write the verb form next to the nouns. 1 mark for each correct answer.

noun	verb
1 appearance	_____
2 complaint	_____
3 advice	_____
4 confirmation	_____
5 recovery	_____

5 Complete the sentences using the words and phrases in the box. You will not need to use all the words. 1 mark for each correct answer.

| limb medication infectious diseases vaccinations surgery transplant cure treatment side-effects |

1 Coughs and sneezes spread _____.
2 She has been on _____ since returning from her trip to Las Vegas.
3 My wife is going to the Caribbean, so she needs to make sure that she is up to date with her _____.
4 He underwent a successful heart _____ after he had a number of serious heart attacks.
5 There is no _____ for your mother's illness, I'm afraid.

GRAMMAR FOR WRITING (10 marks)

6 Change the verbs in sentences 1–10 into the passive using the correct form of *be* and the past participle.

1 Dogs can _____ (train) to detect cancer in humans.
2 Last week he _____ (advise) by his doctor to take more exercise.
3 White blood vessels _____ (produce) by the bones.
4 Some cancers can _____ (cure) by a combination of chemo- and radiotherapy.
5 These chemicals _____ (release) into the blood during times of stress.
6 The risk of disease _____ (increase) by obesity.
7 The cells _____ (transplant) into the surviving tissue in the operation yesterday.
8 He was a heavy smoker all his life. His lungs _____ (damage) by many years of smoking.
9 The initial diagnosis _____ (confirm) by the results of the test last month.
10 The stethoscope _____ (invent) by Rene Laennec in 1816.

ACADEMIC WRITING SKILLS (10 marks)

7 Complete this description of a process using the sequencing words and phrases in the box. You will not need to use all the words and phrases. You may not use any word or phrase more than once. 2 marks for each correct answer.

| to begin with following this finally as well as the second stage is when then this also is then However, |

The process of digesting a cheese sandwich is quite complicated. [1]_____, when you chew a cheese sandwich, the teeth grind down the cheese and the bread. Enzymes in your saliva [2]_____ break down the food to make it pass down the throat more easily. [3]_____ the food reaches the stomach, it is churned in the stomach acid. [4]_____, the cheese is digested by an enzyme called pepsin. Any remaining food [5]_____ passed down to the duodenum, where the remainder of the carbohydrates are broken down.

TOTAL __/50

WRITING TASK 1 MODEL ANSWER

Compare and contrast the two sharks in the diagram.

The diagram gives information about two kinds of large tropical shark, the whale shark and the tiger shark.

The sharks have a number of differences in terms of size, shape and colour. The whale shark is a much larger animal than the tiger shark. It is six metres longer than its smaller cousin and eight and a half (8.5) tonnes heavier. Both sharks are similar in shape. However, their skin patterns are different. The whale shark has dots on its body, the tiger shark has stripes.

The sharks are also different in terms of their diet, behaviour and conservation status. The whale shark eats very small animals like plankton and krill, whereas the tiger shark has a diet of larger sea creatures such as tuna, dolphins and turtles. This may explain why the tiger shark attacks humans, which are the same size as the food it normally eats. In terms of conservation, the whale shark is more endangered than the tiger shark.

Overall, it is clear that the whale shark is a much larger animal, but it is a gentle giant, whereas the smaller tiger shark is much more dangerous.

ADDITIONAL WRITING TASK 1

Compare and contrast two similar animals (e.g. a German shepherd dog and a labrador, or a sparrow and a thrush or a tiger and a lion).

_____

_____

_____

_____

_____

_____

_____

_____

_____

_____

_____

_____

_____

WRITING TASK 2 MODEL ANSWER

Describe the laws and traditions concerning weddings in your country. Have there been any changes in recent years?

Weddings in China

Weddings are very important occasions in my country. They are vital social events which join two families together to celebrate the new marriage. In this essay, I will describe the law concerning marriage where I live, outline the customs and traditions of a typical wedding and show how weddings have changed in recent years.

Marriage reform was a priority in the People's Republic of China following its establishment in 1949. Laws were designed to end forced marriages and the sale of women. The Cultural Revolution of the1960s and 1970s introduced fundamental changes to marriage in China. The Second Marriage Law of 1980 states that men must be at least twenty-two years old and women twenty on the day of the wedding. The law does not require any formal wedding vows.

On the morning of the wedding day, women perform a hair dressing ritual for the bride. The bride's hair is tied up in a bun, symbolizing her entry into adulthood. A similar ceremony is also performed on the groom. Then there is a procession from the groom's house to collect the bride. Bridesmaids may try to block the groom's way and ask him questions about the bride. The couple may serve tea to the bride's parents before the wedding ceremony. The ceremony itself is simple, and is followed by the reception and dinner.

Some modern innovations are now quite common. Wedding albums featuring photographs of the bride and groom in different costumes are very popular.

ADDITIONAL WRITING TASK 2

Describe the traditions concerning an important festival in your country. How have these traditions changed over the years?

_____

_____

_____

_____

_____

_____

_____

_____

_____

_____

_____

WRITING TASK 3 MODEL ANSWER

Should museums be free or should visitors pay for admission? Discuss.

Some people think it is important that museums are free, to provide education for children. However, others argue that museums are entertainment so visitors should be charged to view the collections. This essay will present the arguments in favour of and against charging for museums. I will argue that museums should be free because of their educational value for children.

Those in favour of entry fees to museums have some valid arguments. Governments have to decide how to prioritize their resources, and it is important to fund schools, policing and health care. These should be more important than art, dinosaurs and historic artefacts. Museums can be expensive to build and maintain, and the day-to-day running costs can be a major drain on public funds. While some museums cater for a broad section of the population, many contain collections of interest to relatively few people. It is a good idea to open such collections to the whole world by putting them online, and this would also save a lot of money.

However, many people argue that governments should fund museums. They help bring history alive and can motivate children to learn more and study harder. Many state-owned museums have seen a huge increase in the numbers of visitors since they stopped charging admission fees. Much money is still collected through voluntary contributions and revenue is also derived from gift shops and museum cafés. In fact the whole city benefits whenever people come to visit its museums.

In conclusion, although museums are expensive, it seems to me that governments should pay for them. If they do not fund museums, the most important objects from the country will be sold abroad and children will not be able to see what their country was like in the past.

ADDITIONAL WRITING TASK 3

Should the internet be available to everyone or should there sometimes be restrictions?

_____

_____

_____

_____

_____

_____

_____

_____

_____

_____

_____

_____

_____

_____

WRITING TASK 4 MODEL ANSWER

Describe the traffic problems in this city and outline the advantages and disadvantages of the suggested solutions. Which of these solutions is the most suitable?

The map shows the traffic problems of a busy city.

Many of the people in this city have to travel to their offices and schools on the other side of the river from where they live, so the city suffers from very bad traffic congestion. This makes people late, wastes fuel and adds to pollution in the city. The main problem is that there is only one main road. The problem is made worse because there is only one bridge. To make matters worse, there is a junction near the housing area where traffic builds up in the morning when people commute to work and take their children to school and in the evening when workers return home and parents collect their children.

One solution is to build more bridges over the river. However, the cost would be prohibitive and they might also become congested.

Another solution is to build a railway line from the residential area to the city centre. This would reduce traffic, but it would be expensive to build, as it would also require the building of a new bridge.

A slightly cheaper solution is to run a Personal Rapid Transit (PRT) system of electric cars to and around the city. Such systems are computer-controlled to ensure that not all cars arrive at the same junction at the same time. Although they are expensive to set up, the running costs are minimal.

To sum up, the main problem with this city is the bottleneck caused by the single road, the lack of bridges and the congestion and pollution these cause. Overall, a Personal Rapid Transit system is the best solution to this problem. It would both reduce congestion and be the most environmentally friendly choice. Unless a PRT system is installed soon, city life will become impossible.

ADDITIONAL WRITING TASK 4

Compare and contrast the advantages and disadvantages of public and private transport.

WRITING TASK 5 MODEL ANSWER

Outline the human causes of climate change. What effects will these have on the planet?

Human activity is having a major effect on the environment, which will cause many problems for human and animal life in the future. This essay will set out the main causes of climate change and the effects of human activity on the environment.

Humans are affecting the climate in a number of ways. The most obvious cause of climate change is the carbon dioxide released by burning fossil fuels. Another cause is deforestation, which is the result of logging, subsistence farming and intensive cattle farming in vast areas of land that were previously the rain forests so crucial to our planet's survival. Deforestation causes arid conditions, increases greenhouse gases and reduces the planet's ability to cope with increasing pollution. Another major cause of climate change is the migration of people from rural to urban areas, which leads to much higher temperatures in densely populated urban areas.

The effects of climate change are already visible as glaciers melt and the polar ice caps shrink. These have led to rising sea levels but this is only the beginning. As global temperatures increase further, more glaciers in Alaska and other polar regions will melt, adding billions of tonnes of water to the sea. This will raise sea levels even higher and submerge low-lying islands. It will also lead to flooding in coastal cities and the erosion of coastlines.

Human activity is clearly causing the climate to change and, as a result, this is having a number of effects on the planet. It is important that we try to reduce our negative impact on the planet as much as possible – for example, by using renewable energy instead of fossil fuels – before it is too late.

ADDITIONAL WRITING TASK 5

Think of an environmental problem facing your country. What are the reasons for this problem? What will the consequences be if no solution is found?

_____

_____

_____

_____

_____

_____

_____

_____

_____

_____

WRITING TASK 6 MODEL ANSWER

What can people do to live longer? What can a government do to increase the average life expectancy of its country's citizens?

The average world lifespan is 70, but how you live your life can add or remove years from this number. Smoking, drinking alcohol and overeating can cause numerous health problems. By making changes to their lifestyle, people can increase their chances of a longer, healthier life. There are also a number of measures that governments can take to increase national life expectancy.

Individuals can take three important steps to live longer and improve their health. Firstly, they can improve their fitness through regular sport and other forms of exercise. Secondly, eating a more balanced diet that provides sufficient carbohydrates for energy, protein to build muscle and good quality fats such as omega 3s and 6s can help people stay healthy. A balanced diet will also increase the chances of getting the recommended daily allowance (RDA) of vitamins and minerals. Lastly, making some sacrifices, for instance quitting smoking and avoiding excessive consumption of alcohol, will have a very positive effect on health.

Governments can help increase their citizens' average life expectancy by financing educational campaigns so that people understand the health benefits of exercise and the risks involved in smoking and drinking. Governments can also tax unhealthy foods, alcohol and tobacco and ban smoking in public places, something that has had a very positive effect on health in many countries. Finally, governments can promote sports and outdoor pursuits to encourage people to have a more active lifestyle.

In conclusion, there are a number of things people and governments can do to increase the health and lengthen life expectancy of the population. Education about the benefits of a healthy lifestyle is key, but more drastic measures such as taxes and outright bans may also be needed.

ADDITIONAL WRITING TASK 6

How can people in your country be encouraged to live healthier lives?

_____

_____

_____

_____

_____

_____

_____

_____

_____

WRITING TASK 7 MODEL ANSWER

Choose one new area of technology or invention and outline its advantages and disadvantages.

One of the most important inventions in recent years has been the smartphone, the result of years of innovation in the fields of personal computing and wireless communication. However, this technology has caused major changes in the way we live, and used thoughtlessly can lead to anti-social behaviour. This essay will argue that the advantages of smartphones outweigh the disadvantages, but that smartphone owners must treat their devices with caution.

Smartphones offer numerous benefits. The main advantage is permanent access to the Internet, which is far more important for most users than the ability to make phone calls. This gives workers the possibility of continuing their work outside of the office, allowing for a more flexible lifestyle and better use of otherwise 'dead time'. Away from work, people can communicate with friends via instant messaging services and social networks. They can enjoy mobile games and can access all the music they could ever want.

However, these advantages come at a cost. Perhaps the biggest concern with smartphones is their effect on the individual user. Wherever you go in public you will see people glued to their screens, nervously checking their emails and flicking through friends' status updates. There is a joke at the moment which goes, 'My friends are coming over tonight to play with their mobile phones'. Another point against smartphones is the blurring of personal and professional lives. They are also expensive to buy and to use, and they become outdated almost immediately.

Used with caution, smartphones can be a wonderful asset. However, we must remember that the world is not entirely digital, and that we could all benefit from some downtime to enjoy offline friendships and the world around us.

ADDITIONAL WRITING TASK 7

Choose one area of new technology. How does this technology benefit you? Are there any possible disadvantages involved in its use?

_____

_____

_____

_____

_____

_____

_____

_____

Fashion is harmful. Discuss.

The fashion industry is worth billions of dollars and creates millions of jobs around the world. However, its critics argue that fashion encourages us to spend money on things we do not need, is harmful to the environment and exploits workers in developing countries. This essay will argue that these views are simplistic, and that both the global economy and those societies it maintains would be worse off without fashion.

The speed of change in the fashion world means that we buy new clothes unnecessarily. This means that more cotton needs to be produced, resulting in more intensive agriculture, which in turn leads to environmental damage. However, stopping production in developing countries would deprive millions of workers of a vital source of income. It would have a trickle down effect on local economies as governments would receive fewer taxes.

Many clothes are produced in factories with poor safety standards. The people who work in them are paid low wages, while the international clothing companies make huge profits. However, the fashion industry provides jobs in factories and in primary industries such as wool and cotton. Rather than keeping the same clothes year after year, we have a duty to the global economy to regularly update our wardrobes.

Critics argue that it is wrong to throw away clothing just because it is out of fashion. However, fashion is an art form that gives pleasure to millions. It allows people to express themselves and stand out from the crowd.

To conclude, fashion may have some negative impact on the environment, but this is true of all major industries. It brings in revenue to governments, both in developing countries and in the industrialized world. Fashion gives pleasure to consumers and provides employment for workers. To destroy fashion would be to destroy lives.

ADDITIONAL WRITING TASK 8

Discuss the consequences of a global ban on branded fashion.

_____

_____

_____

_____

_____

_____

_____

_____

_____

_____

WRITING TASK 9 MODEL ANSWER

The graphs show the retail price and annual sales of two different types of television. Describe both graphs and explain the data.

The data shows the retail price of television sets (TVs) between 2000 and 2010, and how many TVs were sold during that period.

The first graph shows how the price of both traditional cathode ray tube (CRT) TVs and the more modern liquid crystal display (LCD) TVs fell dramatically over the decade. The average LCD TV retailed at approximately £1,000 at the turn of the century, but ten years later this had dropped to roughly £200. In contrast, CRT TVs sold for over £300 in 2000, but had fallen to just over £100 by 2010. From 2005 the prices of both types of TV fell dramatically.

The second graph gives information about unit sales of both CRT and LCD TVs. As with graph 1, 2005 was a key date and saw the beginning of a sharp rise in the sales of LCD TVs. By 2010, sales had increased from a little over a million in 2000 to ten times that figure. This is in stark contrast to the dramatic fall in sales the of CRT TVs, from roughly five million in 2000 to less than half a million by the end of the decade. In 2007, LCD TVs finally became more popular than CRT TVs following a brief period of roughly equal sales.

Overall, it seems clear that the decrease in the price of LCD TVs in 2005 brought about a huge increase in sales, while a similar decrease in CRT prices did not result in increased sales. The two graphs show how new technology at the right price can quickly replace a previously successful product.

ADDITIONAL WRITING TASK 9

Use the Internet to research global sales of laptop and desktop computers over the past ten years. Draw a graph based on your research and write an explanation of the data.

_____

_____

_____

_____

_____

_____

_____

_____

_____

_____

_____

WRITING TASK 10 MODEL ANSWER

Write a four-paragraph description of this flow chart, explaining how the body responds to changes in temperature.

The flow chart shows how body temperature in human beings is regulated in an area of the brain called the hypothalamus.

When the body temperature rises above the ideal temperature of 37 degrees Celsius, messages are sent from heat sensors in the skin to the hypothalamus. This information is then processed, triggering three major chemical processes. First of all sweating increases so that air can cool the skin down. Then blood is sent to the skin where it is cooler and the metabolism slows. The body then loses heat and a signal is sent to the brain to stop the processes.

When the temperature of the body falls below the ideal temperature of 37 degrees Celsius, the hypothalamus is alerted by heat sensors in the skin and three different processes begin. Shivering starts, blood is diverted away from the skin and the metabolism increases. As soon as the body gains heat again, a signal is sent back to the brain, which then stops these processes.

The flow chart shows how the brain controls two of the many complex actions in our body without our knowledge.

ADDITIONAL WRITING TASK 10

Describe the various stages from discovering an illness to returning home from hospital.

_____

_____

_____

_____

_____

_____

_____

_____

_____

_____

_____

_____

_____

_____

ACKNOWLEDGEMENTS

I would like to thank Sue Ullstein for her excellent editorial work, Barry Tadman for his support during the writing of this book and Kate Hansford for giving me the opportunity to work on this project. I would also like to thank Carmen Konzett for her love, friendship and support, and for always being ready to discuss teaching ideas, materials development and EFL. Special thanks to our baby boy, Felix, whose gorgeous smile and infectious laugh is the most wonderful start to every day.

Matt Firth

Publisher acknowledgements

The publishers are extremely grateful to the following people and their learners for reviewing and trialling this course during its development. The course has benefited hugely from your insightful comments, advice and feedback.

Mr M.K. Adjibade, King Saud University, Saudi Arabia; Canan Aktug, Bursa Technical University, Turkey; Olwyn Alexander, Heriot Watt University, UK; Valerie Anisy, Damman University, Saudi Arabia; Anwar Al-Fetlawi, University of Sharjah, UAE; Laila Al-Qadhi, Kuwait University, Kuwait; Tahani Al-Taha, University of Dubai, UAE; Ozlem Atalay, Middle East Technical University, Turkey; Seda Merter Ataygul, Bursa Technical University Turkey; Harika Altug, Bogazici University, Turkey; Kwab Asare, University of Westminster, UK; Erdogan Bada, Cukurova University, Turkey; Cem Balcikanli, Gazi University, Turkey; Gaye Bayri, Anadolu University, Turkey; Meher Ben Lakhdar, Sohar University, Oman; Emma Biss, Girne American University, UK; Dogan Bulut, Meliksah University, Turkey; Sinem Bur, TED University, Turkey; Alison Chisholm, University of Sussex, UK; Dr. Panidnad Chulerk , Rangsit University, Thailand; Sedat Cilingir, Bilgi University, Istanbul, Turkey; Sarah Clark, Nottingham Trent International College, UK; Elaine Cockerham, Higher College of Technology, Muscat, Oman; Asli Derin, Bilgi University, Turkey; Steven Douglass, University of Sunderland, UK; Jacqueline Einer, Sabanci University, Turkey; Basak Erel, Anadolu University, Turkey; Hande Lena Erol, Piri Reis Maritime University, Turkey; Gulseren Eyuboglu, Ozyegin University, Turkey; Muge Gencer, Kemerburgaz University, Turkey; Jeff Gibbons, King Fahed University of Petroleum and Minerals, Saudi Arabia; Maxine Gilway, Bristol University, UK; Dr Christina Gitsaki, HCT, Dubai Men's College, UAE; Sam Fenwick, Sohar University, Oman; Peter Frey, International House, Doha, Qatar; Neil Harris, Swansea University, UK; Vicki Hayden, College of the North Atlantic, Qatar; Ajarn Naratip Sharp Jindapitak, Prince of Songkla University, Hatyai, Thailand; Joud Jabri-Pickett, United Arab Emirates University, Al Ain, UAE; Aysel Kilic, Anadolu University, Turkey; Ali Kimav, Anadolu University, Turkey; Bahar Kiziltunali, Izmir University of Economics, Turkey; Kamil Koc, Ozel Kasimoglu Coskun Lisesi, Turkey; Ipek Korman-Tezcan, Yeditepe University, Turkey; Philip Lodge, Dubai Men's College, UAE; Iain Mackie, Al Rowdah University, Abu Dhabi, UAE; Katherine Mansfield, University of Westminster, UK; Kassim Mastan, King Saud University, Saudi Arabia; Elspeth McConnell, Newham College, UK; Lauriel Mehdi, American University of Sharjah, UAE; Dorando Mirkin-Dick, Bell International Institute, UK; Dr Sita Musigrungsi, Prince of Songkla University, Hatyai, Thailand; Mark Neville, Al Hosn University, Abu Dhabi, UAE; Shirley Norton, London School of English, UK; James Openshaw, British Study Centres, UK; Hale Ottolini, Mugla Sitki Kocman University, Turkey; David Palmer, University of Dubai, UAE; Michael Pazinas, United Arab Emirates University, UAE; Troy

Priest, Zayed University, UAE; Alison Ramage Patterson, Jeddah, Saudi Arabia; Paul Rogers, Qatar Skills Academy, Qatar; Josh Round, Saint George International, UK; Harika Saglicak, Bogazici University, Turkey; Asli Saracoglu, Isik University, Turkey; Neil Sarkar, Ealing, Hammersmith and West London College, UK; Nancy Shepherd, Bahrain University, Bahrain; Jonathan Smith, Sabanci University, Turkey; Peter Smith, United Arab Emirates University, UAE; Adem Soruc, Fatih University Istanbul, Turkey; Dr Peter Stanfield, HCT, Madinat Zayed & Ruwais Colleges, UAE; Maria Agata Szczerbik, United Arab Emirates University, Al Ain, UAE; Burcu Tezcan-Unal, Bilgi University, Turkey; Dr Nakonthep Tipayasuparat, Rangsit University, Thailand; Scott Thornbury, The New School, New York, USA; Susan Toth, HCT, Dubai Men's Campus, Dubai, UAE; Melin Unal, Ege University, Izmir, Turkey; Aylin Unaldi, Bogaziçi University, Turkey; Colleen Wackrow, Princess Nourah bint Abdulrahman University, Riyadh, Saudi Arabia; Gordon Watts, Study Group, Brighton UK; Po Leng Wendelkin, INTO at University of East Anglia, UK; Halime Yildiz, Bilkent University, Ankara, Turkey; Ferhat Yilmaz, Kahramanmaras Sutcu Imam University, Turkey.

Special thanks to Peter Lucantoni for sharing his expertise, both pedagogical and cultural.

Special thanks also to Michael Pazinas for writing the Research projects which feature at the end of every unit. Michael has first-hand experience of teaching in and developing materials for the paperless classroom. He has worked in Greece, the Middle East and the UK. Prior to his current position as Curriculum and Assessment Coordinator for the Foundation Program at the United Arab Emirates University he was an English teacher for the British Council, the University of Exeter and several private language institutes. Michael is also a graphic designer, involved in instructional design and educational eBook development.

Photos

p.8: (1) © Eric Limon/Shutterstock; p.8: (2) © szefai/Shutterstock; p.8: (3) © Steven Vidler/Eurasia Press/Corbis. All other video stills are by kind permission of © Discovery Communication, LLC 2014.

Dictionary

Cambridge dictionaries are the world's most widely used dictionaries for learners of English. Available at three levels (Cambridge Essential English Dictionary, Cambridge Learner's Dictionary and Cambridge Advanced Learner's Dictionary), they provide easy-to-understand definitions, example sentences, and help in avoiding typical mistakes. The dictionaries are also available online at dictionary.cambridge.org. © Cambridge University Press, reproduced with permission.

Corpus

Development of this publication has made use of the Cambridge English Corpus (CEC). The CEC is a multi-billion word computer database of contemporary spoken and written English. It includes British English, American English and other varieties of English. It also includes the Cambridge Learner Corpus, developed in collaboration with Cambridge English Language Assessment. Cambridge University Press has built up the CEC to provide evidence about language use that helps to produce better language teaching materials.

Typeset by Integra.